Algebra Readiness Builders

Algebra 2

Katherine Patten LaChance and Rhonda Brady

Copyright and Reproduction of Materials

Algebra Readiness Educators, LLC have spent numerous hours writing and editing our books. We have designed this book as a reproducible book.

The reproduction rights grant permission to the purchaser of this book to reproduce copies only for the students in a teacher's classroom.

This right does not extend to other teachers, to the entire grade level of teachers, to the entire campus, or to the entire school district. We allow the copying of this book only for student use.

Algebra Readiness Educators, LLC
P.O. Box 2188
Orange, Texas 77631

www.AlgebraReadinessEducators.com

klachance@AREducators.com

rbrady@AREducators.com

Please honor our copyright.

How To Get The Best Results

Our books are designed to recycle skills necessary for algebra readiness. When used effectively, students practice skills until they become automatic allowing for deeper understanding of future mathematical concepts.

- Introduce builder # 1 as a homework assignment on the first day of school. This will set expectations for the year!
- Assign the builders as homework each day Monday through Thursday.
- Utilize 20 minutes a day of class time during the first week to introduce and work through the builders homework assignment.
- Average students are able to complete builder assignments in 15 minutes by the third week of school.
- Have the worked-out keys projected as the students enter the classroom so they can check and correct the previous night's assignment.
- Remember that skills are mastered over time; re-work only problems requested by students.
- Students **MUST** be held accountable for completed and corrected builder assignments.

Having spent several years searching for a resource that spirals the necessary skills for success in math, we decided to write our own. Our students' scores on the state mandated test improved dramatically after the implementation of our builders. Enjoy the same success by implementing builders as your daily homework assignments.

Acknowledgements

We extend our deep gratitude and appreciation to the following people:

Della McFerrin Alford

Della is a mathematics teacher and lives in Bridge City, Texas with her husband Avery. She has two daughters Lyndalyn and Amanda.

Della Graduated from Lamar University Beaumont, Texas in 1979 with a Bachelor's Degree in Mathematics. Della has 34 years teaching experience.

Della was the driving force behind the Algebra 2 Builders and has worked tirelessly to make the book into what is has become. We are grateful to her for the many contributions to our series of books and her knowledge of how students learn.

" Having a multitude of problems, with step-by-step solutions is crucial to enhancing the learning experience of those studying Algebra II."

Della Alford 5-11-2013

Cliff, Christopher and **Marianne LaChance** and **Phil** and **Rachel Brady**. Endured many hours of neglect so we could complete our books.

Elizabeth R. Patten. Encouraged and supported us in numerous ways. Without her help, our books would still be just our homework assignments.

Christopher LaChance. Designed our book covers and gave much needed technology support.

Ricky Ryan Offered suggestions and feedback on what needed to be included in our builders.

Student Testimonials

"Math has always been my weakest subject. I am constantly struggling to retain the information. The Algebra 2 Builders have helped me so much, I took them for granted in Algebra 1, but they have become a blessing in Algebra 2. The Builders helped me remember things from Algebra 1 and have honed my skills on units we learned in Algebra 2. The only thing that has helped me maintain my A in Algebra 2 is the Builders. They are the extra practice that everyone can benefit from".

"The Algebra Builders were very helpful, even though I didn't like doing them. They helped me prepare for the lessons we would have in the future. At the beginning of the year, we did not have them and Algebra seemed really hard. When we started using them, Algebra was easier and my grades went up."

"I was always a lazy student, and made ok grades without trying. When I started Algebra 1, I struggled. Mrs. LaChance introduced the Algebra Builders, and it really helped with my understanding of what I just learned and things we had already learned. They were easy and quick assignments, I hope we have something like this next year."

Algebra 2 Builder # 1

Name:______________________________

Solve Equations

$4 - 3(2x - 5) = 6x - 7$

Solve Inequalities

Solve, show your answer graphically, with set builder and interval notation.

$4x + 5 < 6x - 7$

Evaluate Expressions

$3x - 2(3 - 4x)$ when $x = 4$

Literal Equations

$PV = nRT$ Solve for T

Word Problems

Footballs cost $22.00 each. The Athletic Director has $277.00 in his budget to spend on footballs. There is a $13.00 shipping fee per order. How many footballs can the Athletic Director order?

Relations/Functions

Determine if the relation is a function. Find the domain and range.

Function: Yes No

Domain:

Range:

x	y
-1	-2
0	-1
1	0
	1

Vocabulary

Domain
Range
Function
Solution
Equation
Inequality

__________________ is the set of first elements in ordered pair or table.

__________________ a value for the variable or an ordered pair that makes an equation true.

__________________ is a type of problem that often has a set of answers and can be written in interval notation.

__________________ a relation in which every input has exactly one output.

Representing Functions as Graphs

Change to slope intercept form $y = mx + b$, find the slope. Use {-2, -1, 0, 1, 2} for the x values. Make a table, plot the points and graph. Find the y-intercept by setting x to 0; then find the x-intercept by setting y to 0. **$3x - y = 4$**

x	y

x-int=_____

y-int=_____ m=_____

Distributive Property

$-6k^3 - 3k - 8k(2k^2 + 5)$

$(x - 2y)(7x - 2y)$

Algebra 2 Builder # 2

Name:______________________________

Solve Equations

$5x - \frac{1}{5} = 2x - \frac{3}{5}$

Solve Inequalities

Solve, show your answer graphically, with set builder and interval notation.

$2 - (4x + 3) \geq 7$

Evaluate Expressions

$x^2 - 3x + 5$ when $x = -2$

Literal Equations

$M = \frac{Mol}{L}$ Solve for Mol

Relations/Functions

Determine if the relation is a function. Find the domain and range.

Function: Yes No

Domain:

Range:

Word Problems

Harry works for a major sporting goods distributor. He earns a base salary of $30,000 per year and 5% commision on his sales. How much will Harry need to sell to earn $50,000 by the end of the year?

Vocabulary

Domain
Range
Function
Solution
Equation
Inequality

__________________ is the set of second elements in ordered pair or table.

__________________ a mathematical statement that shows two expressions are equivalent.

__________________ a value for the variable or an ordered pair that makes an equation true.

__________________ a relation in which every input has exactly one output.

Representing Functions as Graphs

Change to slope intercept form $y = mx + b$, find the slope. Use {-2, -1, 0, 1, 2} for the x values. Make a table, plot the points and graph. Find the y-intercept by setting x to 0; then find the x-intercept by setting y to 0. **$-3x + 3y = 6$**

x	y

x-int=_____

y-int=_____ m=_____

Distributive Property

$-3k^3 + 8k - 8k(6k^2 - 4)$

$(3x - 5)(2x + 7)$

Algebra 2 Builder # 3

Name:______________________________

Solve Equations

$3(2x - 5) - x = 5(x - 3)$

Solve Inequalities

Solve, show your answer graphically, with set builder and interval notation.

$-2(3x + 4) \leq 5(x - 3)$

Evaluate Expressions

$3x^2 + 4y^2$ when x = -2 and y = 3

Literal Equations

$F_g = G\left(\frac{m_1 m_2}{d^2}\right)$ Solve for m_2

Word Problems

Paul's age is 8 years less than 5 times Sarah's age. The sum of their ages is 64. Find Paul's age.

Relations/Functions

Determine if the relation is a function. Find the domain and range.

Function: Yes No

Domain:

Range:

X	Y
-3	4
-1	-2
0	3
2	7
2	-1

Vocabulary

Domain
Range
Function
Solution
Equation
Inequality

_________________ a relation in which every input has exactly one output.

_________________ is the set of first elements in ordered pair or table.

_________________ is a type of problem that often has a set of answers and can be written in interval notation.

_________________ a value for the variable or an ordered pair that makes an equation true.

Representing Functions as Graphs

Change to slope intercept form y = mx + b find the slope. Use {-2, -1, 0, 1, 2} for the x values. Make a table, plot the points and graph. Find the y-intercept by setting x to 0; then find the x-intercept by setting y to 0. **2x – y = 4**

x	y

x-int=_____

y-int=_____ m=_____

Distributive Property

$-3m^3 - m - 2m(5m^2 + 4)$

$(5 - x)(7 + 3x)$

Algebra 2 Builder # 4

Name:______________________________

Solve Equations

$5(2x - 3) = 3(x - 4) + 5x$

Solve Inequalities

Solve, show your answer graphically, with set builder and interval notation.

$3(2x - 4) + 5 \leq 2 - 3(3 - 2x)$

Evaluate Expressions

$\frac{2x+3y+4}{3x-y}$ when x = 2 and y = -3

Literal Equations

$V_1M_1 = V_2M_2$ Solve for M_2

Word Problems

The smaller of two numbers is 2 less than 3/4 the larger. The sum of the two numbers is 47. Find the value of the numbers.

Relations/Functions

Determine if the relation is a function. Find the domain and range.

Function: Yes No

Domain:

Range:

X	Y
-2 → -3	
3 → 9	
4 → 9	
6 → 12	

Vocabulary

Domain
Range
Function
Solution
Equation
Inequality

________________ a value for the variable or an ordered pair that makes an equation true.

________________ is a type of problem that often has a set of answers and can be written in interval notation.

________________ a mathematical statement that shows two expressions are equivalent.

________________ is the set of second elements in ordered pair or table.

Representing Functions as Graphs

y
9 8 7 6 5 4 3 2 1 0 -1 -2 -3 -4 -5 -6 -7 -8 -9
-9 -8 -7 -6 -5 -4 -3 -2 -1 0 1 2 3 4 5 6 7 8 9 x

Change to slope intercept form y = mx + b, find the slope. Use {-2, -1, 0, 1, 2} for the x values. Make a table, plot the points and graph. Find the y-intercept by setting x to 0; then find the x-intercept by setting y to 0. **-4x + 2y = 6**

x	y

x-int=_____

y-int=_____ m=_____

Distributive Property

$4k(-5m - 2k) + 5k(-2m - 3k)$

$5x(3x^2 + 3x - 4)$

Algebra 2 Builder # 5

Name:____________________________

Solve Equations	$5(2x - 3) - x = 3(3x - 4)$	Solve Inequalities	Solve, show your answer graphically, with set builder and interval notation. $3x > -15$ and $4x < 16$
Evaluate Expressions	$\frac{3x-2y-1}{x-3y}$ when x = -2 and y = 3	Literal Equations	$\frac{V_1}{T_1} = \frac{V_2}{T_2}$ Solve for V_2
Relations/Functions	Determine if the relation is a function. Use set builder and interval notation for the domain and range. Function: Yes No Domain: Range:	Word Problems	A large candy bar costs 35 cents more than a small candy bar. Marianne wants to write an equation for the approximate cost of 5 small candy bars and 3 large candy bars. If the total cost of the candy is around $5.50, solve for the approximate cost of a large candy bar and a small candy bar.

Vocabulary

Domain
Range
Function
Solution
Equation
Inequality

_______________ is the set of second elements in ordered pair or table.

_______________ a relation in which every input has exactly one output.

_______________ a value for the variable or an ordered pair that makes an equation true.

_______________ is the set of first elements in ordered pair or table.

Representing Functions as Graphs

Change to slope intercept form. Find the y-intercept and the slope. Graph the function. Then find the x-intercept by setting y to 0. **$6x - 3y = 9$**

x-int=__________ y-int = _______ m = _______

Distributive Property

$(2x^2 - 5y)(3x + 4y^2)$

$(x - 3)(2x^2 - 4x + 5)$

Algebra 2 Builder # 6

Name:______________________________

Solve Equations

$\frac{1}{2}(10x + 14) = \frac{2}{3}(21 - 3x)$

Solve Inequalities

Solve, show your answer graphically, with set builder and interval notation.

$4x > -16$ and $5x + 2 \leq 7$

Evaluate Expressions

$(2x)^2 - xy^2$ when $x = -4$ and $y = 5$

Literal Equations

$E = mc^2$ Solve for c

Word Problems

The product of 15 and a number n is at most 45. What is the largest possible number?

Relations/Functions

Determine if the relation is a function. Use set builder and interval notation for the domain and range.

Function: Yes No

Domain:

Range:

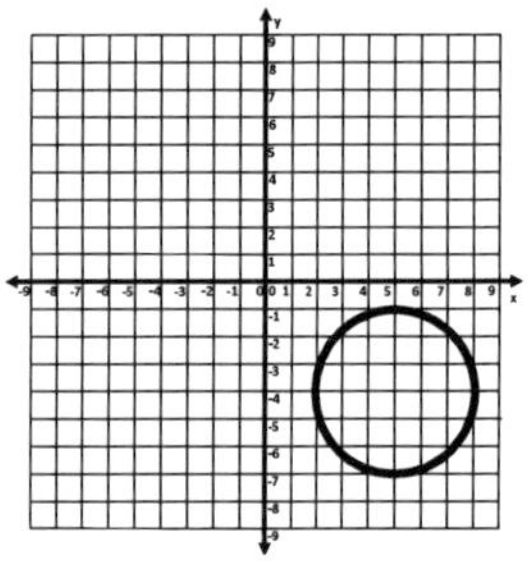

Vocabulary

Domain
Range
Function
Solution
Equation
Inequality

_______________ a mathematical statement that shows two expressions are equivalent.

_______________ is the set of second elements in ordered pair or table.

_______________ is a type of problem that often has a set of answers and can be written in interval notation.

_______________ is the set of first elements in ordered pair or table.

Representing Functions as Graphs

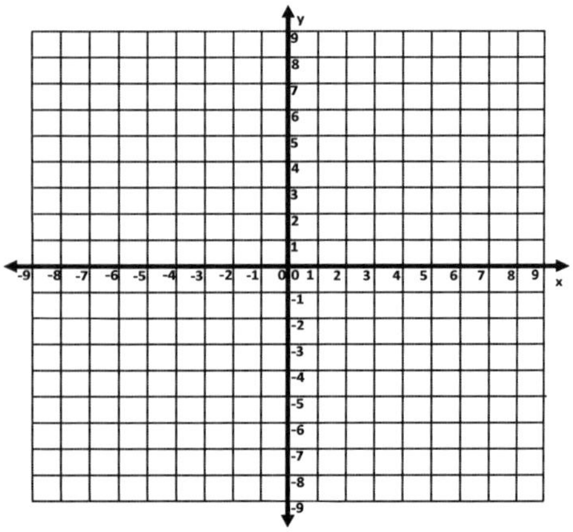

Change to slope intercept form. Find the y-intercept and the slope. Graph the function. Then find the x-intercept by setting y to 0. $4x + 8y = -16$

x-int=__________ y-int = ________ m = ________

Distributive Property

$(3x - 4)(3x + 4)$

$(x - 4)(3x^2 + 2x - 1)$

Algebra 2 Builder # 7

Name:______________________________

Solve Equations	$4.3w + 3.1 = 3.2(w + 2)$
Solve Inequalities	Solve, show your answer graphically, with set builder and interval notation. $5x \le -15$ or $3x > 12$
Evaluate Expressions	$\frac{a^2 - 2ab + 2}{3a^2b}$ a = -2 and b= 3
Literal Equations	$\frac{1}{f} = \frac{1}{d_1} + \frac{1}{d_0}$ Solve for f
Word Problems	Ann bowled 115,121,125,118 and 122 in five games. What must Ann bowl in the sixth game so that she will have an average score of 120 for the six games?
Relations/Functions	Determine if the relation is a function. Use set builder and interval notation for the domain and range. Function: Yes No Domain: Range:

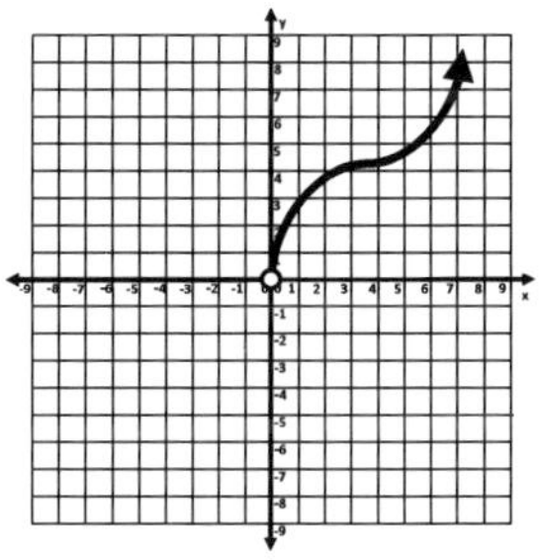

Vocabulary

Domain
Range
Function
Solution
Equation
Inequality

_______________ a value for the variable or an ordered pair that makes an equation true.

_______________ a mathematical statement that shows two expressions are equivalent.

_______________ is the set of first elements in ordered pair or table.

_______________ is the set of second elements in ordered pair or table.

Representing Functions as Graphs

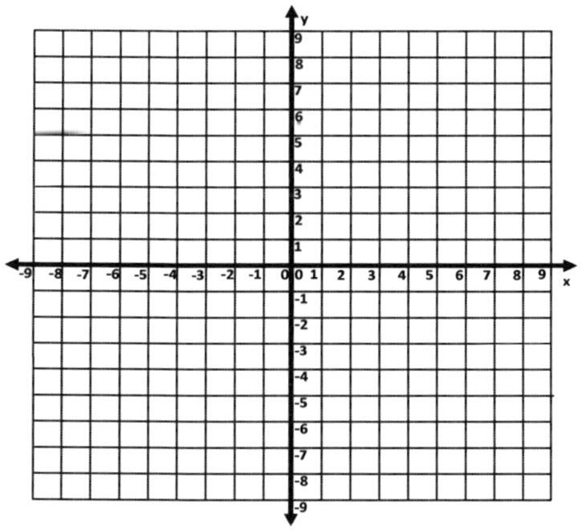

Change to slope intercept form. Find the y-intercept and the slope. Graph the function. Then find the x-intercept by setting y to 0. $2x + 3y = -9$

x-int = __________ y-int = ________ m = ________

Distributive Property

$(2x + 5y)(2x - 5y)$

$(x - 2)(x + 3)(x - 1)$

Algebra 2 Builder # 8

Name:____________________________

Solve Equations

$3(4x - 3) - x = -5(2x - 4)$

Solve Inequalities

Solve, show your answer graphically, with set builder and interval notation.

$7x < -7$ or $-3x \geq 12$

Evaluate Expressions

$2x^2 \div (6 + 2x) + 4$ when $x = -4$

Literal Equations

$KE = \frac{1}{2}mv^2$ Solve for v

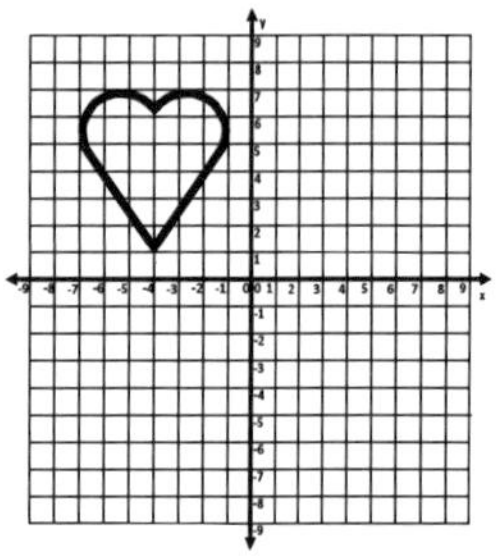

Word Problems

A rectangular tablecloth is 15 inches longer than it is wide. If Lisa has at most 242 inches of lace to sew around the tablecloth. What is the greatest possible width of the tablecloth?

Relations/Functions

Determine if the relation is a function. Use set builder and interval notation for the domain and range.

Function: Yes No

Domain:

Range:

Vocabulary

Domain
Range
Function
Solution
Equation
Inequality

____________________ is a type of problem that often has a set of answers and can be written in interval notation.

____________________ a relation in which every input has exactly one output.

____________________ is the set of second elements in ordered pair or table.

____________________ mathematical statement that two expressions are equivalent.

Representing Functions as Graphs

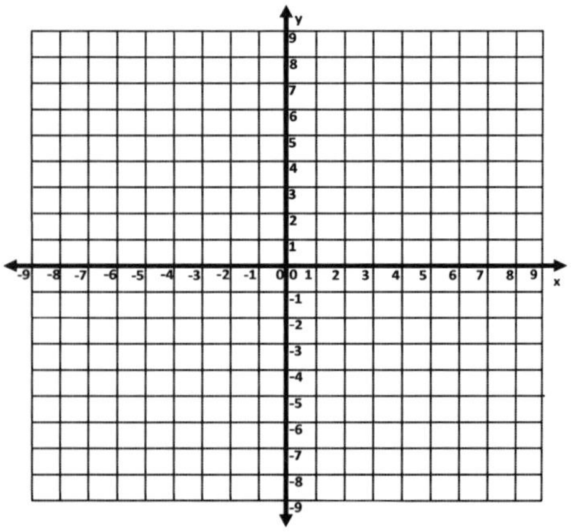

Change to slope intercept form. Find the y-intercept and the slope. Graph the function. Then find the x-intercept by setting y to 0.

$\frac{2}{3}x + \frac{1}{3}y = 2$

x-int = __________ y-int = ________ m = ________

Distributive Property

$(4x - 1)^2$

$(2x + 3)(3x + 2)(4x - 1)$

Algebra 2 Builder # 9 Name:______________________

Transformations

The graph of y = f(x) is on the coordinate grid, use the graph to perform the transformation below.

A. Graph g(x) = f(x) + 3

B. Explain the transformation in words.

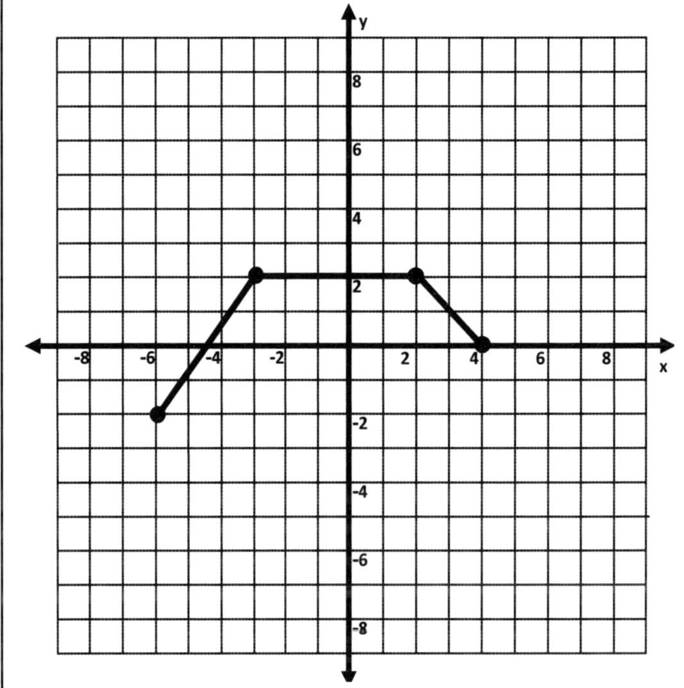

Vocabulary

Commutative Property
Associative Property
Distributive Property
Additive Inverse Property
Multiplicative Inverse Property
Continuous Function
Discrete Function
Inverse Function

__________________ A function that results from interchanging the domain and range values of a one to one function.

__________________ For all real numbers a and b, a + b = b + a or ab = ba.

__________________ A function whose graph consist of separate points.

__________________ For all real numbers a, b, and c, (a + b) + c = a + (b + c) or (ab)c = a(bc)

Parent Functions

Write the equation and graph the parent linear function.

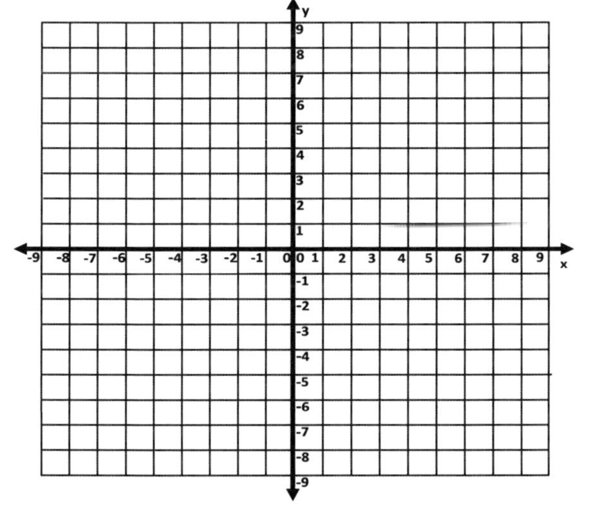

Express the domain and range in set builder and interval notation for the parent function above.

Domain:

Range:

Graphing Inequalities

Graph $y > -2x + 3$

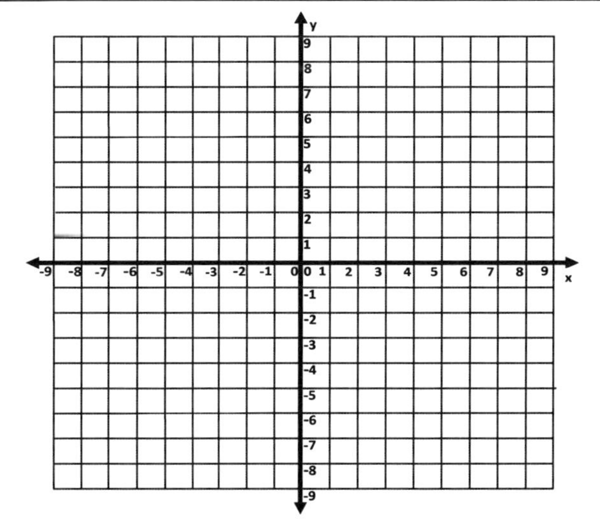

Function Notation

If f(x) = 3x + 5, find f(2).

Algebra 2 Builder # 10

Name:______________________________

Transformations

The graph of y = f(x) is on the coordinate grid, use the graph to perform the transformation below.

A. Graph $g(x) = f(x - 2)$

B. Explain the transformation in words.

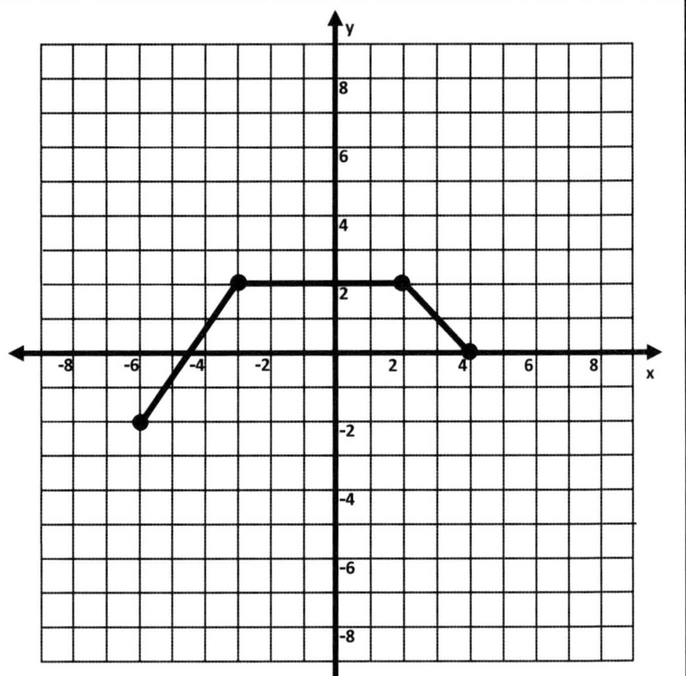

Vocabulary

Commutative Property
Associative Property
Distributive Property
Additive Inverse Property
Multiplicative Inverse Property
Continuous Function
Discrete Function
Inverse Function

______________________ For all real numbers a, b and c, $a(b + c) = ab + ac$.

______________________ A function whose graph has no gaps or breaks.

______________________ For all real number a, $a \cdot \frac{1}{a} = 1$, $a \neq 0$.

______________________ For all real numbers a, $a + (-a) = 0$.

Parent Functions

Write the equation and graph the parent quadratic function.

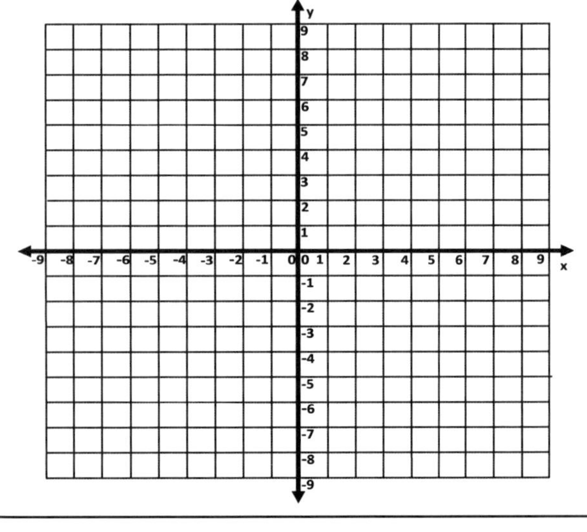

Express the domain and range in set builder and interval notation for the parent function above.

Domain:

Range:

Graphing Inequalities

Graph $y \leq 3x - 5$

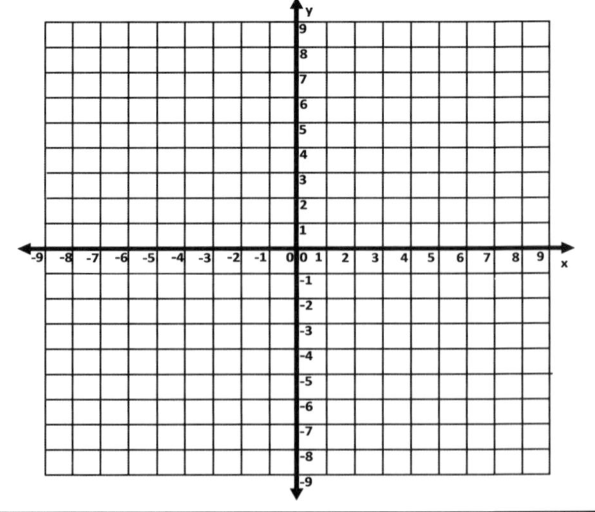

Function Notation

If $f(x) = 2x^2 + 3x + 7$, find f(-1).

Algebra 2 Builder # 11

Name:________________________

Transformations

The graph of y = f(x) is on the coordinate grid, use the graph to perform the transformation below.

A. Graph g(x) = -f(x)

B. Explain the transformation in words.

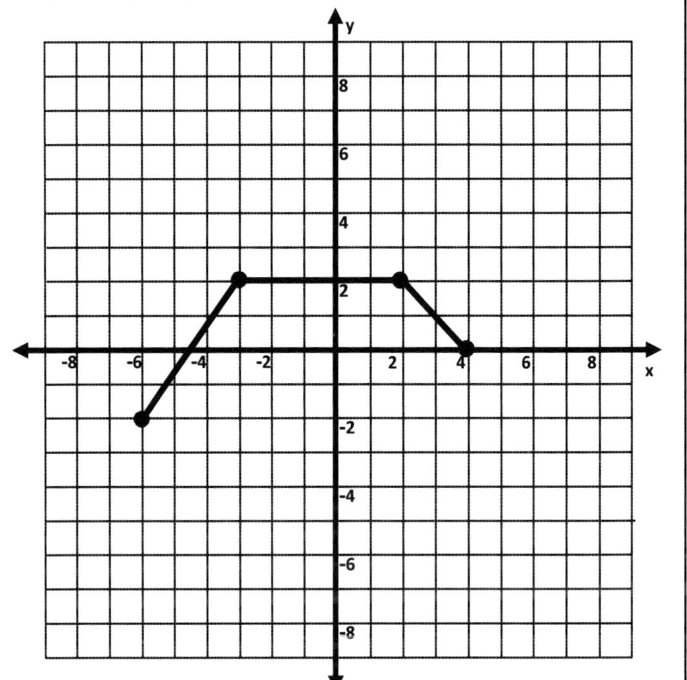

Vocabulary

Commutative Property
Associative Property
Distributive Property
Additive Inverse Property
Multiplicative Inverse Property
Continuous Function
Discrete Function
Inverse Function

____________________ For all real numbers a, a + (-a) = 0.

____________________ A function that results from interchanging the domain and range values of a one to one function.

____________________ For all real number a, $a \cdot \frac{1}{a} = 1, \quad a \neq 0.$

____________________ For all real numbers a, b, and c, (a + b) + c = a + (b + c) or (ab)c = a(bc)

Parent Functions

Write the equation and graph the parent absolute value function.

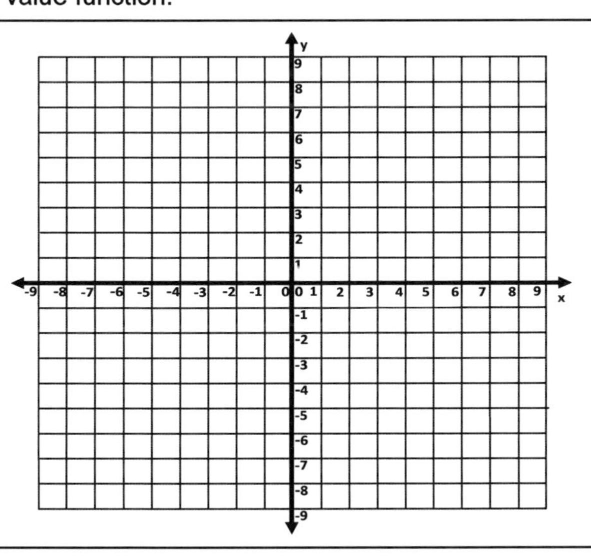

Express the domain and range in set builder and interval notation for the parent function above.

Domain:

Range:

Graphing Inequalities

Graph $4x + 2y > 3$

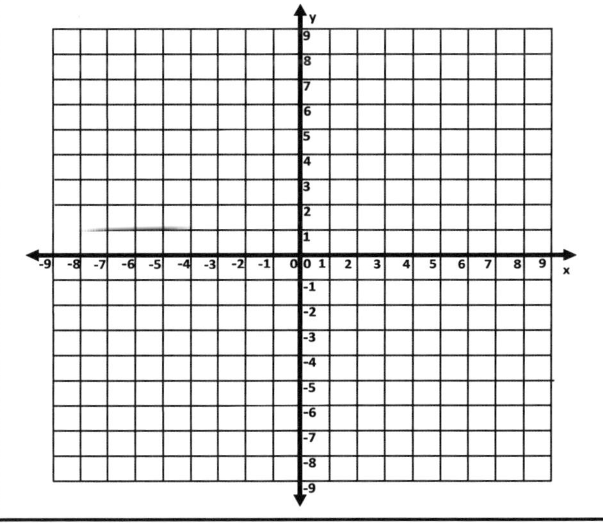

Function Notation

If $f(x) = 2|4x - 5| + 7$, find f(1/2).

Algebra 2 Builder # 12

Name:______________________

Transformations

The graph of y = f(x) is on the coordinate grid, use the graph to perform the transformation below.

A. Graph g(x) = f(-x)

B. Explain the transformation in words.

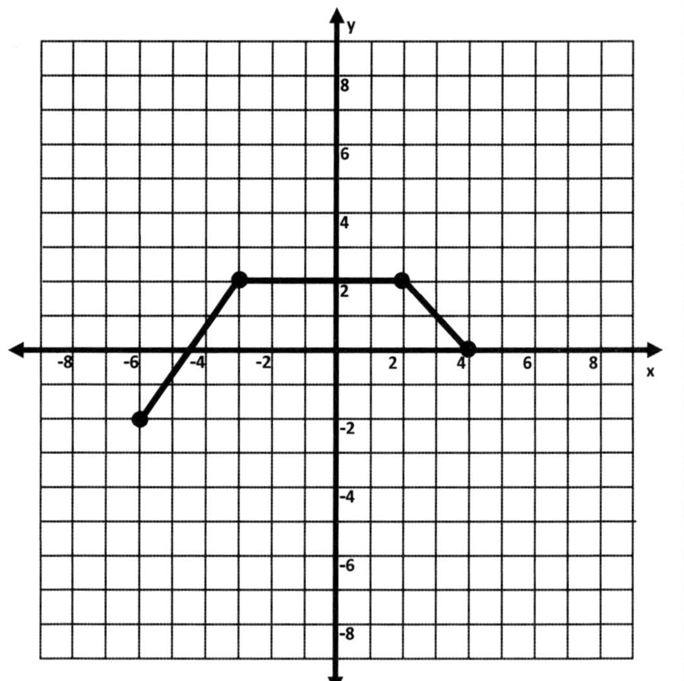

Vocabulary

Commutative Property
Associative Property
Distributive Property
Additive Inverse Property
Multiplicative Inverse Property
Continuous Function
Discrete Function
Inverse Function

________________ For all real numbers a and b, a + b = b + a or ab = ba.

________________ A function whose graph has no gaps or breaks.

________________ A function whose graph consist of separate points.

________________ For all real numbers a, b and c, a(b + c) = ab + ac.

Parent Functions

Write the equation and graph the parent square root function.

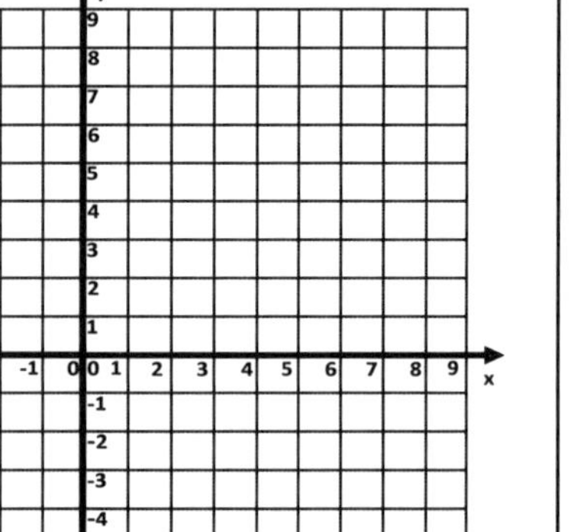

Express the domain and range in set builder and interval notation for the parent function above.

Domain:

Range:

Graphing Inequalities

Graph 3x – 6y ≤ 12

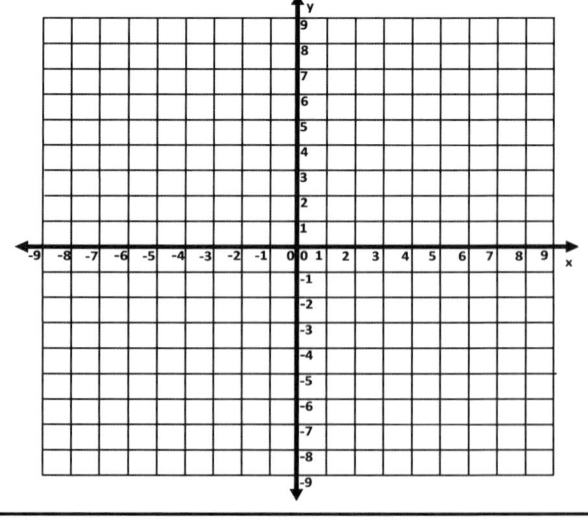

Function Notation

If f(x) = $-|2x + 3|$, find f(-5).

Algebra 2 Builder # 13

Name:________________________

Transformations

The graph of y = f(x) is on the coordinate grid, use the graph to perform the transformation below.

A. Graph g(x) = f(2x)

B. Explain the transformation in words.

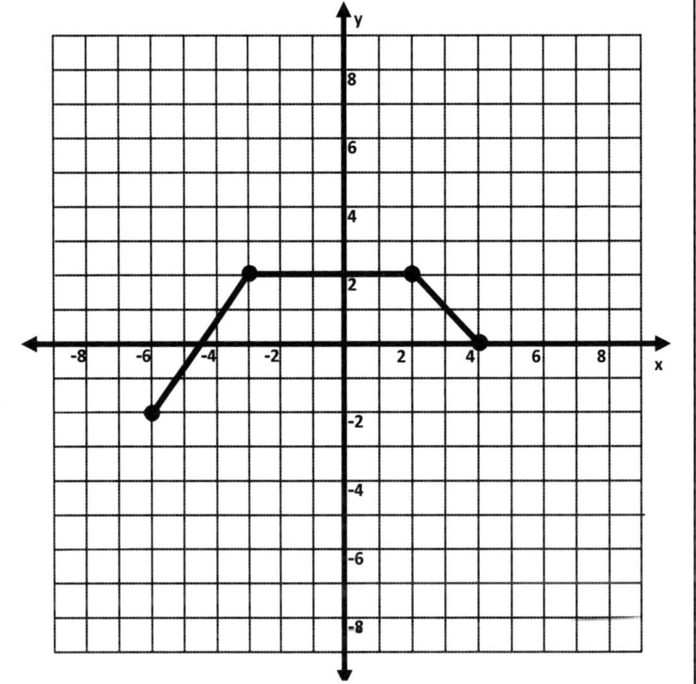

Vocabulary

Commutative Property
Associative Property
Distributive Property
Additive Inverse Property
Multiplicative Inverse Property
Continuous Function
Discrete Function
Inverse Function

________________ For all real numbers a, b, and c, (a + b) + c = a + (b + c) or (ab)c = a(bc)

________________ For all real numbers a, b and c, a(b + c) = ab + ac.

________________ A function whose graph has no gaps or breaks.

________________ A function whose graph consist of separate points.

Parent Functions

Write the equation and graph the parent rational function.

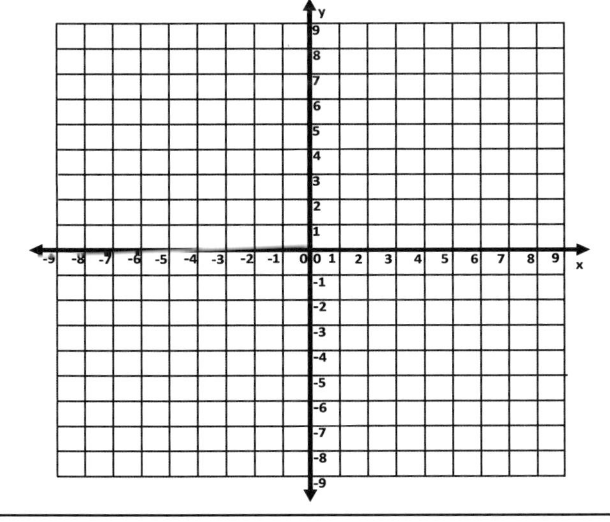

Express the domain and range in set builder and interval notation for the parent function above.

Domain:

Range:

Graphing Inequalities

Graph $y > |x|$

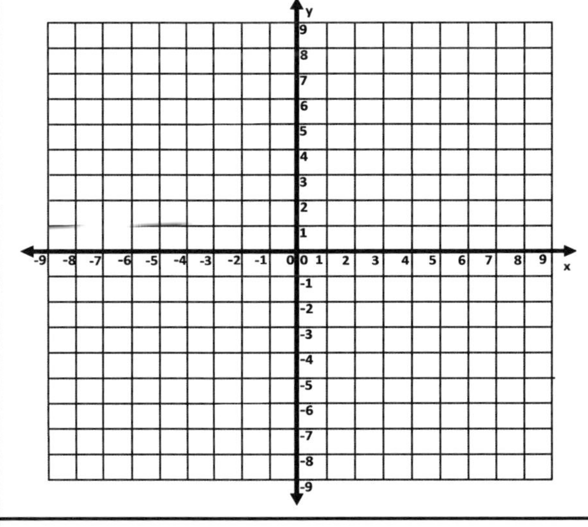

Function Notation

If $f(x) = \frac{x+3}{2x-5}$, find f(3).

Algebra 2 Builder # 14

Name:______________________________

Transformations

The graph of y = f(x) is on the coordinate grid, use the graph to perform the transformation below.

A. Graph g(x) = 2f(x)

B. Explain the transformation in words.

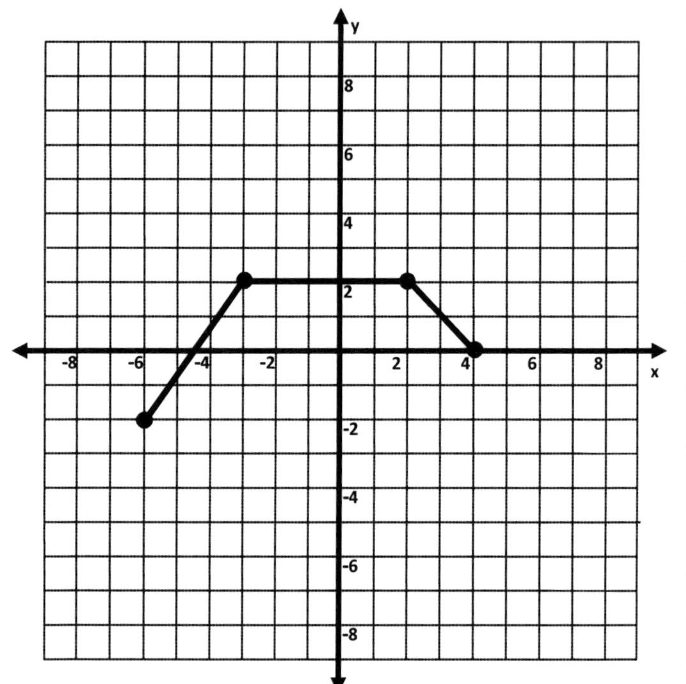

Vocabulary

Commutative Property
Associative Property
Distributive Property
Additive Inverse Property
Multiplicative Inverse Property
Continuous Function
Discrete Function
Inverse Function

_____________________ For all real numbers a and b, a + b = b + a or ab = ba.

_____________________ For all real numbers a, a + (-a) = 0.

_____________________ A function that results from interchanging the domain and range values of a one to one function.

_____________________ For all real number a, $a \cdot \frac{1}{a} = 1$, $a \neq 0$.

Parent Functions

Write the equation and graph the parent cube root function.

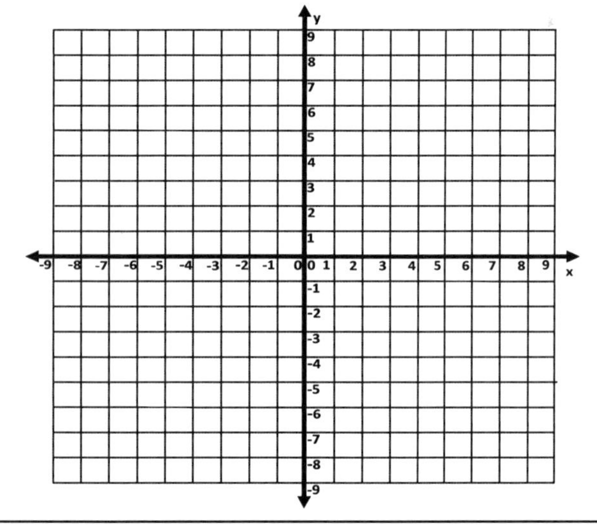

Express the domain and range in set builder and interval notation for the parent function above.

Domain:

Range:

Graphing Inequalities

Graph $y \leq |x| - 4$

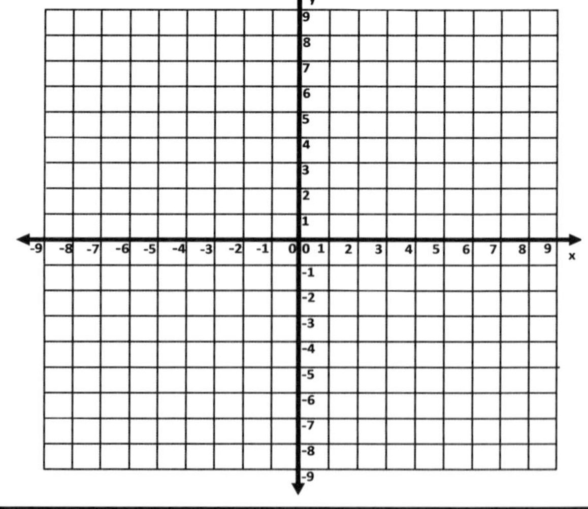

Function Notation

If $f(x) = \frac{x+4}{3x-2}$, find $f(\frac{1}{2})$.

Algebra 2 Builder # 15

Name:____________________________

Transformations

The graph of y = f(x) is on the coordinate grid, use the graph to perform the transformation below.

A. Graph g(x) = f(x – 3) + 2

B. Explain the transformation in words.

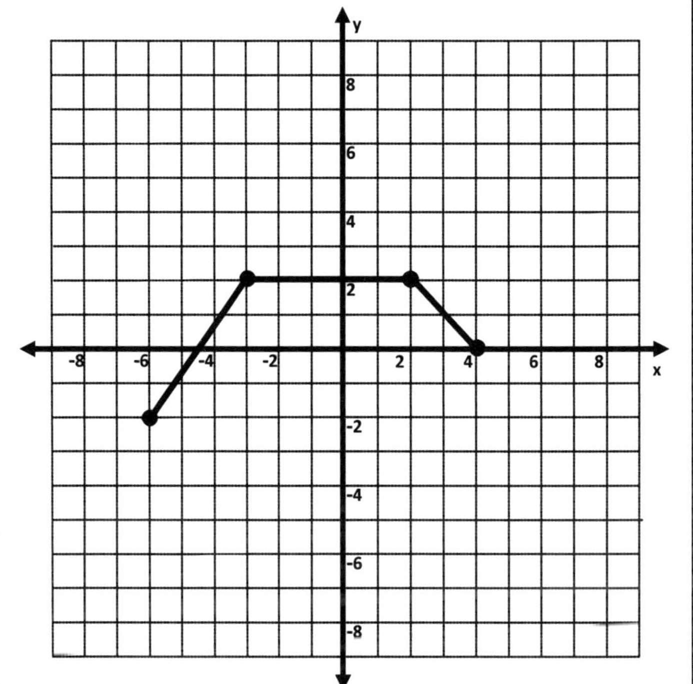

Vocabulary

Commutative Property
Associative Property
Distributive Property
Additive Inverse Property
Multiplicative Inverse Property
Continuous Function
Discrete Function
Inverse Function

__________________ A function that results from interchanging the domain and range values of a one to one function.

__________________ For all real numbers a and b, a + b = b + a or ab = ba.

__________________ A function whose graph consist of separate points.

__________________ For all real numbers a, b, and c, (a + b) + c = a + (b + c) or (ab)c = a(bc)

Parent Functions

Write the equation and graph the parent quadratic function.

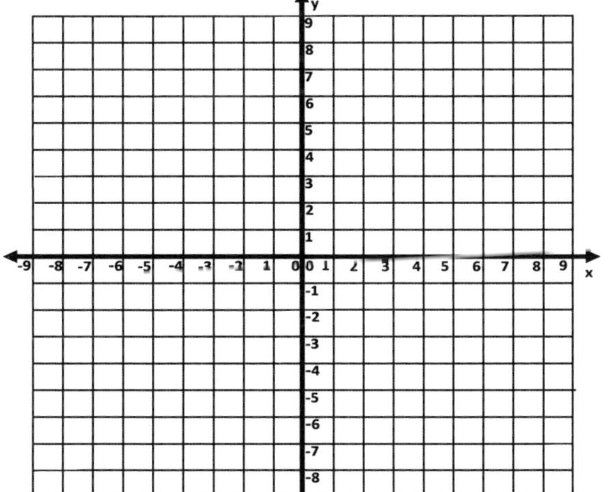

Express the domain and range in set builder and interval notation for the parent function above.

Domain:

Range:

Graphing Inequalities

Graph y > $|x| + 2$

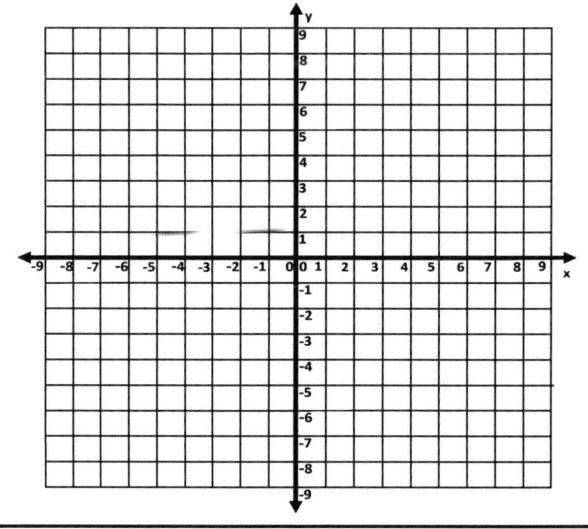

Function Notation

If f(x) = $\frac{x^2 + 5x - 4}{x + 2}$, find f(-2).

Algebra 2 Builder # 16

Name:______________________________

Transformations

The graph of y = f(x) is on the coordinate grid, use the graph to perform the transformation below.

A. Graph g(x) = ½ f(x)

B. Explain the transformation in words.

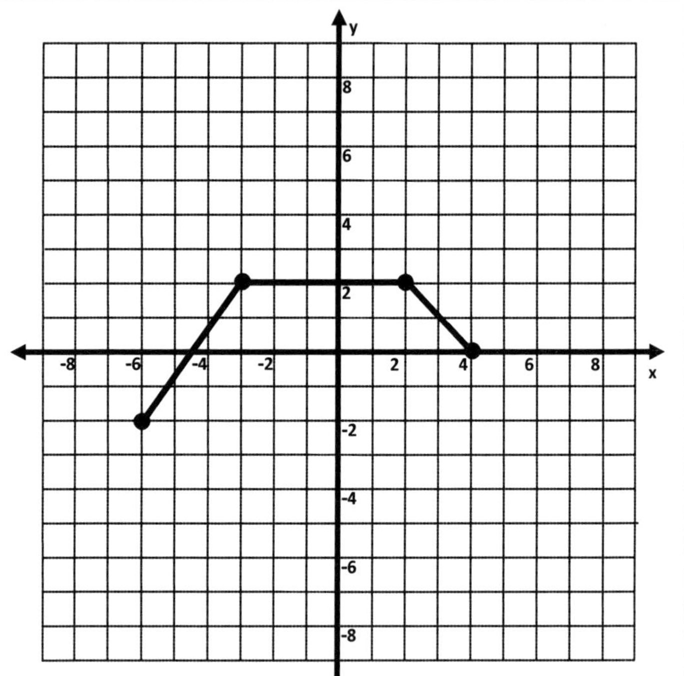

Vocabulary

Commutative Property
Associative Property
Distributive Property
Additive Inverse Property
Multiplicative Inverse Property
Continuous Function
Discrete Function
Inverse Function

____________________ For all real numbers a, b and c, a(b + c) = ab + ac.

____________________ A function whose graph has no gaps or breaks.

____________________ For all real number a, $a \cdot \frac{1}{a} = 1, \quad a \neq 0.$

____________________ For all real numbers a, a + (-a) = 0.

Parent Functions

Write the equation and graph the parent cubic function.

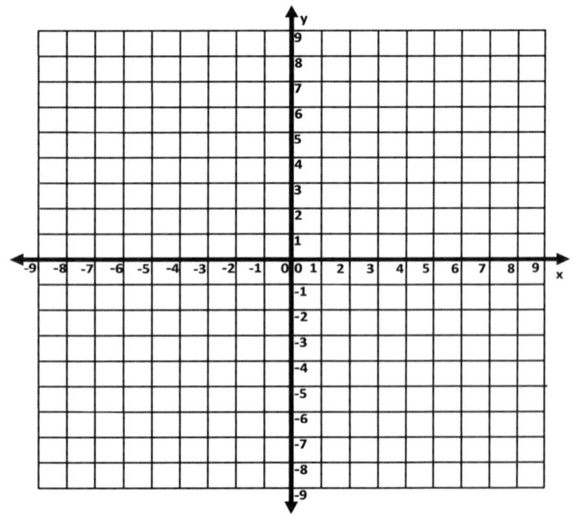

Express the domain and range in set builder and interval notation for the parent function above.

Domain:

Range:

Graphing Inequalities

Graph $y \leq -|x|$

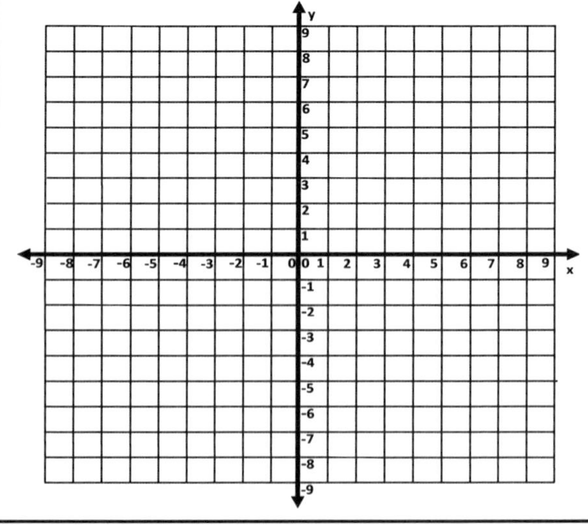

Function Notation

If $f(x) = \frac{x^2 - 9}{x^2 - 4}$, find f(3).

Algebra 2 Builder # 17

Name:____________________

Scatter Plots

x	1	5	7	-2	4	3
y	6	3	1	9	4	5

A. Make a scatterplot of the data.
B. Find the correlation coefficient r and the line of best fit.

C. Predict the value of y when x = 10. __________

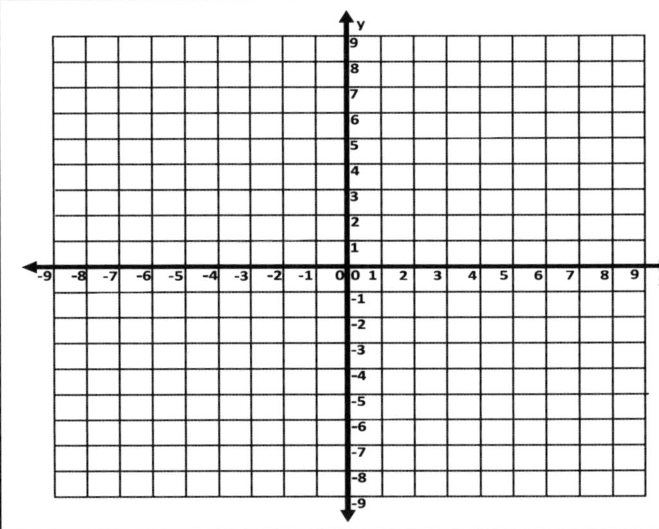

Transformations

Graph: $y = x^2 + 1$

Name the parent function:

Explain the transformation in words:

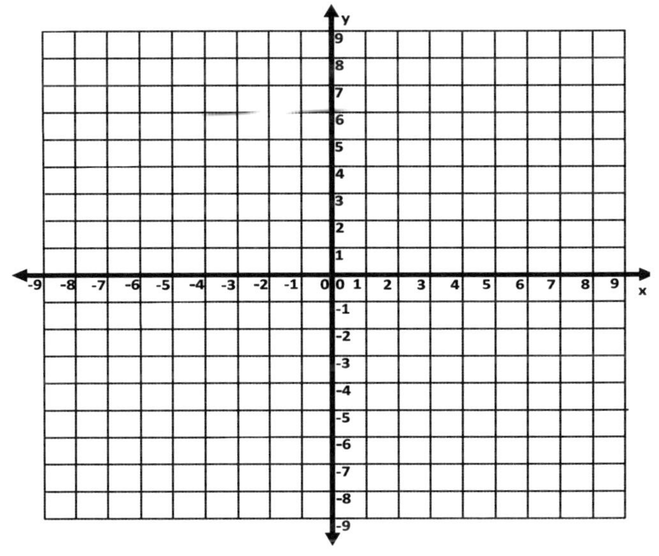

Inverse Functions

Given the table, find the inverse.

Original

x	y
2	8
3	9
4	10
5	11
6	12

Inverse

x	y

Writing Equations of Lines

Write an equation of a line in slope intercept form, that passes through the points (2 , 1) and (3 , 5).

Vocabulary

Parallel Lines
Perpendicular Lines
Scatter Plot
Parent Function
Transformations
Representations
Slope
Discrete Function
Continuous Function

_______________ The ratio of the vertical change (rise) to the horizontal change (run).

_______________ Lines that have the same slope.

_______________ A graph with points plotted to find the relationship between two sets of data.

_______________ A function whose graph consist of separate points.

Algebra 2 Builder # 18

Name:____________________________

Scatter Plots

x	-2	-1	0	1	2
y	9	0	-5	-6	-3

A. Make a scatterplot of the data.
B. Find the quadratic regression equation.

C. Predict the value of x when y = 49. __________

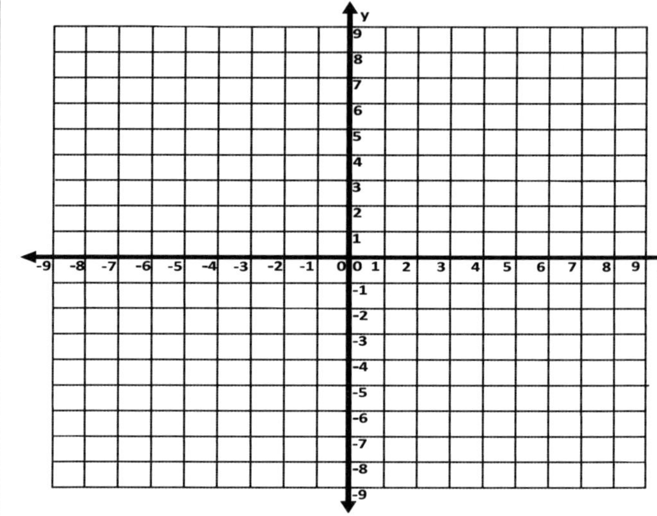

Transformations

Graph: $f(x) = \sqrt{x-4}$

Name the parent function:

Explain the transformation in words:

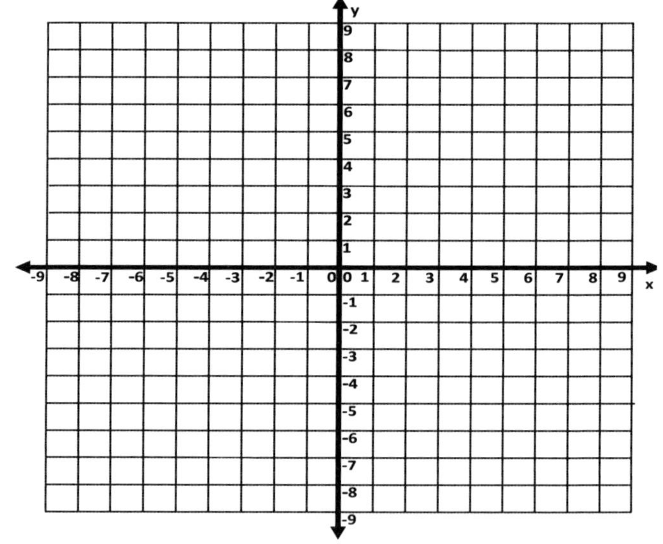

Inverse Functions

Given the equation below, find the inverse.

2x + 3y = 6

Writing Equations of Lines

Write an equation of a line in standard form that passes through the point (3,1) and is parrallel to the line **y = 3x + 4.**

Vocabulary

Parallel Lines
Perpendicular Lines
Scatter Plot
Parent Function
Transformations
Representations
Slope
Discrete Function
Continuous Function

____________________ Lines whose slopes are negative reciprocals.

____________________ The most basic function in a family of functions.

____________________ Ways to manipulate a graphs, size, shape, position or orientation.

____________________ Models, graphs, equations, tables and verbal descriptions of data.

Algebra 2 Builder # 19

Name:____________________________

Scatter Plots

x	-4	-2	0	1	-3	-1
y	-6.6	5	-5	1.4	5.8	-1.2

A. Make a scatterplot of the data.
B. Find the cubic regression equation.

C. Predict the value of y when x = -7. __________

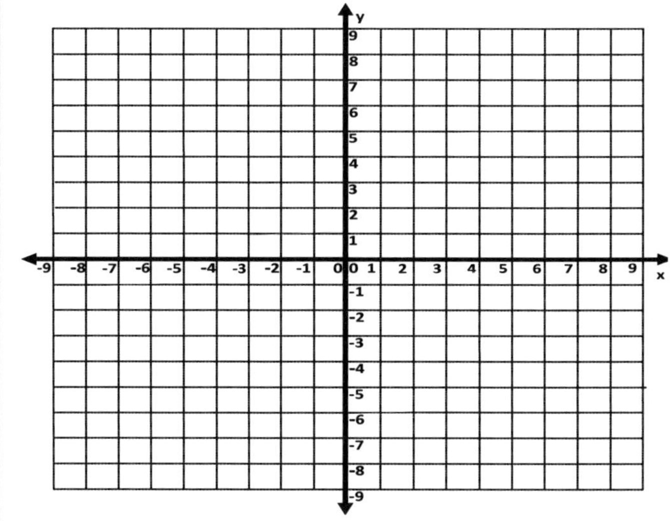

Transformations

Graph: $y = |x - 4| + 2$

Name the parent function:

Explain the transformation in words:

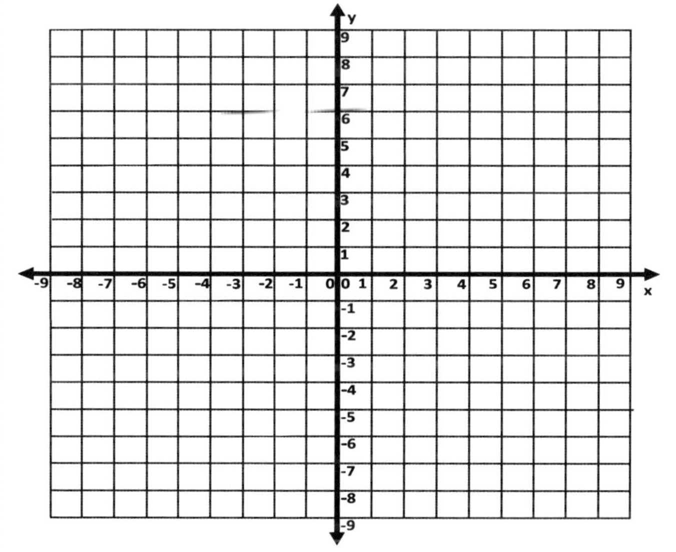

Inverse Functions

Given the graph, graph the inverse.

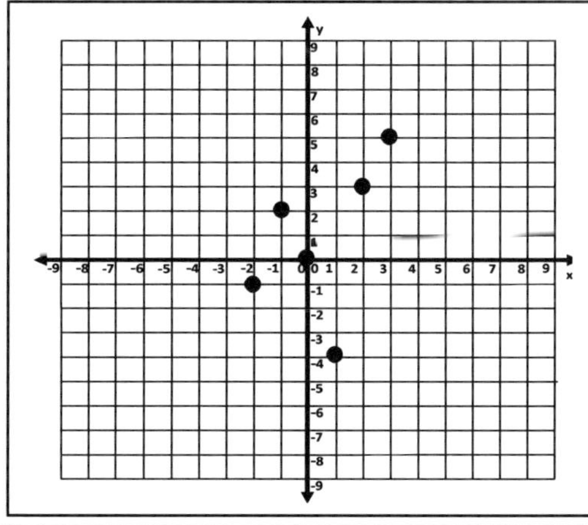

Writing Equations of Lines

Write an equation of a line in slope intercept form that passes through the point (-1,2) and is perpendicular to the line **2x + 4y = 8**

Vocabulary

Parallel Lines
Perpendicular Lines
Scatter Plot
Parent Function
Transformations
Representations
Slope
Discrete Function
Continuous Function

__________________ The ratio of the vertical change (rise) to the horizontal change (run).

__________________ Lines that have the same slope.

__________________ A graph with points plotted to find the relationship between two sets of data.

__________________ A funtion whose graph has no gaps or breaks.

Algebra 2 Builder # 20 Name:________________________

Scatter Plots

x	-6	-3	1	0
y	0.01	0.17	7.74	3

A. Make a scatterplot of the data.
B. Find the exponential regression equation.

C. Predict the value of y when x = 3.2 _________

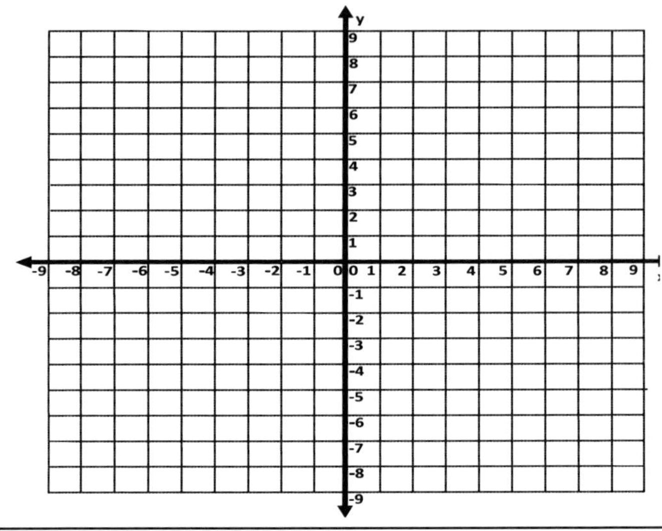

Transformations

Graph: $f(x) = 2x^3$

Name the parent function:

Explain the transformation in words:

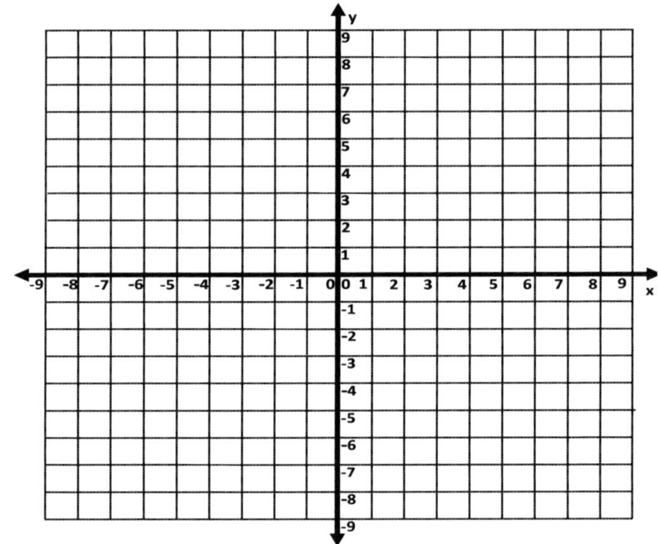

Inverse Functions

Given the equation $y = \sqrt{x} + 2$ find the inverse.

Writing Equations of Lines

Write the equation of the line shown in the graph in slope intercept form.

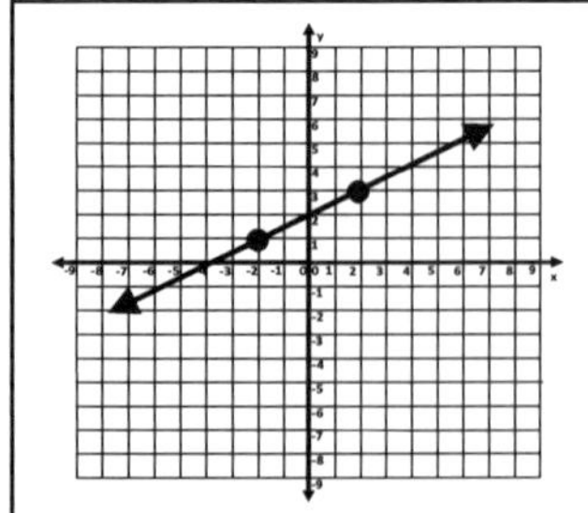

Vocabulary

Parallel Lines
Perpendicular Lines
Scatter Plot
Parent Function
Transformations
Representations
Slope
Discrete Function
Continuous Function

_______________ Lines whose slopes are negative reciprocals.

_______________ Ways to manipulate a graphs, size, shape, position or orientation.

_______________ Models, graphs, equations, tables and verbal descriptions of data.

_______________ The most basic function in a family of functions.

Algebra 2 Builder # 21

Name:____________________________

Discrete/Continuous Functions

Write and graph the functions described. Express the domain and range in set builder notation. State if the function is discrete or continuous.

A dog trots at an average speed of 4.5 mph. The function d(x) gives the distance in miles the dog trots in x hours.

Function:

Domain:

Range:

Discrete or Continuous:

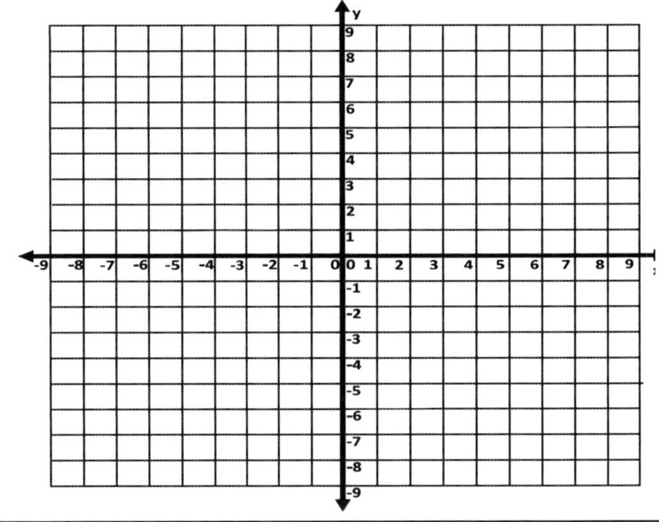

Transformations

Graph: $y = \sqrt[3]{2x}$

Name the parent function:

Explain the transformation in words:

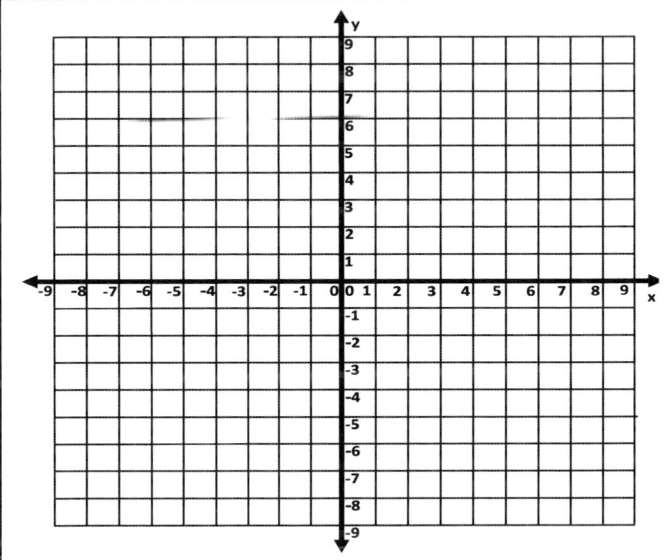

Inverse Functions

Given the graph, graph the inverse.

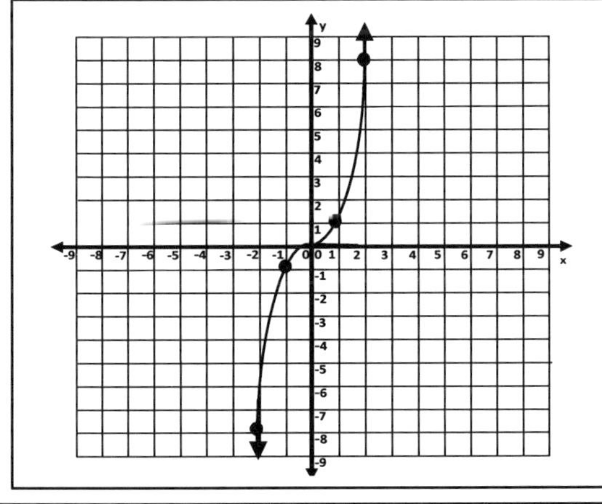

Writing Equations of Lines

Write an equation of a line in standard form that passes through the point (-1,3) and is perpendicular to the line that passes through (3,7) and (4,7).

Vocabulary

Parallel Lines
Perpendicular Lines
Scatter Plot
Parent Function
Transformations
Representations
Slope
Discrete Function
Continuous Function

____________________ Lines that have the same slope.

____________________ The ratio of the vertical change (rise) to the horizontal change (run).

____________________ A graph with points plotted to find the relationship between sets of data.

____________________ A function whose graph consist of separate points.

Algebra 2 Builder # 22

Name:______________________________

Discrete/Continuous Functions

Write and graph the functions described. Express the domain and range in set builder notation. State if the function is discrete or continuous.

An ice cream cone cost $2.50. The functions C(x) gives the cost of purchasing x number of cones.

Function:

Domain:

Range:

Discrete or Continuous:

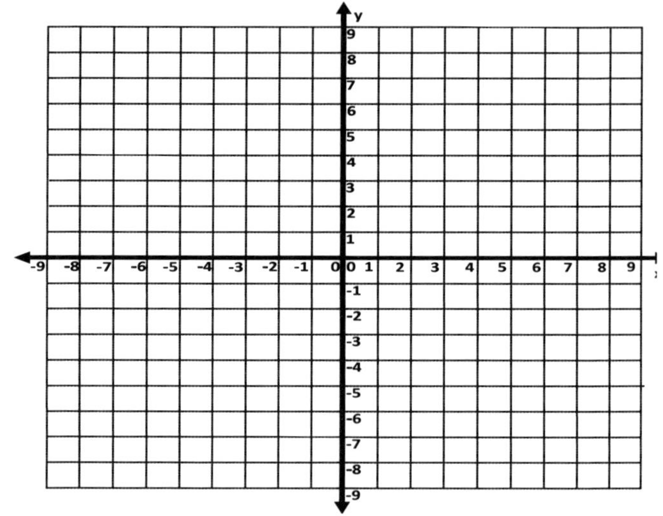

Transformations

Graph: $f(x) = 3x + 4$

Name the parent function:

Explain the transformation in words:

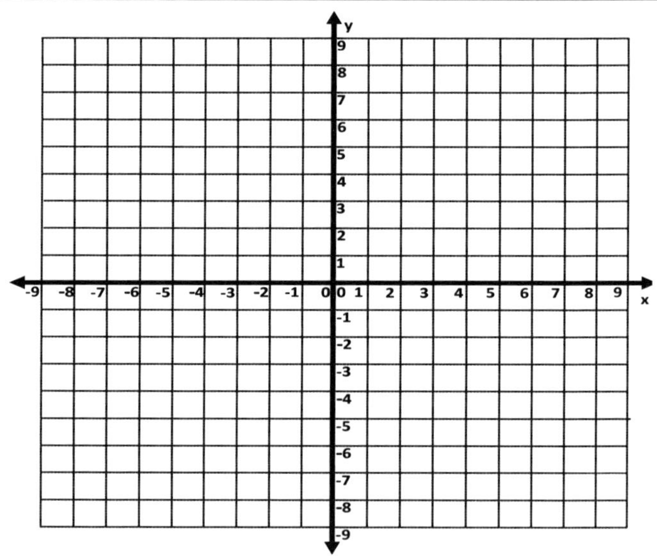

Inverse Functions

Given the equation below, find the inverse.

$f(x) = x^2 + 3$ for $x \geq 0$

Writing Equations of Lines

Write the equation of the line in slope intercept form with the given properties.

x	-5	-2	1
y	9	4	-1

Vocabulary

Parallel Lines
Perpendicular Lines
Scatter Plot
Parent Function
Transformations
Representations
Slope
Discrete Function
Continuous Function

____________________ Models, graphs, equations, tables and verbal descriptions of data.

____________________ Lines whose slopes are negative reciprocals.

____________________ The most basic function in a family of functions.

____________________ Ways to manipulate a graphs, size, shape, position or orientation.

Algebra 2 Builder # 23

Name:_______________________________

Discrete/Continuous Functions

Write and graph the functions described. Express the domain and range in set builder notation. State if the function is discrete or continuous.

Chris drops $3 into his piggy bank every week. The function p(x) gives the total amount of money in the piggy bank after x weeks.

Function:

Domain:

Range:

Discrete or Continuous:

Transformations

Graph: $y = 2^x + 1$

Name the parent function:

Explain the transformation in words:

Inverse Functions

Given the equation below find the inverse.

$f(x) = (x-2)^2 + 1$ for $x \leq 0$

Writing Equations of Lines

A mechanic charges $20.00 an hour, h for labor plus parts. If the parts cost $217.00, write a linear equation that will find the total cost, c.

Vocabulary

Parallel Lines
Perpendicular Lines
Scatter Plot
Parent Function
Transformations
Representations
Slope
Discrete Function
Continuous Function

_________________ The ratio of the vertical change (rise) to the horizontal change (run).

_________________ A graph with points plotted to find the relationship between two sets of data.

_________________ Lines that have the same slope.

_________________ A function whose graph has not gaps or breaks.

Algebra 2 Builder # 24

Name:_______________________________

Discrete/Continuous Functions

Write and graph the functions described. Express the domain and range in set builder notation. State if the function is discrete or continuous.

The open bathroom faucet uses 3 gallons per minute. The function f(x) gives the volume of water used after x minutes.

Function:

Domain:

Range:

Discrete or Continuous:

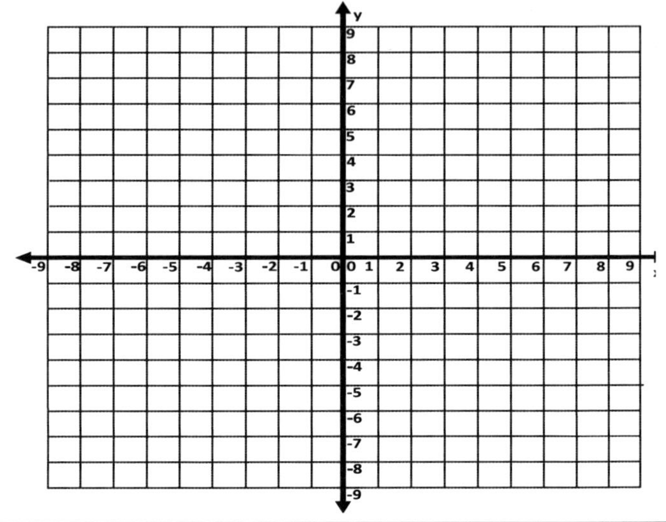

Transformations

Graph: $f(x) = \frac{1}{x-2}$

Name the parent function:

Explain the transformation in words:

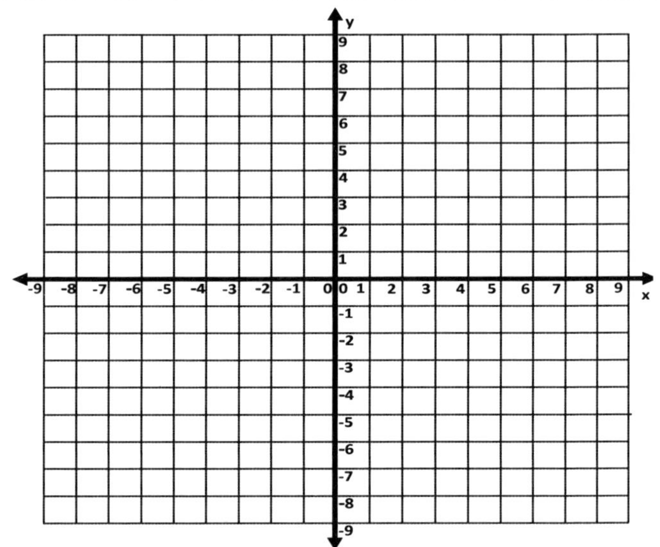

Inverse Functions

Given the graph below, graph the inverse.

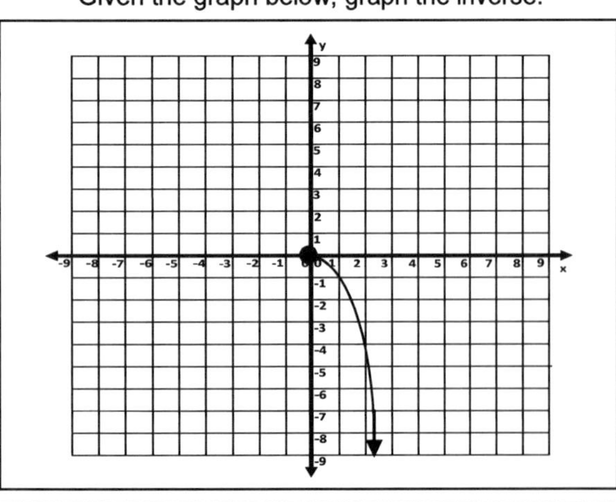

Writing Equations of Lines

The river is rising at a constant rate. On day 5, the river is at 6 feet, and on day 10 the river is at 8 feet. Write a linear equation to find the height of the river, h after d, days.

Vocabulary

Parallel Lines
Perpendicular Lines
Scatter Plot
Parent Function
Transformations
Representations
Slope
Discrete Function
Continuous Function

____________________ Lines whose slopes are negative reciprocals.

____________________ The most basic function in a family of functions.

____________________ Models, graphs, equations, tables and verbal descriptions of data.

____________________ Ways to manipulate a graphs, size, shape, position or orientation.

Algebra 2 Builder # 25

Name:______________________________

System of Equations

Solve the system of equations by graphing, then classify the system as consistent and independent, consistent and dependent, or inconsistent.

$3x + 2y = 6$
$2x - 4y = 20$

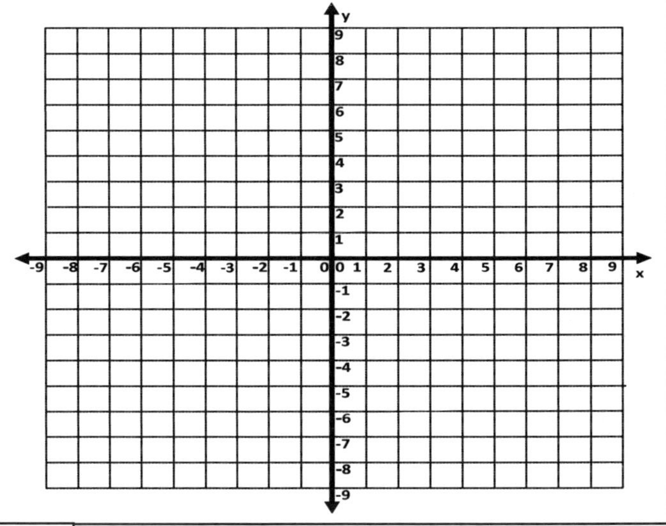

Factoring

Factor completely.

$3x^2 + 6x$ $\qquad$ $x^2 - 16$

Simplify Radicals

Simplify the radical.

$\sqrt{8}$ $\qquad$ $2\sqrt{40}$

Vocabulary

Vertex form of a quadratic function
System of Equations
Linear programming
Discriminant
Radical
Standard form of a quadratic function
Complex Number
Polynomial

__________________ a part of the quadratic formula that is used to determine the number and type of roots of a quadratic equation.

__________________ a method of finding a minimum or maximum value of a linear function, that satisfies a given set of constraints.

__________________ an expression in the form $\sqrt{b}$ or the $\sqrt[n]{b}$ where b is a number or an expression, and n is an integer greater than 2.

__________________ a set of two or more equations that have two or more variables.

Graphing System of Inequalities

Graph the system of inequalitites.

$x > 4$
$y \leq 2$

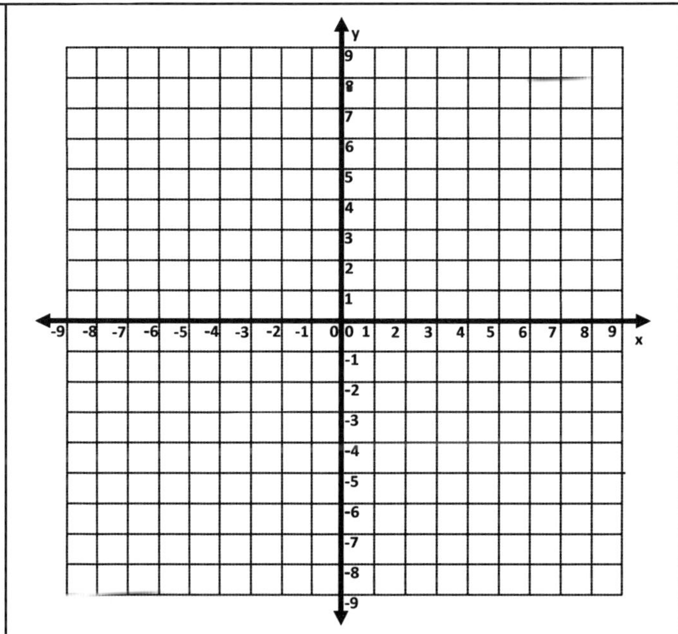

Algebra 2 Builder # 26   Name:______________________

System of Equations

Solve the system of equations by substitution, then classify the system as consistent and independent, consistent and dependent, or inconsistent.

5x + y = 4
6x – y = 7

Solve the system of equations by elimination, then classify the system as consistent and independent, consistent and dependent, or inconsistent.

x + y = -4
3x + y = 6

Factoring

Factor completely.

$x^2 – 25$ $x^2 – 5x – 6$

Simplify Radicals

Simplify the radical.

$\sqrt{32}$ $4\sqrt{27}$

Vocabulary

- Vertex form of a quadratic function
- System of Equations
- Linear programming
- Discriminant
- Radical
- Standard form of a quadratic function
- Complex Number
- Polynomial

______________ a monomial or a sum of monomials.

______________ a number written in the form a + bi where a and b are real numbers and i = $\sqrt{-1}$.

______________ a quadratic function written in the form f(x) = a(x – h)^2 + k.

______________ a quadratic function written in the form f(x) = ax^2 + bx + c

Graphing System of Inequalities

Graph the system of inequalitites.

$y > |x|$
y – 5x ≤ 5

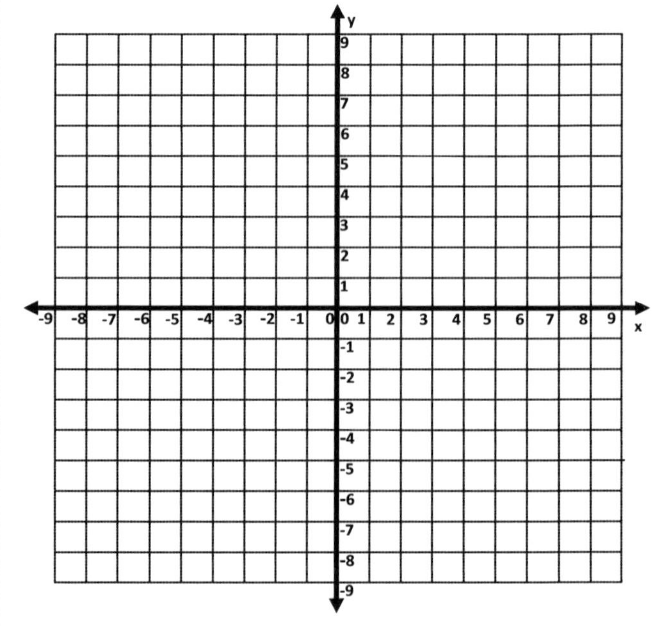

Algebra 2 Builder # 27

Name:______________________________

System of Equations

Solve the system of equations by substitution, then classify the system as consistent and independent, consistent and dependent, or inconsistent.

$2x - 4y = -8$
$2y = x + 4$

Solve the system of equations by elimination, then classify the system as consistent and independent, consistent and dependent, or inconsistent.

$3x + 4y = 7$

$6x - 8y = -18$

Factoring

Factor completely.

$5x^3 + 7x^2 + x$

$x^4 - 16$

Simplify Radicals

Simplify the radical.

$\frac{\sqrt{6}}{\sqrt{5}}$

$\frac{\sqrt{18}}{\sqrt{4}}$

Vocabulary

Vertex form of a quadratic function
System of Equations
Linear programming
Discriminant
Radical
Standard form of a quadratic function
Complex Number
Polynomial

______________________ a part of the quadratic formula that is used to determine the number and type of roots of a quadratic equation.

______________________ a method of finding a minimum or maximum value of a linear function, that satisfies a given set of constraints.

______________________ an expression in the form $\sqrt{b}$ or the $\sqrt[n]{b}$ where b is a number or an expression, and n is an integer greater than 2.

______________________ a set of two or more equations that have two or more variables.

Graphing System of Inequalities

Graph the system of inequalitites.

$y - 2x < 7$
$y + 2x > -1$

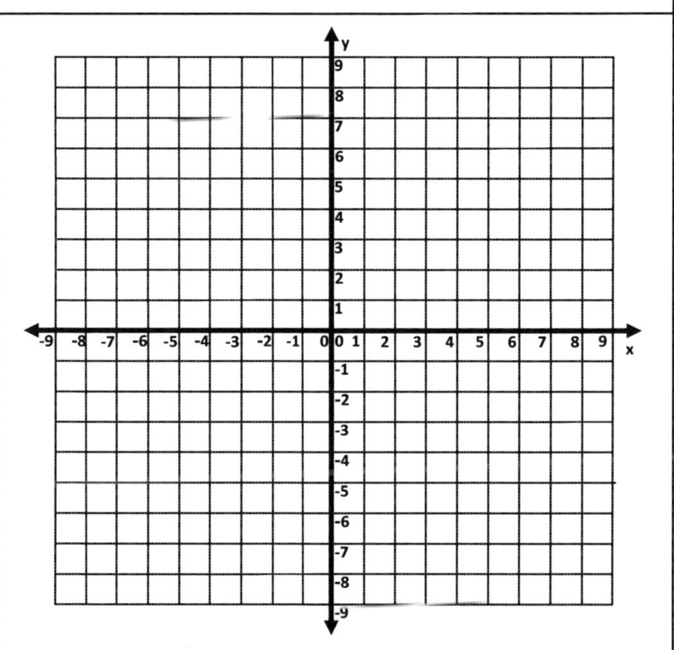

Algebra 2 Builder # 28

Name:______________________________

System of Equations

Show the augmented matrix you would put into your calculator. What is the solution when you use **rref** on your calculator?

$7x - 5y = 20$
$-8x - 3y = 12$

Write the matrix equation for the system then use the inverse matrix to solve the system.

$y = 2x - 6$
$5x = y + 9$

Factoring

Factor completely.

$6x^2 + 17x + 12$ $\qquad$ $x^4 - 4x^2$

Simplify Radicals

Simplify the radical.

$$\frac{2+\sqrt{5}}{3-\sqrt{5}}$$

Vocabulary

- Vertex form of a quadratic function
- System of Equations
- Linear programming
- Discriminant
- Radical
- Standard form of a quadratic function
- Complex Number
- Polynomial

____________________ a monomial or a sum of monomials.

____________________ a quadratic function written in the form $f(x) = ax^2 + bx + c$

____________________ a number written in the form a + bi where a and b are real numbers and i = $\sqrt{-1}$.

____________________ a quadratic function written in the form $f(x) = a(x - h)^2 + k$.

Graphing System of Inequalities

Graph the system of inequalitites.

$y < -|x - 2|$
$x - 2y \leq 4$

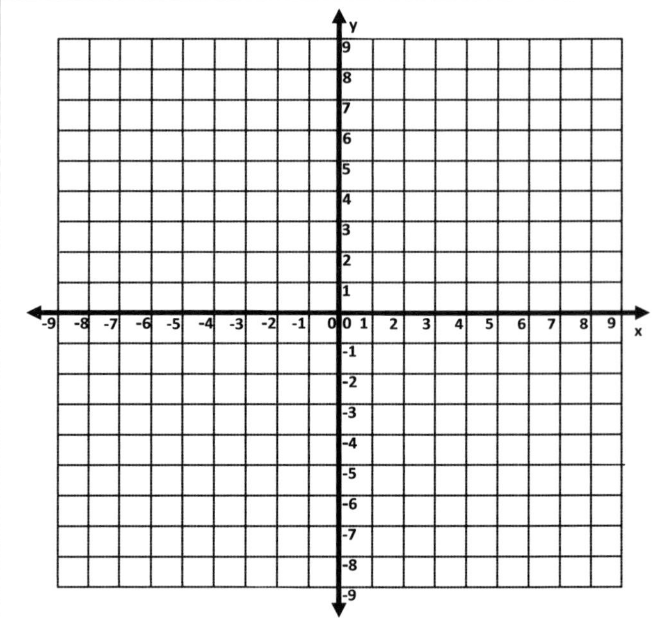

Algebra 2 Builder # 29 Name:_______________________

System of Equations

Lyndalyn and Amanda are going to the movies with friends. Lyndalyn bought 3 bags of popcorn and 5 candy bars for $21.00. Amanda bought 5 bags of popcorn and 5 candy bars for $32.50. How much does each bag of popcorn and each candy bar cost? Solve using the elimination method.

Factoring

Factor completely.

$x^2 - 6x + 9$ $4x^2 - 4y^2$

Simplify Radicals

Simplify the radical.

$$\frac{4-\sqrt{3}}{-2+\sqrt{3}}$$

Vocabulary

Vertex form of a quadratic function
System of Equations
Linear programming
Discriminant
Radical
Standard form of a quadratic function
Complex Number
Polynomial

_______________ a method of finding a minimum or maximum value of a linear function, that satisfies a given set of constraints.

_______________ a part of the quadratic formula that is used to determine the number and type of roots of a quadratic equation.

_______________ an expression in the form $\sqrt{b}$ or the $\sqrt[n]{b}$ where b is a number or an expression, and n is an integer greater than 2.

_______________ a set of two or more equations that have two or more variables.

Linear Programming

Find the minimum value of the objective function subject to the the given constraints.

Objective Function: C = 2x + 5y

Constraints: $x \geq 0$ $y \leq 0$
$x \leq 6$ $y \geq \frac{1}{2}x - 4$

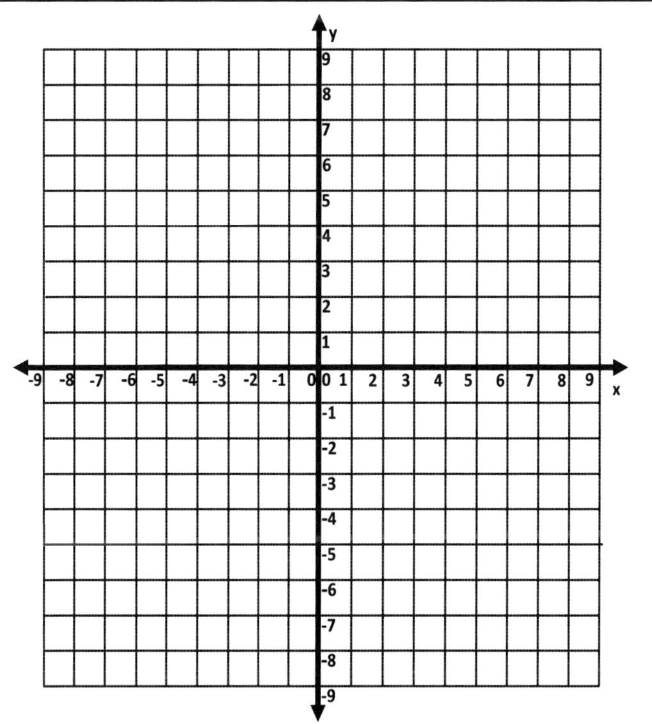

Algebra 2 Builder # 30 Name:______________________

System of Equations

At the theater, orchestra seats cost $20.00 more than balcony seats. If a company buys 25 orchestra seats and 30 balcony seats, the total cost would be $1875.00. What would be the price for one orchestra seat and one balcony seat? Solve using the substitution method.

Factoring

Factor completely.

$x^3 - 8$ $x^3 + 8$

Simplify Radicals

Simplify the radical.

$$\frac{-2-4\sqrt{7}}{-5-2\sqrt{7}}$$

Vocabulary

Vertex form of a quadratic function
System of Equations
Linear programming
Discriminant
Radical
Standard form of a quadratic function
Complex Number
Polynomial

__________________ a quadratic function written in the form $f(x) = a(x - h)^2 + k$.

__________________ a monomial or a sum of monomials.

__________________ a number written in the form a + bi where a and b are real numbers and $i = \sqrt{-1}$.

__________________ a quadratic function written in the form $f(x) = ax^2 + bx + c$

Linear Programming

Find the maximum value of the objective function subject to the the given constraints.

Objective Function: P = 2x + 3y

Constraints: $x \geq 2$ $y \geq 3$

$$y \leq -\frac{1}{2}x + 7$$

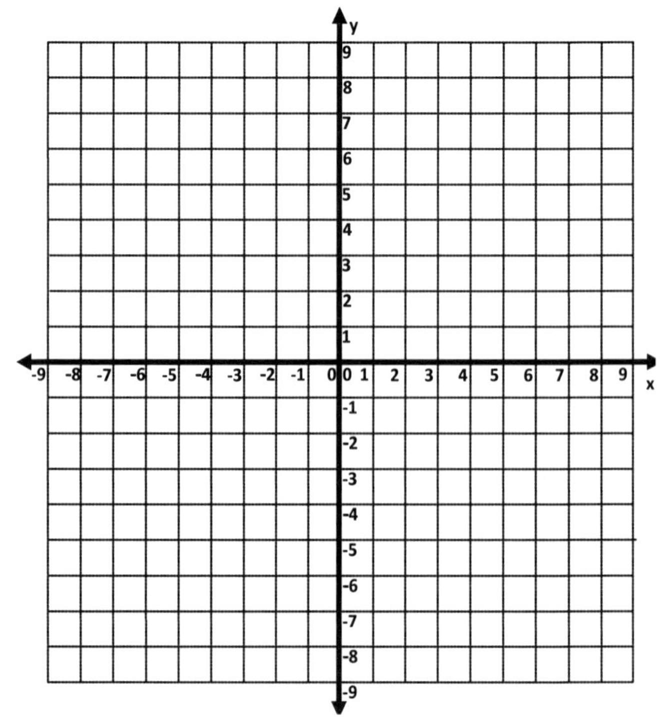

Algebra 2 Builder # 31 Name:______________________________

<table>
<tr><td>System of Equations</td><td colspan="3">Mrs. West invested $6000.00 into 2 accounts. One account earns 1.5% simple interest and the other account earns 2% simple interest. How much did she invest in each account if in 1 year she earned $110.00 in interest? Solve using an augmented matrix.</td></tr>
<tr><td>Factoring</td><td>Factor completely.
$2x^3 + 54$ $-3x^3 + 24$</td><td>Simplify Radicals</td><td>Simplify the radical.
$\sqrt{-25}$ $2\sqrt{-8}$</td></tr>
<tr><td>Vocabulary</td><td>Vertex form of a quadratic function
System of Equations
Linear programming
Discriminant
Radical
Standard form of a quadratic function
Complex Number
Polynomial</td><td colspan="2">__________________ a part of the quadratic formula that is used to determine the number and type of roots of a quadratic equation.
__________________ an expression in the form $\sqrt{b}$ or the $\sqrt[n]{b}$ where b is a number or an expression, and n is an integer greater than 2.
__________________ a set of two or more equations that have two or more variables.
__________________ a method of finding a minimum or maximum value of a linear function, that satisfies a given set of constraints.</td></tr>
<tr><td>Linear Programming</td><td>Zach is the manager at a seafood restaurant. Zach orders at most 100 fish every day. He needs at least 40 but no more than 70 catfish and at least 30 tilapia. Catfish cost $5 each and tilapia cost $4 each. How many of each fish should he order to minimize his daily cost?</td><td colspan="2">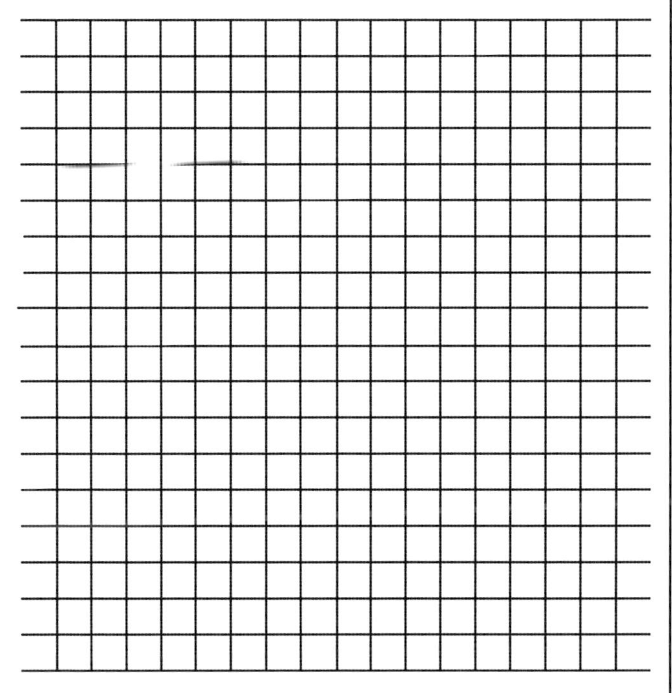</td></tr>
</table>

Algebra 2 Builder # 32 Name:________________________

System of Equations

Mrs. McDonald has a farm with ducks and pigs. There are 27 heads and 84 legs. How many ducks and pigs are on Mrs. McDonalds farm? Solve using an inverse matrix.

Factoring

Factor completely.

$5x^3 - 2x^2 - 20x + 8$

Simplify Radicals

Simplify the radical.

$3\sqrt{-27}$ $-4\sqrt{-54}$

Vocabulary

Vertex form of a quadratic function
System of Equations
Linear programming
Discriminant
Radical
Standard form of a quadratic function
Complex Number
Polynomial

____________________ a quadratic function written in the form $f(x) = a(x - h)^2 + k$.

____________________ a monomial or a sum of monomials

____________________ a quadratic function written in the form $f(x) = ax^2 + bx + c$.

____________________ a number written in the form a + bi where a and b are real numbers and $i = \sqrt{-1}$.

Linear Programming

Renee makes jewelry and it takes her 2 hours to make a bracelet and 4 hours to make a necklace. She can work at most 120 hours a month. It cost $2 to make a bracelet and $8 to make a necklace. Renee wants to spend no more than $160 a month on supplies. A local store buys 5 of each type of jewelry each month. If Renee makes a profit of $15 on a bracelet and $40 on a necklace, how many bracelets and necklaces should she make each month to maximize her profit?

Algebra 2 Builder # 33

Name:______________________________

Simplify Radicals	$2\sqrt{3} + 3\sqrt{3}$	**Complex Numbers**	Write the expression as a complex number in standard form. $(5 - 6i) - (-2 - 3i)$
Factoring Quadratics	Solve by factoring. $x^2 - 4x - 5 = 0$	**Completing the Square**	Solve by completing the square. $x^2 - 4x - 5 = 0$
Quadratic Formula	Solve by the Quadratic Formula. $x^2 - 4x - 5 = 0$	**Discriminant**	Find the discriminant, then determine the nature of the roots. $x^2 + 4x + 4 = 0$

Vocabulary

Zero(s) of a Function	______________	For a quadratic equation, the expression under the radical in the quadratic formula.
Axis of Symmetry	______________	The shape of the graph of a quadratic function.
Parabola	______________	Value(s) of x for which f(x) = 0.
Discriminant	______________	The line that divides the graph into equal halves.
Rational Number		
Irrational Number		
Conjugate		
Vertex of a Parabola		

Algebra 2 Builder # 34 Name:______________________________

Simplify Radicals	$\sqrt{12}+\sqrt{27}$	**Complex Numbers**	Write the expression as a complex number in standard form. $3(2-4i)-2(3+5i)$
Factoring Quadratics	Solve by factoring. $x^2-4x-21=0$	**Completing the Square**	Solve by completing the square. $x^2-4x-21=0$
Quadratic Formula	Solve by the Quadratic Formula. $x^2-4x-21=0$	**Discriminant**	Find the discriminant, then determine the nature of the roots. $3x^2+7x+8=0$

Vocabulary	Zero(s) of a Function Axis of Symmetry Parabola Discriminant Rational Number Irrational Number Conjugate Vertex of a Parabola	________________ A number that can be expressed as the ratio of two integers and the denominator cannot equal zero. ________________ Two binomials that are the same except the middle signs are opposite. ________________ A number that neither repeats or terminates. ________________ The maximum or minimum point on a parabola.

Algebra 2 Builder # 35

Name:______________________________

Simplify Radicals	$\sqrt{16x^2y} - x\sqrt{25y}$	**Complex Numbers**	Write the expression as a complex number in standard form. $(2 - 3i)^2$
Factoring Quadratics	Solve by factoring. $2x^2 + 5x - 12 = 0$	**Completing the Square**	Solve by completing the square. $x^2 - 6x = 7$
Quadratic Formula	Solve by the Quadratic Formula. $3x^2 - 4x + 1 = 0$	**Discriminant**	Find the discriminant, then determine the nature of the roots. $2x^2 - 5x - 3 = 0$

Vocabulary

Zero(s) of a Function
Axis of Symmetry
Parabola
Discriminant
Rational Number
Irrational Number
Conjugate
Vertex of a Parabola

_________________ The shape of the graph of a quadratic function.

_________________ For a quadratic equation, the expression under the radical in the quadratic formula.

_________________ The line that divides the graph into equal halves.

_________________ Value(s) of x for which f(x) = 0.

Algebra 2 Builder # 36

Name:______________________________

Simplify Radicals	$2\sqrt{27x^3 y^5} - 4xy\sqrt{3xy^3}$	**Complex Numbers**	Write the expression as a complex number in standard form. $\frac{3-2i}{1+i}$
Factoring Quadratics	Solve by factoring. $15x^2 + 34x + 15 = 0$	**Completing the Square**	Solve by completing the square. $x^2 - 6x + 3 = 0$
Quadratic Formula	Solve by the Quadratic Formula. $x^2 + 2x + 3 = 0$	**Discriminant**	Find the discriminant, then determine the nature of the roots. $2x^2 - 3x - 4 = 0$

Vocabulary

Zero(s) of a Function
Axis of Symmetry
Parabola
Discriminant
Rational Number
Irrational Number
Conjugate
Vertex of a Parabola

_______________ The maximum or minimum point on a parabola.

_______________ Two binomials that are the same except the middle signs are opposite.

_______________ A number that can be expressed as the ratio of two integers and the denominator cannot equal zero.

_______________ A number that neither repeats or terminates.

Algebra 2 Builder # 37 Name:______________________________

Simplify Radicals	$\sqrt[3]{18} \cdot \sqrt[3]{6}$	**Complex Numbers**	Write the expression as a complex number in standard form. $\dfrac{4-3i}{-2+i}$
Solve by Factoring	Find the real zeros. $x^4 - 16 = 0$	**Completing the Square**	Solve by completing the square. $x^2 - 4x + 5 = 0$
Quadratic Formula	Solve by the Quadratic Formula. $2x^2 - 5x = -7$	**Discriminant**	Find the discriminant, then determine the nature of the roots. $\frac{1}{2}x^2 + 8x - 4 = 0$

Vocabulary	Zero(s) of a Function Axis of Symmetry Parabola Discriminant Rational Number Irrational Number Conjugate Vertex of a Parabola	______________ The shape of the graph of a quadratic function. ______________ Value(s) of x for which f(x) = 0. ______________ The line that divides the graph into equal halves. ______________ For a quadratic equation, the expression under the radical in the quadratic formula.

Algebra 2 Builder # 38 **Name:**___________________________

Simplify Radicals	$\sqrt[3]{4x^2y} \cdot \sqrt[3]{6xy^4}$	**Complex Numbers**	Write the expression as a complex number in standard form. $\frac{-3-2i}{1-3i}$
Solve by Factoring	Find the real zeros. $x^3 - 8 = 0$	**Completing the Square**	Solve by completing the square. $x^2 - 5x + 2 = 0$
Quadratic Formula	Solve by the Quadratic Formula. $3x^2 + 6x = 5$	**Discriminant**	Find the discriminant, then determine the nature of the roots. $x^2 - 5x + 2 = 0$

Vocabulary

Zero(s) of a Function
Axis of Symmetry
Parabola
Discriminant
Rational Number
Irrational Number
Conjugate
Vertex of a Parabola

_______________ A number that neither repeats or terminates.

_______________ The maximum or minimum point on a parabola.

_______________ A number that can be expressed as the ratio of two integers and the denominator cannot equal zero.

_______________ Two binomials that are the same except the middle signs are opposite.

Algebra 2 Builder # 39

Name:____________________________

<table>
<tr><td>Simplify Radicals</td><td>$\sqrt[3]{\frac{2}{3}}$</td><td>Complex Numbers</td><td>Write the expression as a complex number in standard form.
$\frac{(3+i)-(2+3i)}{(1-3i)-(3-2i)}$</td></tr>
<tr><td>Solve by Factoring</td><td>Find the real zeros.
$x^3 + x^2 - 4x - 4 = 0$</td><td>Completing the Square</td><td>Solve by completing the square.
$5x^2 + 20x = 10$</td></tr>
<tr><td>Quadratic Formula</td><td>Solve by the Quadratic Formula.
$\frac{x-1}{x-3} = \frac{2}{x+1}$</td><td>Discriminant</td><td>Find the discriminant, then determine the nature of the roots.
$x^2 - 6x + 9 = 0$</td></tr>
<tr><td>Vocabulary</td><td>Zero(s) of a Function
Axis of Symmetry
Parabola
Discriminant
Rational Number
Irrational Number
Conjugate
Vertex of a Parabola</td><td colspan="2">________________ The shape of the graph of a quadratic function.
________________ Value(s) of x for which f(x) = 0.
________________ The line that divides the graph into equal halves.
________________ For a quadratic equation, the expression under the radical in the quadratic formula.</td></tr>
</table>

Algebra 2 Builder # 40

Name:____________________________

Simplify Radicals

$\sqrt[3]{\frac{3y^2}{4x}}$

Complex Numbers

Write the expression as a complex number in standard form.

$\frac{2(1-i)-3(1+2i)}{3(2+3i)-(3+4i)}$

Solve by Factoring

Find the real zeros.

$2x^3 + 5x^2 + 6x + 15 = 0$

Completing the Square

Solve by completing the square

$\frac{1}{2}x^2 + 4x = -2$

Quadratic Formula

Solve by the Quadratic Formula

$\frac{x-2}{2x+3} = \frac{x-5}{x+3}$

Discriminant

Find the discriminant, then determine the nature of the roots.

$5x^2 + 8x + 9 = 0$

Vocabulary

Zero(s) of a Function Axis of Symmetry Parabola Discriminant Rational Number Irrational Number Conjugate Vertex of a Parabola	____________	A number that neither repeats or terminates.
	____________	Two binomials that are the same except the middle signs are opposite.
	____________	The maximum or minimum point on a parabola.
	____________	A number that can be expressed as the ratio of two integers and the denominator cannot equal zero.

Algebra 2 Builder # 41

Name:______________________________

Vertex Form

Write in vertex form.

$f(x) = x^2 - 4x + 5$

Exponent Rules

$x^5 \cdot x^3$

$\frac{x^8}{x^2}$

Solve Quadratic Inequalities

Solve algebraically.

$x^2 - 8x < 0$

Vertex

Use $-\frac{b}{2a}$ to find the vertex.

$f(x) = x^2 - 2x + 3$

Graph Quadratics

$f(x) = (x - 6)(x - 2)$

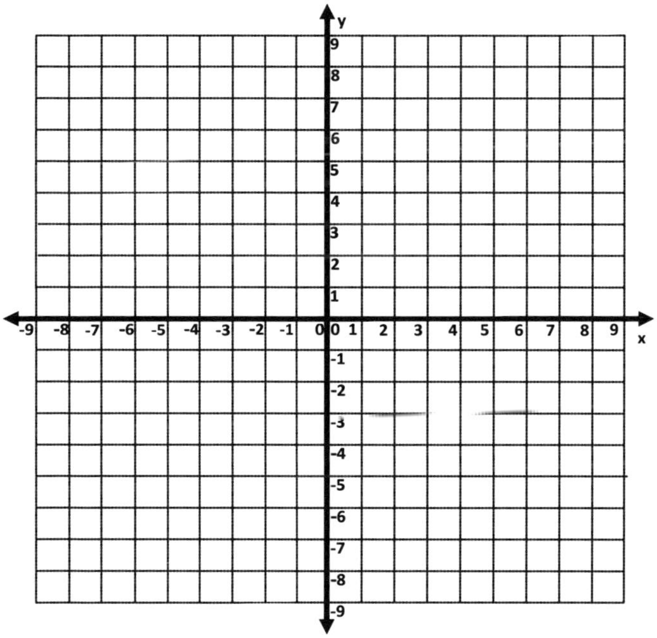

Vocabulary

Product of Powers Property

Power of a Power Property

Power of a Quotient Property

Quotient of Powers Property

Power of a Product Property

Negative Exponent Property

Zero Exponent Property

____________________________ $a^m a^n = a^{m+n}$

____________________________ $\frac{a^m}{a^n} = a^{m-n}$ $a \neq 0$

____________________________ $(ab)^m = a^m b^m$

____________________________ $a^0 = 1$ $a \neq 0$

Algebra 2 Builder # 42

Name:______________________________

Vertex Form	Write in vertex form. $f(x) = x^2 - 8x - 7$	**Exponent Rules**	$(x^5)^2$ $3x^0$
Solve Quadratic Inequalities	Solve algebraically. $x^2 - 5x \geq 6$	**Vertex**	Use $-\frac{b}{2a}$ to find the vertex. $y = 2x^2 + 4x + 9$
Graph Quadratics	$y = (x - 2)^2 - 4$		Coordinate grid: x from -9 to 9, y from -9 to 9

Vocabulary

Product of Powers Property
Power of a Power Property
Power of a Quotient Property
Quotient of Powers Property
Power of a Product Property
Negative Exponent Property
Zero Exponent Property

______________________ $a^{-n} = \frac{1}{a^n}$ or $\frac{1}{a^{-n}} = a^n$ $a \neq 0$

______________________ $\left(\frac{a}{b}\right)^n = \frac{a^n}{b^n}$ $b \neq 0$

______________________ $(a^m)^n = a^{mn}$

______________________ $\frac{a^m}{a^n} = a^{m-n}$ $a \neq 0$

Algebra 2 Builder # 43 Name:______________________________

Vertex Form	Write in vertex form. $y = 2x^2 + 8x + 5$	**Exponent Rules**	$(2xy^2)^3$ $(5x^2y)^2$
Solve Quadratic Inequalities	Solve algebraically. $x^2 \leq 4x$	**Vertex**	Use $-\frac{b}{2a}$ to find the vertex. $f(x) = 3x^2 + 6x + 7$
Graph Quadratics	$y = x^2 + 4x + 4$		[coordinate grid, x and y from -9 to 9]

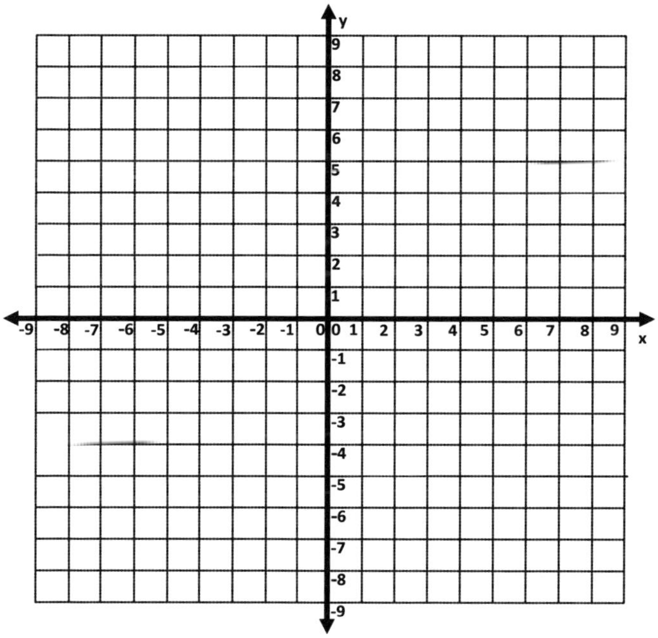

Vocabulary

Product of Powers Property	______________	$(ab)^m = a^m b^m$
Power of a Power Property		
Power of a Quotient Property	______________	$a^0 = 1 \quad a \neq 0$
Quotient of Powers Property	______________	$a^m a^n = a^{m+n}$
Power of a Product Property		
Negative Exponent Property	______________	$\frac{a^m}{a^n} = a^{m-n} \quad a \neq 0$
Zero Exponent Property		

Algebra 2 Builder # 44

Name:____________________________

Vertex Form	Write in vertex form. $f(x) = -3x^2 - 6x - 5$	**Exponent Rules**	$(x^{-3}y^{-4})^{-2}$ $\qquad \frac{x^{-5}}{y^{-3}}$
Solve Quadratic Inequalities	Solve algebraically. $2x^2 - 2x - 4 > 0$	**Vertex**	Use $-\frac{b}{2a}$ to find the vertex. $y = x^2 - 5x + 7$
Graph Quadratics	$f(x) = -x^2 - 2x + 8$		

Vocabulary

- Product of Powers Property
- Power of a Power Property
- Power of a Quotient Property
- Quotient of Powers Property
- Power of a Product Property
- Negative Exponent Property
- Zero Exponent Property

________________ $\frac{a^m}{a^n} = a^{m-n}$ $\quad a \neq 0$

________________ $\left(\frac{a}{b}\right)^n = \frac{a^n}{b^n}$ $\quad b \neq 0$

________________ $a^{-n} = \frac{1}{a^n}$ or $\frac{1}{a^{-n}} = a^n$ $\quad a \neq 0$

________________ $(a^m)^n = a^{mn}$

Algebra 2 Builder # 45 Name:______________________________

Vertex Form	Write in vertex form. $f(x) = \frac{1}{2}x^2 + 4x + 5$	**Exponent Rules**	$\frac{2x^{-2}y^{-3}}{4x^{6}y^{-2}}$ $\frac{9x^{-6}y^{4}}{3x^{-2}y^{0}}$
Solve Quadratic Inequalities	Solve algebraically. $\frac{1}{2}x^2 + 5x > -8$	**Vertex**	Use $-\frac{b}{2a}$ to find the vertex. $y = -2x^2 - 4x + 7$
Graph Quadratics	$f(x) = (x - 3)(x + 1)$		

Vocabulary

Product of Powers Property
Power of a Power Property
Power of a Quotient Property
Quotient of Powers Property
Power of a Product Property
Negative Exponent Property
Zero Exponent Property

______________________ $a^0 = 1 \quad a \neq 0$

______________________ $\frac{a^m}{a^n} = a^{m-n} \quad a \neq 0$

______________________ $a^m a^n = a^{m+n}$

______________________ $(ab)^m = a^m b^m$

Algebra 2 Builder # 46

Name:____________________________

Vertex Form

Write in vertex form.

$y = -\frac{1}{3}x^2 + 2x - 5$

Exponent Rules

$(2xy^{-2})(3x^2y^{-3})^{-2}$

$(x^{1/2}y^{1/4})^2$

Solve Quadratic Inequalities

Solve algebraically.

$2x^2 < 6x + 20$

Vertex

Use $-\frac{b}{2a}$ to find the vertex.

$f(x) = x^2 + 3x + 8$

Graph Quadratics

$y = -(x-1)^2 - 3$

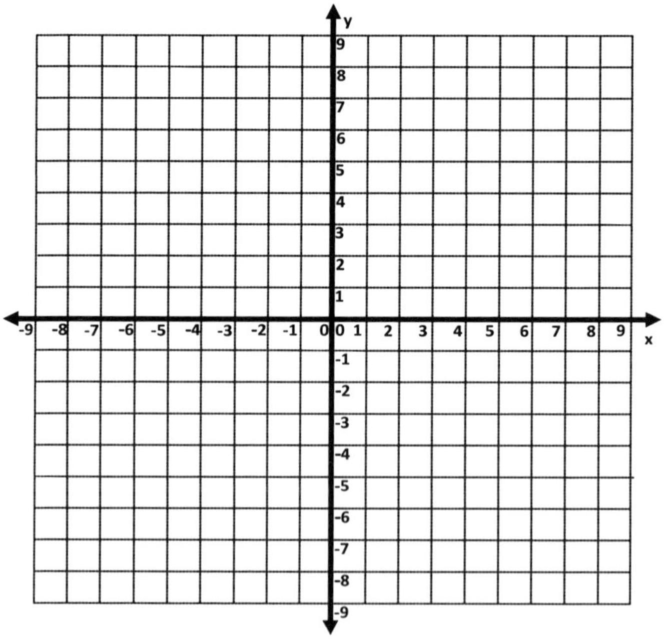

Vocabulary

Product of Powers Property	________________	$a^{-n} = \frac{1}{a^n}$ or $\frac{1}{a^{-n}} = a^n \quad a \neq 0$
Power of a Power Property		
Power of a Quotient Property	________________	$\frac{a^m}{a^n} = a^{m-n} \quad a \neq 0$
Quotient of Powers Property		
Power of a Product Property	________________	$\left(\frac{a}{b}\right)^n = \frac{a^n}{b^n} \quad b \neq 0$
Negative Exponent Property		
Zero Exponent Property	________________	$(a^m)^n = a^{mn}$

Algebra 2 Builder # 47

Name:______________________________

Vertex Form

Write in vertex form.

$f(x) = x^2 - 5x + 7$

Exponent Rules

$(5x^0y^3)(-3x^{-3}y^{-2})^{-2}$

$(x^{-4})^{1/2}$

Solve Quadratic Inequalities

Solve algebraically.

$4x^2 - 5x + 4 \le 3x^2 - 7x + 7$

Vertex

Use $-\frac{b}{2a}$ to find the vertex.

$f(x) = \frac{1}{2}x^2 - 4x + 2$

Graph Quadratics

$y = x^2 - 2x - 3$

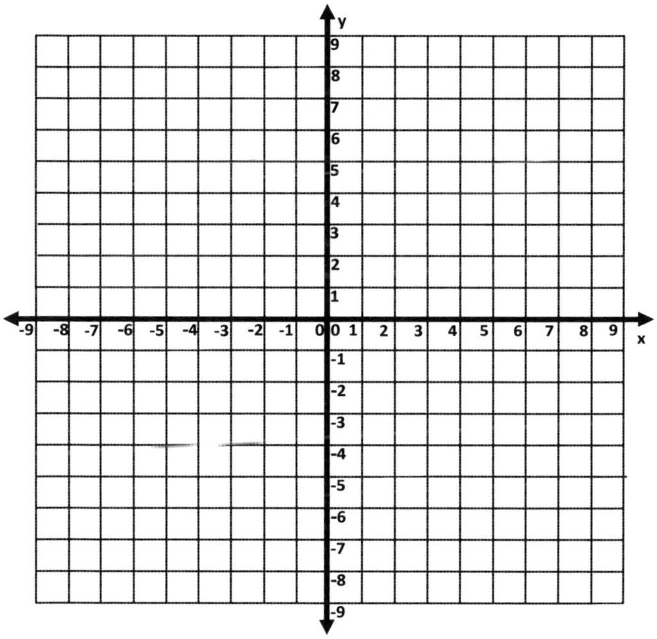

Vocabulary

Product of Powers Property
Power of a Power Property
Power of a Quotient Property
Quotient of Powers Property
Power of a Product Property
Negative Exponent Property
Zero Exponent Property

____________________ $a^m a^n = a^{m+n}$

____________________ $a^0 = 1 \quad a \neq 0$

____________________ $\frac{a^m}{a^n} = a^{m-n} \quad a \neq 0$

____________________ $(ab)^m = a^m b^m$

Algebra 2 Builder # 48

Name:______________________________

Vertex Form

Write in vertex form.

$f(x) = 2x^2 - 3x + 5$

Exponent Rules

$\left(\frac{x^2y^{-3}}{4x^3y^2}\right)^{-2}$

$\frac{x^{2/3}\ y}{4x^{1/3}\ y^{1/2}}$

Solve Quadratic Inequalities

Solve algebraically.

$2x^2 + 7x + 1 \geq 2x + 4$

Vertex

Use $-\frac{b}{2a}$ to find the vertex.

$f(x) = -\frac{1}{4}x^2 + 8x + 2$

Graph Quadratics

$f(x) = -2(x-3)^2 + 1$

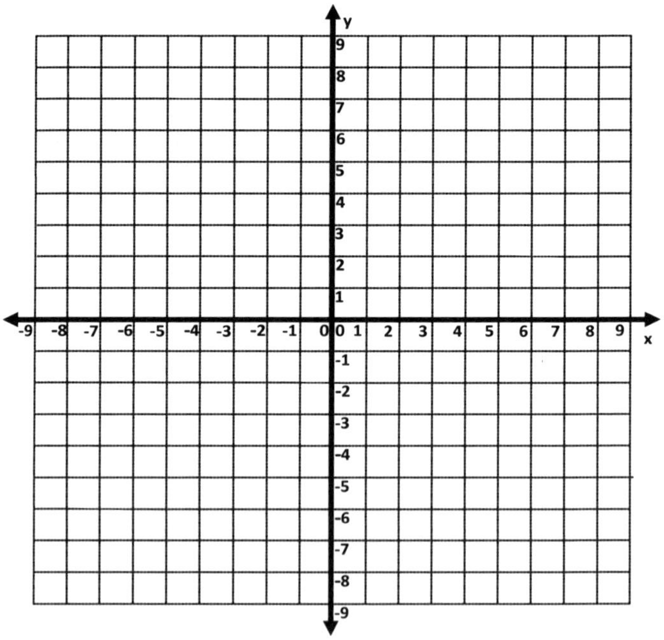

Vocabulary

Product of Powers Property	______________	$a^{-n} = \frac{1}{a^n}$ or $\frac{1}{a^{-n}} = a^n$ $a \neq 0$
Power of a Power Property		
Power of a Quotient Property	______________	$(a^m)^n = a^{mn}$
Quotient of Powers Property		
Power of a Product Property	______________	$\frac{a^m}{a^n} = a^{m-n}$ $a \neq 0$
Negative Exponent Property		
Zero Exponent Property	______________	$\left(\frac{a}{b}\right)^n = \frac{a^n}{b^n}$ $b \neq 0$

Algebra 2 Builder # 49

Name:______________________________

Solve Radicals by Graphing	Use a graphing calculator. Round to the nearest hundredth. $\sqrt{x+2} = 3$	**Solve Radicals Algebraically**	Check for extraneous solutions. $\sqrt{x+2} = 4$
Square Root Inequalities	Solve using a table on the calculator. $3\sqrt{x} - 1 \geq 8$	**Rational Expressions**	Simplify. $\frac{x^2 - 5x + 6}{x^2 - 6x + 8}$
Inverse Functions	Find $f^{-1}(x)$. Find the domain and range of f(x) and $f^{-1}(x)$. Write in set builder and interval notation. $f(x) = \sqrt{x+3}$	**Long Division**	$(3x^4 + 4x^3 - 3x + 1) \div (3x + 4)$

Vocabulary

Zero(s) of a Function
Domain
Range
Extraneous Solution
Radical
Radicand
End Behavior
Inverse Function

____________________ a function that results from interchanging the domain and range values of a one to one function.

____________________ is the set of first elements in ordered pair or table.

____________________ is the set of second elements in ordered pair or table.

____________________ value(s) of x for which f(x) = 0.

Algebra 2 Builder # 50

Name:______________________________

Solve Radicals by Graphing	Use a graphing calculator. Round to the nearest hundredth. $\sqrt{2x-8} = 2.3$	**Solve Radicals Algebraically**	Check for extraneous solutions. $\sqrt{4x+2} - 5 = 3$
Square Root Inequalities	Solve using a table on the calculator. $\sqrt{x-3} \le 1$	**Rational Expressions**	Simplify. $\frac{x^2-1}{x^2+3x-4} \cdot \frac{x^2+6x+8}{x^3-1}$
Inverse Functions	Find $f^{-1}(x)$. Find the domain and range of f(x) and $f^{-1}(x)$. Write in set builder and interval notation. $f(x) = \sqrt{x} + 1$	**Long Division**	$(x^3 - 3x^2 + 2x - 5) \div (x^2 - 1)$

Vocabulary	Zero(s) of a Function Domain Range Extraneous Solutions Radical Radicand End Behavior Inverse Function	______________ solutions that do not check. ______________ the number or expression under the radical sign. ______________ the behavior of the graph of a function as x approaches negative infinity or positive infinity. ______________ an expression of the form $\sqrt{b}$ or $\sqrt[n]{b}$ where b is a number or expression.

Algebra 2 Builder # 51

Name:______________________________

Solve Radicals by Graphing	Use a graphing calculator. Round to the nearest hundredth. $\sqrt[3]{x-5} = 1.3$	**Solve Radicals Algebraically**	Check for extraneous solutions. $\sqrt[3]{2x+3} = -2$
Square Root Inequalities	Solve using a table on the calculator. $\sqrt{x+4} - 1 < 2$	**Rational Expressions**	Simplify. $\frac{x^2-5x+6}{x^2-9} \div \frac{x^3-8}{x^2+x-6}$
Inverse Functions	Find $f^{-1}(x)$. Find the domain and range of f(x) and $f^{-1}(x)$. Write in set builder and interval notation. $f(x) = \sqrt{2x+3}$	**Long Division**	$(2x^4 - 14x^3 + 22x^2 - 2x + 1) \div (2x - 4)$

Vocabulary

Zero(s) of a Function
Domain
Range
Extraneous Solutions
Radical
Radicand
End Behavior
Inverse Function

_________________ is the set of second elements in ordered pair or table.

_________________ value(s) of x for which f(x) = 0.

_________________ a function that results from interchanging the domain and range values of a one to one function.

_________________ is the set of first elements in ordered pair or table.

Algebra 2 Builder # 52

Name:____________________________

Solve Radicals by Graphing	Use a graphing calculator. Round to the nearest hundredth. $\sqrt{3x-2} = \sqrt{2x+5}$	**Solve Radicals Algebraically**	Check for extraneous solutions. $\sqrt[3]{3x} - 2 = 2$
Square Root Inequalities	Solve using a table on the calculator. $\sqrt{x-2} > 3$	**Rational Expressions**	Simplify. $\frac{1}{x+2} + \frac{2}{x-3}$
Inverse Functions	Find $f^{-1}(x)$. Find the domain and range of f(x) and $f^{-1}(x)$. Write in set builder and interval notation. $f(x) = \sqrt{x-2} + 1$	**Long Division**	$(x^4 + 4x^3 - 4x + 6) \div (x^2 + 4x + 1)$

Vocabulary

Zero(s) of a Function
Domain
Range
Extraneous Solutions
Radical
Radicand
End Behavior
Inverse Function

________________ the behavior of the graph of a function as x approaches negative infinity or positive infinity.

________________ an expression of the form $\sqrt{b}$ or $\sqrt[n]{b}$ where b is a number or expression.

________________ solutions that do not check.

________________ the number or expression under the radical sign.

Algebra 2 Builder # 53

Name:______________________________

Solve Radicals by Graphing	Use a graphing calculator. Round to the nearest hundredth. $\sqrt{2x+3}-3=\sqrt{x+4}-2$	**Solve Radicals Algebraically**	Check for extraneous solutions. $\sqrt{x+2}=x-4$
Square Root Inequalities	Solve using a graphing calculator. In y1 type left side of the inequality in y2 type the right side of the inequality. 2nd Calc then 5 intersect. $3\sqrt{x}-2<7$	**Rational Expressions**	Simplify. $\frac{1}{x}-\frac{3}{x+3}$
Inverse Functions	Find $f^{-1}(x)$. Find the domain and range of f(x) and $f^{-1}(x)$. Write in set builder and interval notation. $f(x)=x^2-5 \quad x\leq 0$	**Synthetic Division**	$(x^3+4x^2+5x+7)\div(x-3)$

Vocabulary	Zero(s) of a Function Domain Range Extraneous Solutions Radical Radicand End Behavior Inverse Function	______________________ is the set of second elements in ordered pair or table. ______________________ is the set of first elements in ordered pair or table. ______________________ value(s) of x for which f(x) = 0. ______________________ a function that results from interchanging the domain and range values of a one to one function.

Algebra 2 Builder # 54

Name:______________________________

Solve Radicals by Graphing	Use a graphing calculator. Round to the nearest hundredth. $\sqrt[3]{2x+1} = x + 5$	**Solve Radicals Algebraically**	Check for extraneous solutions. $\sqrt{x+3} + 3 = x$
Square Root Inequalities	Solve using a graphing calculator. In y1 type left side of the inequality in y2 type the right side of the inequality. 2nd Calc then 5 intersect. $\sqrt{x+1} > 10$	**Rational Expressions**	Simplify. $\frac{x}{x^2-9} + \frac{2}{x^2+5x+6}$
Inverse Functions	Find $f^{-1}(x)$. Find the domain and range of f(x) and $f^{-1}(x)$. Write in set builder and interval notation. $f(x) = (x+2)^2 \quad x \geq -2$	**Synthetic Division**	$(x^4 - 3x^2 + 2x + 4) \div (x + 2)$

Vocabulary

Zero(s) of a Function
Domain
Range
Extraneous Solutions
Radical
Radicand
End Behavior
Inverse Function

_______________ the number or expression under the radical sign.

_______________ an expression of the form $\sqrt{b}$ or $\sqrt[n]{b}$ where b is a number or expression.

_______________ solutions that do not check.

_______________ the behavior of the graph of a function as x approaches negative infinity or positive infinity.

Algebra 2 Builder # 55

Name:_______________________________

Solve Radicals by Graphing	Use a graphing calculator. Round to the nearest hundredth. $\sqrt[3]{4x-5}+3=x$	**Solve Radicals Algebraically**	Check for extraneous solutions. $\sqrt{5x-5}=\sqrt{2x+4}$
Square Root Inequalities	Solve using graphing calculator. $\sqrt{x+1}+3\geq 5$	**Rational Expressions**	Simplify. $\frac{x+4}{2x^2-2x-12}-\frac{x}{x^2-4}$
Inverse Functions	Find $f^{-1}(x)$. Find the domain and range of f(x) and $f^{-1}(x)$. Write in set builder and interval notation. $f(x)=(x-3)^2+4 \quad x\leq 3$	**Synthetic Division**	$(2x^3-3x^2+x)\div(x-4)$

Vocabulary	Zero(s) of a Function Domain Range Extraneous Solutions Radical Radicand End Behavior Inverse Function	________________ is the set of first elements in ordered pair or table. ________________ value(s) of x for which f(x) = 0. ________________ is the set of second elements in ordered pair or table. ________________ a function that results from interchanging the domain and range values of a one to one function.

Algebra 2 Builder # 56

Name:____________________________

Solve Radicals by Graphing	Use a graphing calculator. Round to the nearest hundredth. $\sqrt{2x} - 1 = \sqrt{3x+1} - 4$	**Solve Radicals Algebraically**	Check for extraneous solutions. $\sqrt{23x+12} = 2x + 3$
Square Root Inequalities	Solve using graphing calculator. $\sqrt{x+3} < 5$	**Rational Expressions**	Simplify. $\frac{3}{x-2} - \frac{4}{x^2 - 4x + 4}$
Inverse Functions	Find $f^{-1}(x)$. Find the domain and range of f(x) and $f^{-1}(x)$. Write in set builder and interval notation. $f(x) = x^2 + 6 \qquad x \geq 0$	**Synthetic Division**	$(3x^4 - 5x + 2) \div (x + 3)$

Vocabulary

Zero(s) of a Function
Domain
Range
Extraneous Solutions
Radical
Radicand
End Behavior
Inverse Function

_______________ the number or expression under the radical sign.

_______________ the behavior of the graph of a function as x approaches negative infinity or positive infinity.

_______________ an expression of the form $\sqrt{b}$ or $\sqrt[n]{b}$ where b is a number or expression.

_______________ solutions that do not check.

Algebra 2 Builder # 57

Name:______________________________

Direct/Inverse Variation

If y varies directly with x, and y = 30 when x = 6, find the equation relating x and y. Then find y when $x = \frac{3}{2}$.

Rational Equations

Solve and then check for extraneous solutions.

$$\frac{1}{x} = \frac{2x}{x+3}$$

Rational Inequalities

Solve the inequality algebraically.

$$\frac{2}{x-3} > 0$$

Graph Rational Functions

Find the vertical and horizontal asymptotes, the x and y intercepts, the domain and range, then graph the equation.

$$y = \frac{1}{x}$$

Vocabulary

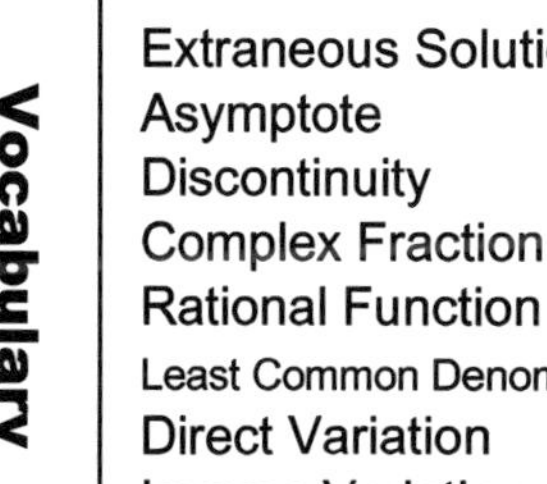

Extraneous Solutions
Asymptote
Discontinuity
Complex Fraction
Rational Function
Least Common Denominator
Direct Variation
Inverse Variation

_______________ a line that a graph closely approaches.

_______________ the relationship of two variables x and y where there is some constant k such that xy = k or $y = \frac{k}{x}$.

_______________ a break in the continuity of a function

_______________ solutions that do not check.

Algebra 2 Builder # 58

Name:______________________________

Direct/Inverse Variation	If y varies inversely with x, and y = 30 when x = 6, find the equation relating x and y. Then find y when x = $\frac{3}{2}$.	**Rational Equations**	Solve and then check for extraneous solutions. $\frac{x-1}{x+3} = \frac{x-5}{x+4}$

Rational Inequalities

Solve the inequality algebraically.

$\frac{2}{x-1} < -2$

Graph Rational Functions

Find the vertical and horizontal asymptotes, the x and y intercepts, the domain and range, then graph the equation.

$y = \frac{1}{x} + 2$

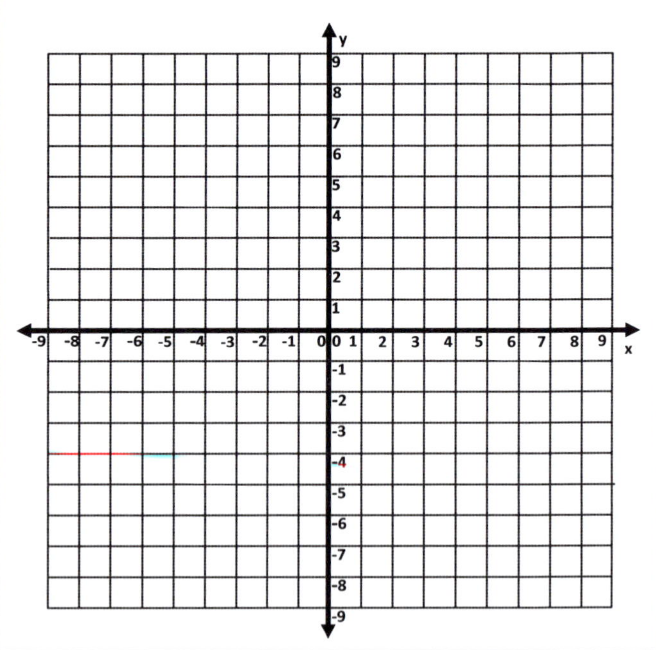

Vocabulary

Extraneous Solutions	______________	a fraction that contains a fraction in the numerator or denominator
Asymptote	______________	a ratio of two polynomial functions where the denominator cannot equal zero.
Discontinuity	______________	the smallest factor that each denominator can divide into evenly.
Complex Fraction	______________	the relationship of 2 variables x and y where there is some constant k such that y = kx.
Rational Function		
Least Common Denominator		
Direct Variation		
Inverse Variation		

Algebra 2 Builder # 59

Name:______________________________

Direct/Inverse Variation	If y varies directly with x, and y = $1/2$ when x = $3/2$, find the equation relating x and y. Then find y when x = 8.	**Rational Equations**	Solve and then check for extraneous solutions. $\frac{1}{x} + \frac{1}{2x} = 3$

Rational Inequalities

Solve the inequality algebraically.

$\frac{3}{x-2} \leq 0$

Graph Rational Functions

Find the vertical and horizontal asymptotes, the x and y intercepts, the domain and range, then graph the equation.

$f(x) = \frac{3}{x} - 2$

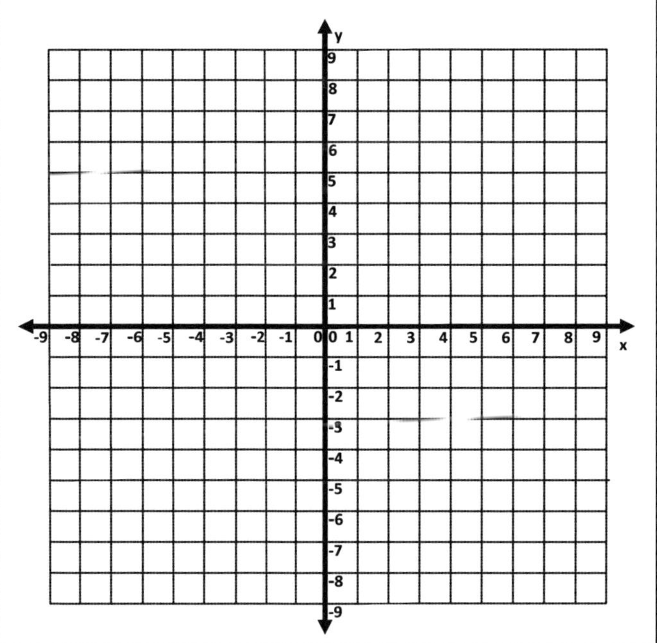

Vocabulary

Extraneous Solutions
Asymptote
Discontinuity
Complex Fraction
Rational Function
Least Common Denominator
Direct Variation
Inverse Variation

_______________ solutions that do not check.

_______________ a line that a graph closely approaches.

_______________ the relationship of two variables x and y where there is some constant k such that xy = k or y = $\frac{k}{x}$.

_______________ a break in the continuity of a function.

Algebra 2 Builder # 60 Name:____________________________

Direct/Inverse Variation	If y varies inversely with x, and y = $1/2$ when x = $3/2$, find the equation relating x and y. Then find y when x = 8.	Rational Equations	Solve and then check for extraneous solutions. $\frac{2}{3x} + \frac{4}{6x} = \frac{x}{3}$

Rational Inequalities	Solve the inequality algebraically. $\frac{3}{x^2 - 4} \geq 0$

Graph Rational Functions	Find the vertical and horizontal asymptotes, the x and y intercepts, the domain and range, then graph the equation. $y = \frac{2}{x-3} + 2$	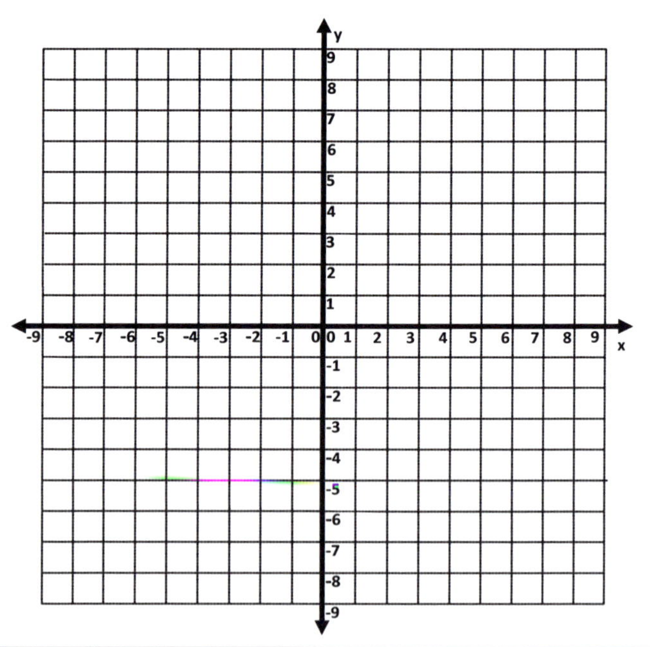

Vocabulary	Extraneous Solutions Asymptote Discontinuity Complex Fraction Rational Function Least Common Denominator Direct Variation Inverse Variation	_______________ the relationship of two variables x and y where there is some constant k such that y = kx. _______________ a fraction that contains a fraction in the numerator or denominator. _______________ a ratio of two polynomial functions where the denominator cannot equal zero. _______________ the smallest factor that each denominator can divide into evenly.

Algebra 2 Builder # 61

Name:______________________________

Direct/Inverse Variation

Use k as the contsant of variation and write an equation for the given relationship

When w varies directly as x and inversely as z.

Rational Equations

Solve and then check for extraneous solutions.

$$\frac{3}{x-2} - 4 = \frac{4}{x-7}$$

Rational Inequalities

Solve the inequality using a table.

$$\frac{-2x-4}{x-3} < 0$$

Graph Rational Functions

Find the vertical and horizontal asymptotes, the x and y intercepts, the domain and range, then graph the equation.

$$g(x) = \frac{2x+3}{x-4}$$

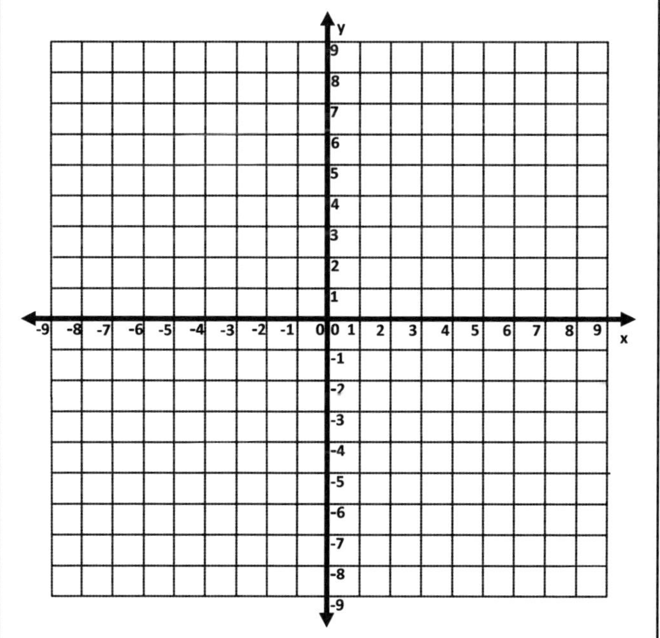

Vocabulary

Extraneous Solutions
Asymptote
Discontinuity
Complex Fraction
Rational Function
Least Common Denominator
Direct Variation
Inverse Variation

________________ a break in the continuity of a function

________________ solutions that do not check.

________________ a line that a graph closely approaches.

________________ the relationship of two variables x and y where there is some constant k such that xy = k or $y = \frac{k}{x}$.

Algebra 2 Builder # 62

Name:______________________________

Direct/Inverse Variation

Use k as the constant of variation and write an equation for the given relationship

When q varies directly as the square of x and inversely as the cube of y.

Rational Equations

Solve and then check for extraneous solutions.

$$\frac{2x}{x^2-4x} = \frac{2}{x-4} + \frac{x-1}{x}$$

Rational Inequalities

Solve the inequality using a table.

$$\frac{-2x-3}{x-4} \geq 0$$

Graph Rational Functions

Find the vertical and horizontal asymptotes, the x and y intercepts, the domain and range, then graph the equation.

$$y = \frac{6}{x^2-x-6}$$

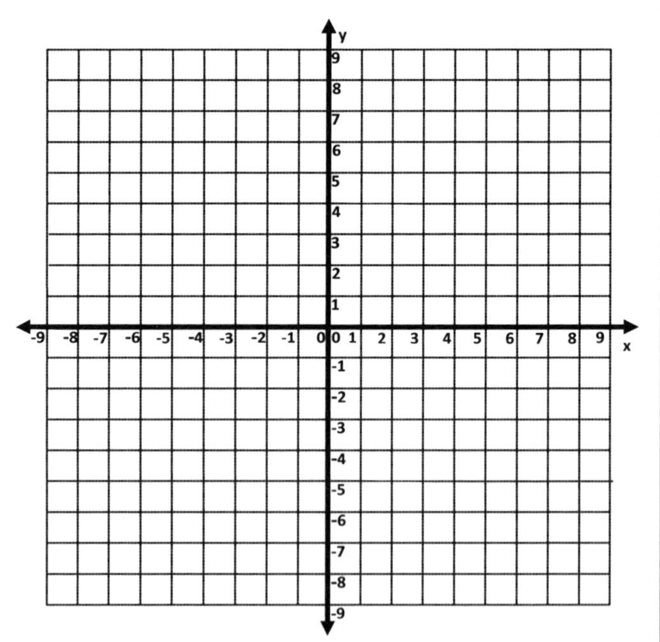

Vocabulary

Extraneous Solutions
Asymptote
Discontinuity
Complex Fraction
Rational Function
Least Common Denominator
Direct Variation
Inverse Variation

_______________ a fraction that contains a fraction in the numerator or denominator.

_______________ the relationship of two variables x and y where there is some constant k such that y = kx.

_______________ a ratio of two polynomial functions where the denominator cannot equal zero.

_______________ the smallest factor that each denominator can divide into evenly.

Algebra 2 Builder # 63

Name:______________________________

Direct/Inverse Variation

Use k as the constant of variation and write an equation for the given relationship

The area of a square varies directly as the square of the length of the side.

Rational Equations

Solve and then check for extraneous solutions.

$$\frac{1}{x-1}+\frac{2}{x+2}=\frac{3}{2}$$

Rational Inequalities

Solve the inequality by graphing.

$$\frac{4x-3}{x-2}>3$$

Graph Rational Functions

Find the vertical and horizontal asymptotes, the x and y intercepts, the domain and range, then graph the equation.

$$f(x)=\frac{x^2-5x-6}{x^2-4}$$

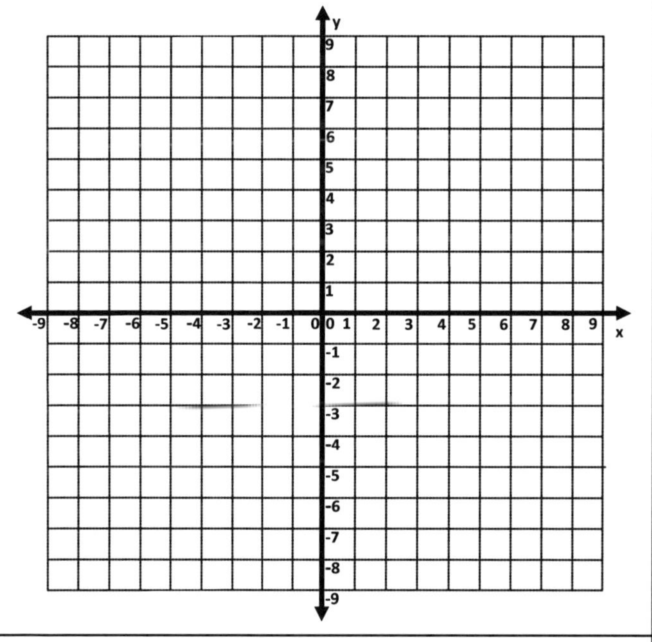

Vocabulary

Extraneous Solutions
Asymptote
Discontinuity
Complex Fraction
Rational Function
Least Common Denominator
Direct Variation
Inverse Variation

_______________ a line that a graph closely approaches.

_______________ solutions that do not check.

_______________ the relationship of two variables x and y where there is some constant k such that xy = k or y = $\frac{k}{x}$.

_______________ a break in the continuity of a function

Algebra 2 Builder # 64

Name:______________________________

Direct/Inverse Variation

Use k as the constant of variation and write an equation for the given relationship

The resistance of an electrical wire and the passage of the current, varies directly as the length of the wire, and inversely as the square of the wire's diameter.

Rational Equations

Solve and then check for extraneous solutions.

$$\frac{3}{x+4} + \frac{x-2}{x} = \frac{5x+1}{7x}$$

Rational Inequalities

Solve the inequality by graphing.

$$\frac{3}{x+2} \leq 1$$

Graph Rational Functions

Find the vertical and horizontal asymptotes, the x and y intercepts, the domain and range, then graph the equation.

$$y = \frac{x^2 - 9}{x^2}$$

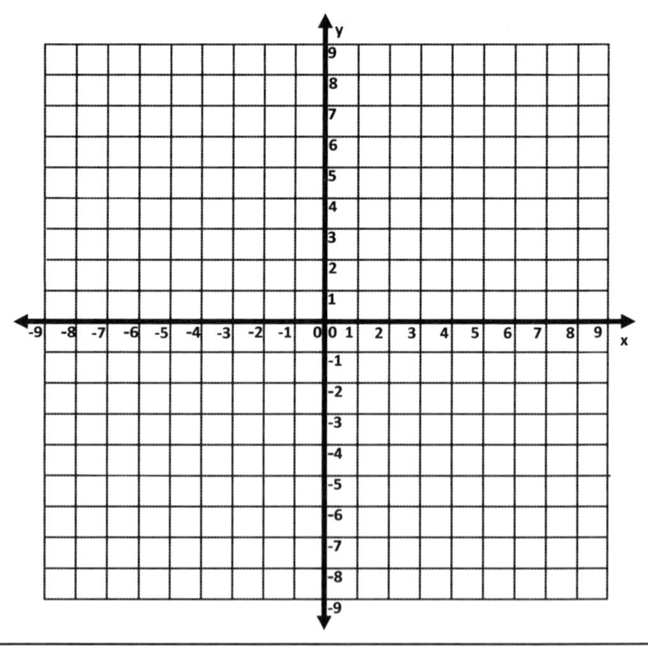

Vocabulary

Extraneous Solutions
Asymptote
Discontinuity
Complex Fraction
Rational Function
Least Common Denominator
Direct Variation
Inverse Variation

________________ a ratio of two polynomial functions where the denominator cannot equal zero.

________________ the relationship of two variables x and y where there is some constant k such that y = kx.

________________ a fraction that contains a fraction in the numerator or denominator.

________________ the smallest factor that each denominator can divide into evenly.

Algebra 2 Builder # 65

Name:______________________________

Evaluate Logarithms

Evaluate without a calculator.

$\log_6 36$ $\quad\quad$ $12^{\log_{12} 3}$

Expand Logarithms

Use properties of logarithms to expand the expression.

$\log xy$

Condense Logarithms

Use properties of logarithms to condense the expression.

$\log_7 x - \log_7 y$

Inverse Functions

Find the inverse of the function.

y = 3^x

Exponential / Log Equations

Solve.

$2^{2x-4} = 16^{x-2}$

Exponential / Log Application

Write an exponential growth model for the given situation.

Sam deposits $700.00 in an account that pays 1.5% annual interest compounded weekly.

Graph Exponential Functions

Find the asymptote, intercepts, the domain and range, then graph.

y = 2^x

Vocabulary

Asymptote
Exponential Function
Exponential Growth
Exponential Decay
Logarithmic Function
Common Logarithm
Natural Logarithm
Natural Base *e*

_______________ a function in which the independent variable is the exponent.

_______________ The inverse of an exponential function.

_______________ An exponential function y = ab^x, where a > 0 and b > 1

_______________ An exponential function y = ab^x, where a > 0 and 0 < b < 1

Algebra 2 Builder # 66

Name:____________________________

Evaluate Logarithms

Evaluate without a calculator.

$\log_8 1$ $\quad\quad$ e^{ln5}

Expand Logarithms

Use properties of logarithms to expand the expression.

$\ln x^2y^3$

Condense Logarithms

Use properties of logarithms to condense the expression.

$2\log x + 3\log y$

Inverse Functions

Find the inverse of the function.

$y = \log_3 x$

Exponential / Log Equations

Solve.

$3^{x+1} = \frac{1^x}{9}$

Exponential / Log Application

Write an exponential decay model for the given situation.

A new car cost $25,000. The value of the car depreciates at a rate of 14% per year.

Graph Exponential Functions

$y = 3^x + 1$ Find the asymptote, intercepts, the domain and range, then graph.

Vocabulary

- Asymptote
- Exponential Function
- Exponential Growth
- Exponential Decay
- Logarithmic Function
- Common Logarithm
- Natural Logarithm
- Natural Base *e*

________________ The Euler number, $e \approx 2.718281828$.

________________ A base 10 logarithm.

________________ A base *e* logarithm denoted by ln.

________________ A line that a graph closely approaches.

Algebra 2 Builder # 67

Name:______________________________

Evaluate Logarithms	Evaluate without a calculator. $\log_3 \frac{1}{27}$ $\log_2 64$	Expand Logarithms	Use properties of logarithms to expand the expression. $\ln 2xy^3$
Condense Logarithms	Use properties of logarithms to condense the expression. $3\log_3 x + 2\log_3 y + \log_3 z$	Inverse Functions	Find the inverse of the function. $y = 2^{x-1}$
Exponential / Log Equations	Solve. $3^{x+1} = 7$	Exponential / Log Application	You deposit $5000.00 in an account that pays 1.25% interest compounded quarterly. After 20 years, what is the balance of the account?

Graph Exponential Functions

Find the asymptote, intercepts, the domain and range, then graph.

$f(x) = 3 \cdot 2^x$

Vocabulary

Asymptote
Exponential Function
Exponential Growth
Exponential Decay
Logarithmic Function
Common Logarithm
Natural Logarithm
Natural Base *e*

_______________ a function in which the independent variable is the exponent.

_______________ An exponential function $y = ab^x$, where $a > 0$ and $0 < b < 1$

_______________ The inverse of an exponential function.

_______________ An exponential function $y = ab^x$, where $a > 0$ and $b > 1$

Algebra 2 Builder # 68

Name:______________________________

Evaluate Logarithms

Evaluate without a calculator.

$\log_{\frac{1}{3}} 27$

$\log_8 4$

Expand Logarithms

Use properties of logarithms to expand the expression.

$\ln \sqrt{xy}$

Condense Logarithms

Use properties of logarithms to condense the expression.

$\ln x - \ln y - \ln z$

Inverse Functions

Find the inverse of the function.

$y = \log x + 1$

Exponential / Log Equations

Solve.

$5^{x-3} = 6^x$

Exponential / Log Application

A new car cost $35,000. The value of the car depreciates at a rate of 12% per year. What is the value of the car in five years?

Graph Exponential Functions

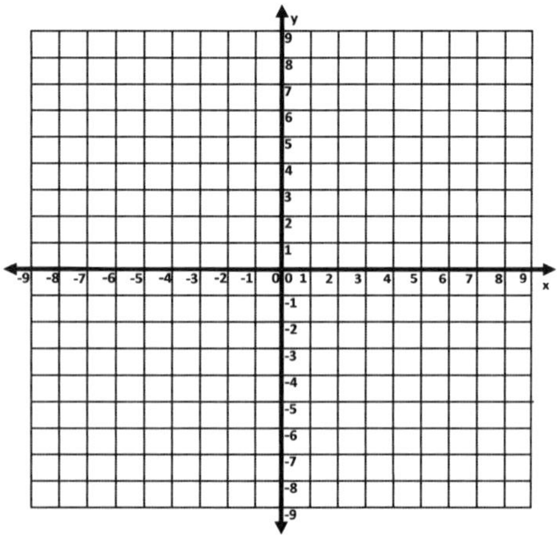

Find the asymptote, intercepts, the domain and range, then graph.

$f(x) = 3\left(\frac{1}{2}\right)^x$

Vocabulary

Asymptote
Exponential Function
Exponential Growth
Exponential Decay
Logarithmic Function
Common Logarithm
Natural Logarithm
Natural Base e

__________________ The Euler number, $e \approx 2.718281828$.

__________________ A line that a graph closely approaches.

__________________ A base 10 logarithm.

__________________ A base e logarithm denoted by ln.

Algebra 2 Builder # 69

Name:____________________________

Evaluate Logarithms

Evaluate using a calculator, round to 4 decimal places.

$\log 5$ $\ln 7$

Expand Logarithms

Use properties of logarithms to expand the expression.

$\log \frac{2x}{y}$

Condense Logarithms

Use properties of logarithms to condense the expression.

$2\ln a - 3\ln b + \ln c$

Inverse Functions

Find the inverse of the function.

$y = 3^x + 2$

Exponential / Log Equations

Solve and check for extraneous solutions.

$\log_5(x - 2) = 2$

Exponential / Log Application

You deposit $6000.00 in an account that pays 1.2% interest compounded quarterly. How long will it take for the account to reach $8000.00?

Graph Logarithmic Functions

Find the asymptote, intercepts, the domain and range, then graph.

$y = \log x$

Vocabulary

- Asymptote
- Exponential Function
- Exponential Growth
- Exponential Decay
- Logarithmic Function
- Common Logarithm
- Natural Logarithm
- Natural Base e

____________ An exponential function $y = ab^x$, where $a > 0$ and $0 < b < 1$

____________ a function in which the independent variable is the exponent.

____________ The inverse of an exponential function.

____________ An exponential function $y = ab^x$, where $a > 0$ and $b > 1$

Algebra 2 Builder # 70

Name:______________________________

Evaluate Logarithms

Evaluate using a calculator, round to 4 decimal places.

$\log 4 + \log 7$

$\ln 3 - \ln 6$

Expand Logarithms

Use properties of logarithms to expand the expression.

$\log_3 \frac{3x^2}{y}$

Condense Logarithms

Use properties of logarithms to condense the expression.

$\frac{1}{2}\log_2 a + 2\log_2 3$

Inverse Functions

Find the inverse of the function.

y = $e^x - 1$

Exponential / Log Equations

Solve and check for extraneous solutions.

$\log_3(2x - 5) = \log_3(x + 7)$

Exponential / Log Application

You deposit $7000.00 in an account that pays 1.25% interest compounded continuously. How long will it take for the account to double?

Graph Logarithmic Functions

Find the asymptote, intercepts, the domain and range, then graph.

y = $\log_2 x$

Vocabulary

- Asymptote
- Exponential Function
- Exponential Growth
- Exponential Decay
- Logarithmic Function
- Common Logarithm
- Natural Logarithm
- Natural Base *e*

________________ A line that a graph closely approaches.

________________ The Euler number, $e \approx 2.718281828$.

________________ A base 10 logarithm.

________________ A base *e* logarithm denoted by ln.

Algebra 2 Builder # 71

Name:____________________________

Evaluate Logarithms

Evaluate using a calculator, round to 4 decimal places.

$\dfrac{\log 5}{\log 6 + \log 7}$ $\dfrac{\ln 3 + \ln 4}{2\ln 5}$

Expand Logarithms

Use properties of logarithms to expand the expression.

$\log_5\left(\frac{x^2\ y^3}{z^4}\right)$

Condense Logarithms

Use properties of logarithms to condense the expression.

$\ln x - 2\ln 4$

Inverse Functions

Find the inverse of the function.

y = $\ln(x+2)$

Exponential / Log Equations

Solve and check for extraneous solutions.

$\log_3(x+2) - \log_3(x-1) = 2$

Exponential / Log Application

A new car cost $35,000.00. The value of the car depreciates at a rate of 12% per year. When will the car be worth $5000.00?

Graph Logarithmic Functions

Find the asymptote, intercepts, the domain and range, then graph.

y = $\log_2 x + 2$

Vocabulary

- Asymptote
- Exponential Function
- Exponential Growth
- Exponential Decay
- Logarithmic Function
- Common Logarithm
- Natural Logarithm
- Natural Base *e*

________________ An exponential function y = ab^x, where a > 0 and 0 < b < 1

________________ a function in which the independent variable is the exponent.

________________ An exponential function y = ab^x, where a > 0 and b > 1

________________ The inverse of an exponential function.

Algebra 2 Builder # 72

Name:____________________________

Evaluate Logarithms	Evaluate using a calculator, round to 4 decimal places. $\log_3 7$ $\log_9 \frac{2}{3}$	**Expand Logarithms**	Use properties of logarithms to expand the expression. $\log \sqrt{\frac{x^3y^5}{2z}}$
Condense Logarithms	Use properties of logarithms to condense the expression. $3\log 2 + 3\log 4 + \frac{1}{2}\log x$	**Inverse Functions**	Find the inverse of the function. $y = 3^{x-2}$
Exponential / Log Equations	Solve and check for extraneous solutions. $\log_3(3x-2) = \log_3(5x-7)$	**Exponential / Log Application**	A new car cost $40,000.00. The value of the car depreciates at a rate of 10% per year. When will the car be worth half of its original cost?

Graph Logarithmic Functions	[coordinate grid, x and y from -9 to 9]	Find the asymptote, intercepts, the domain and range, then graph. $y = \log_2(x+2)$

Vocabulary	Asymptote Exponential Function Exponential Growth Exponential Decay Logarithmic Function Common Logarithm Natural Logarithm Natural Base *e*	________________ A base *e* logarithm denoted by ln. ________________ A line that a graph closely approaches. ________________ The Euler number, $e \approx 2.718281828$. ________________ A base 10 logarithm.

Algebra 2 Builder # 73

Name:____________________________

Graph Parabolas

Write the equation in standard form, find the vertex, how it opens, the focus, the directrix and the length of the latus rectum and graph.

$y = \frac{1}{8}x^2$

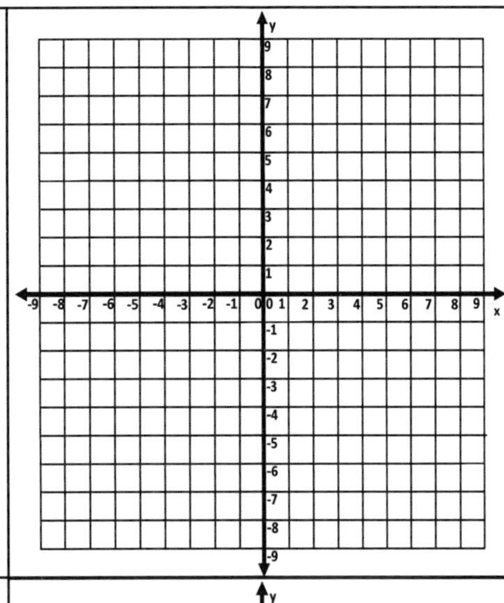

Equations of Parabolas

Write the equation given these conditions.

Vertex (0,0); focus (0,4)

Graph Circles

Write the equation in standard form, find the center and the radius.

$x^2 + y^2 = 25$

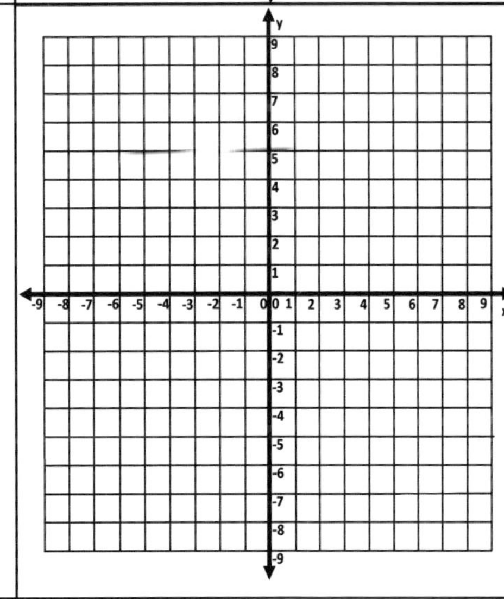

Equations of Circles

Write the equation given these conditions.

Center at the origin; radius is 6

Systems of Equations

Solve.

$x^2 + y^2 = 25$

$y - x = 1$

Vocabulary

Conics
Circle
Center of a Circle
Radius of a Circle
Parabola
Latus Rectum of a Parabola
Focus of a Parabola
Vertex of a Parabola

__________________ A curved formed by the intersection of a plane and double napped cone.

__________________ A locus of points equal distance from a point called the focus and a line called the directrix.

__________________ The locus of points that is equal distance from the center.

__________________ The fixed point on the inside of the parabola.

Algebra 2 Builder # 74

Name:______________________________

Graph Parabolas

Write the equation in standard form, find the vertex, how it opens, the focus, the directrix and the length of the latus rectum and graph.

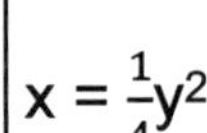

$x = \frac{1}{4}y^2$

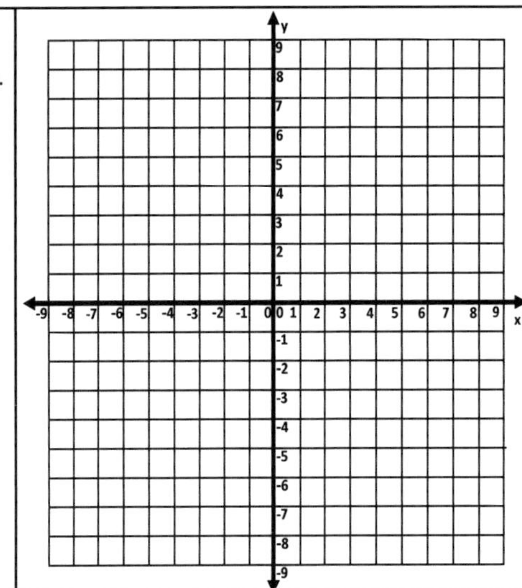

Equations of Parabolas

Write the equation given these conditions.

Vertex (0,0); directrix x = 2

Graph Circles

Write the equation in standard form, find the center and the radius.

$(x - 1)^2 + (y + 2)^2 = 16$

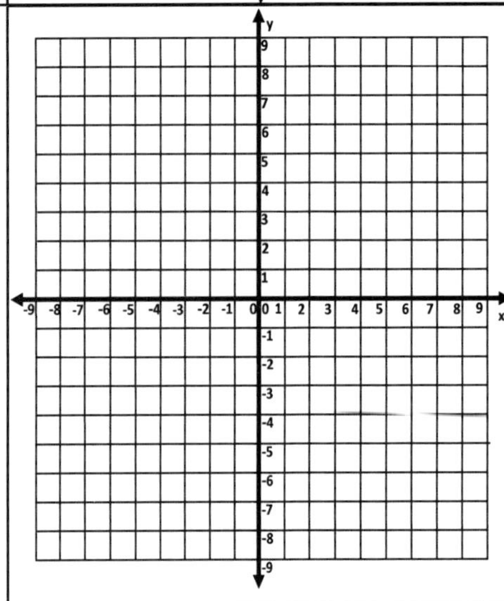

Equations of Circles

Write the equation given these conditions.

Center at (-4,5); radius is 5

Systems of Equations

Solve.

$x^2 + y^2 = 13$

$x - y = 5$

Vocabulary

Conics
Circle
Center of a Circle
Radius of a Circle
Parabola
Latus Rectum of a Parabola
Focus of a Parabola
Vertex of a Parabola

_______________ A chord of a parabola that passes through the focus and is parallel to the directrix.

_______________ A point inside the circle that is the same distance from each point on the circle.

_______________ The turning point on the graph of a parabola.

_______________ The distance from the center of the circle to any point on a circle.

Algebra 2 Builder # 75

Name:______________________________

Graph Parabolas

Write the equation in standard form, find the vertex, how it opens, the focus, the directrix and the length of the latus rectum and graph.

$(y + 2)^2 = -4(x - 4)$

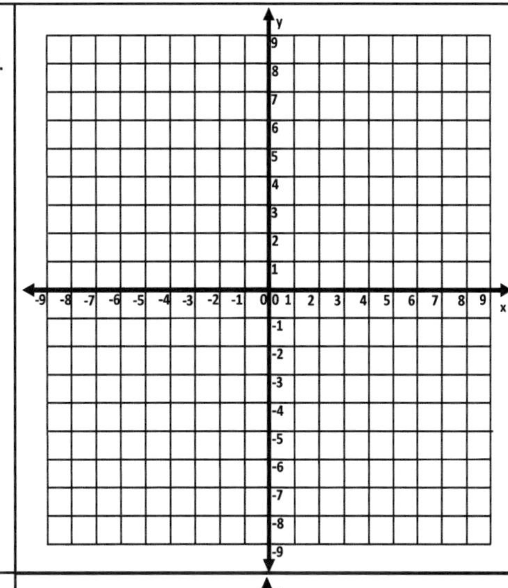

Equations of Parabolas

Write the equation given these conditions.
Vertex (2,1); focus (2,-3)

Graph Circles

Write the equation in standard form, find the center and the radius.

$x^2 + y^2 + 2x - 4y - 4 = 0$

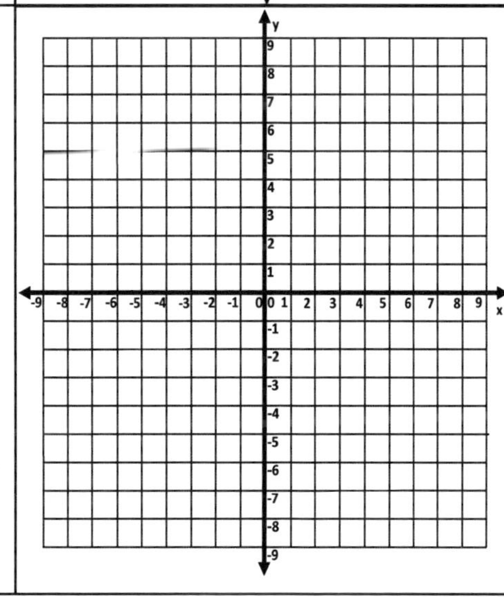

Equations of Circles

Write the equation given these conditions.
Center at (2,3); and passes through the point (3,-1)

Systems of Equations

Solve.

$4x + y^2 = 0$

$3x + y = -1$

Vocabulary

Conics	________________ A curved formed by the intersection of a plane and double napped cone.
Circle	________________ A locus of points equal distance from a point called the focus and a line called the directrix.
Center of a Circle	________________ The locus of points that is equal distance from the center.
Radius of a Circle	________________ The fixed point on the inside of the parabola.
Parabola	
Latus Rectum of a Parabola	
Focus of a Parabola	
Vertex of a Parabola	

Algebra 2 Builder # 76

Name:______________________________

Graph Parabolas

Write the equation in standard form, find the vertex, how it opens, the focus, the directrix and the length of the latus rectum and graph.

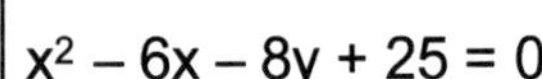

$x^2 - 6x - 8y + 25 = 0$

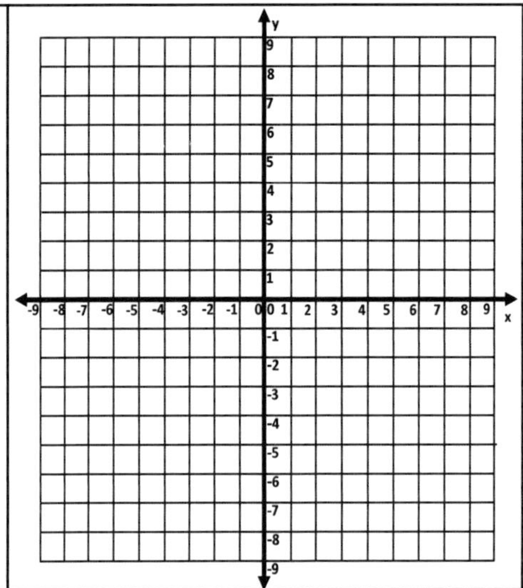

Equations of Parabolas

Write the equation given these conditions.

Focus (2,3); directrix $x = -6$

Graph Circles

Write the equation in standard form, find the center and the radius.

$2x^2 + 2y^2 - 12x + 4y - 12 = 0$

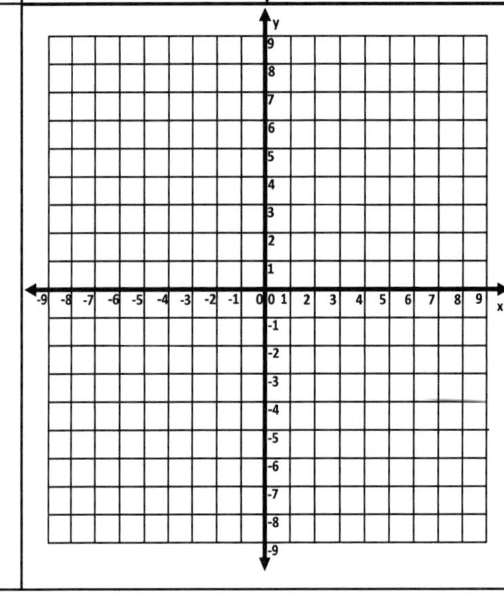

Equations of Circles

Write the equation given these conditions.

Center at (4,-2); and tangent to the x-axis.

Systems of Equations

Solve.

$x^2 + y^2 = 13$

$(x - 5)^2 + y^2 = 18$

Vocabulary

- Conics
- Circle
- Center of a Circle
- Radius of a Circle
- Parabola
- Latus Rectum of a Parabola
- Focus of a Parabola
- Vertex of a Parabola

________________ The distance from the center of the circle to any point on a circle.

________________ A chord of a parabola that passes through the focus and is parallel to the directrix.

________________ The turning point on the graph of a parabola.

________________ A point inside the circle that is the same distance from each point on the circle.

Algebra 2 Builder # 77

Name:____________________________

Graph Ellipse

Write the equation in standard form, find the center, vertices, co-verticies, foci and length of the major and minor axis, then graph.

$$\frac{x^2}{9} + \frac{y^2}{4} = 1$$

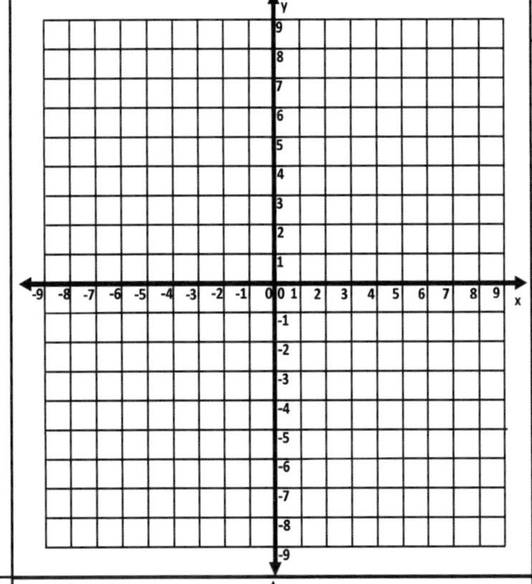

Equations of Ellipse

Write the equation given these conditions.
Center at (0,0); length of the horizontal major axis 16; length of the minor axis 6

Graph Hyperbolas

Write the equation in standard form, find the center, the vertices, slope of the asymptotes, foci, length of transverse axis, then graph.

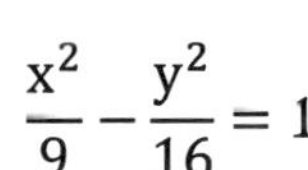

$$\frac{x^2}{9} - \frac{y^2}{16} = 1$$

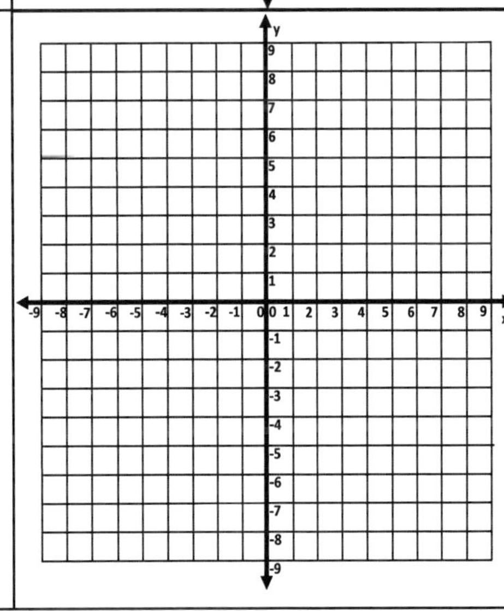

Equations of Hyperbolas

Write the equation given these conditions.
Center at (0,0);
a = 5, c = 7
Vertical transverse axis

Systems of Equations

Solve.

$x^2 + y^2 = 10$

$x^2 - y^2 = -8$

Vocabulary

Ellipse
Major Axis of an Ellipse
Minor Axis of an Ellipse
Vertices of an Ellipse
Foci of an Ellipse
Co-Vertices of an Ellipse
Hyperbola
Transverse Axis of a Hyperbola

__________________ A locus of points P, the difference of whose distance to the foci is constant.

__________________ The line segment between the vertices of a hyperbola.

__________________ The line segment joining the vertices of an ellipse.

__________________ A locus of points P, the sum of whose distance to the foci is constant.

Algebra 2 Builder # 78

Name:____________________________

Graph Ellipse

Write the equation in standard form, find the center, vertices, co-verticies, foci and length of the major and minor axis, then graph.

$9x^2 + 25y^2 = 225$

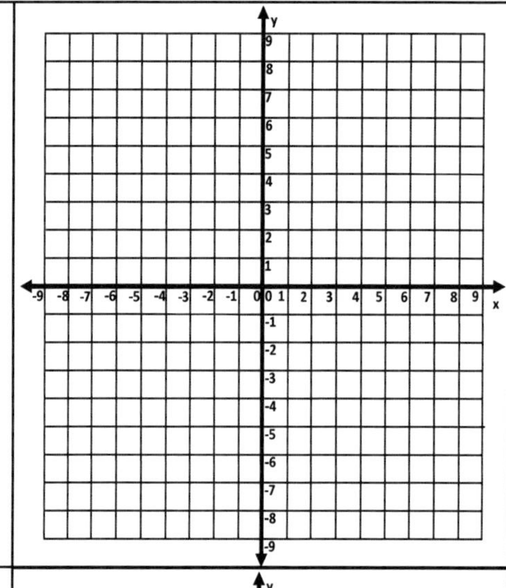

Equations of Ellipse

Write the equation given these conditions.

Center at (-2,3);

a = 4, b = 3

major axis is vertical

Graph Hyperbolas

Write the equation in standard form, find the center, the vertices, slope of the asymptotes, foci, length of transverse axis, then graph.

$-16x^2 + 9y^2 = 144$

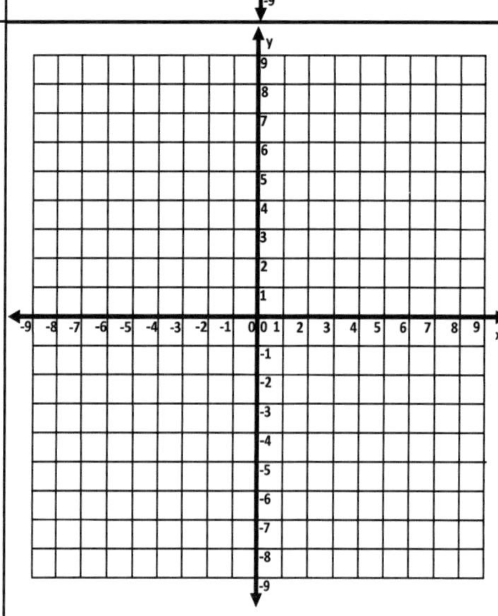

Equations of Hyperbolas

Write the equation given these conditions.

Foci (5,0) and (-5,0)

Vertices (4,0) and (-4,0)

Systems of Equations

Solve.

$2x^2 - y^2 = -7$

$y = 2x - 5$

Vocabulary

Ellipse
Major Axis of an Ellipse
Minor Axis of an Ellipse
Vertices of an Ellipse
Foci of an Ellipse
Co-Vertices of an Ellipse
Hyperbola
Transverse Axis of a Hyperbola

________________ The line segment between the co-vertices of an ellipse.

________________ Where the major axis intersects the ellipse.

________________ Where the minor axis intersects the ellipse.

________________ Two fixed points inside the ellipse on the major axis.

Algebra 2 Builder # 79

Name:______________________________

Graph Ellipse

Write the equation in standard form, find the center, vertices, co-verticies, foci and length of the major and minor axis, then graph.

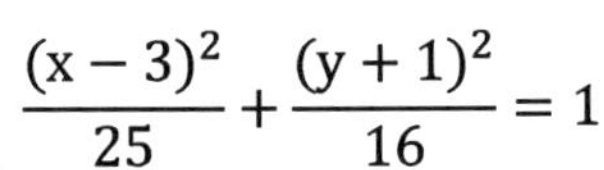

$$\frac{(x-3)^2}{25}+\frac{(y+1)^2}{16}=1$$

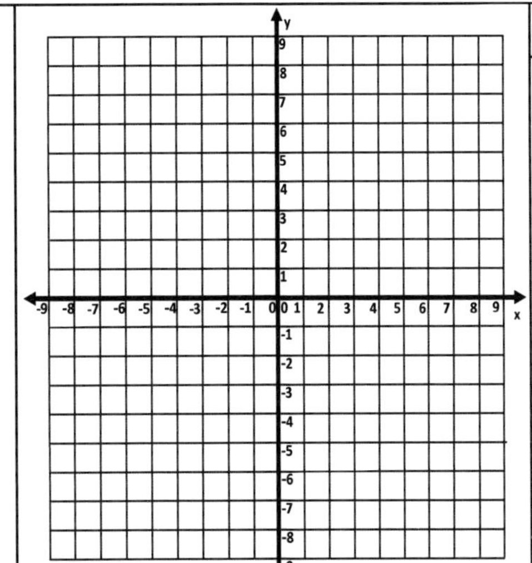

Equations of Ellipse

Write the equation given these conditions.
Foci (0,4) and (0,-4)
Length of major axis 10

Graph Hyperbolas

Write the equation in standard form, find the center, the vertices, slope of the asymptotes, foci, length of transverse axis, then graph.

$$\frac{(y-1)^2}{4}-\frac{(x+2)^2}{4}=1$$

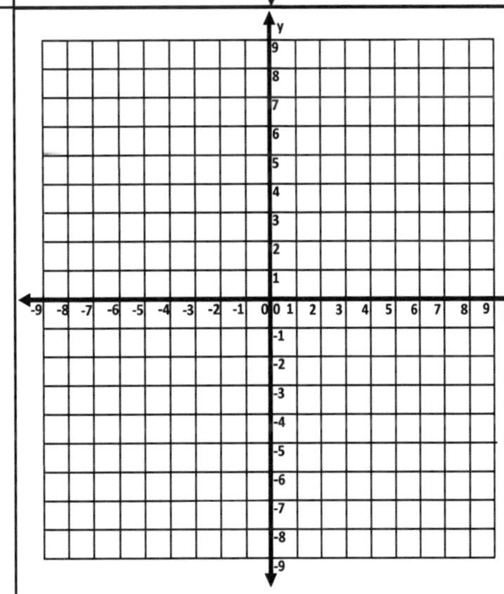

Equations of Hyperbolas

Write the equation given these conditions.
Foci (0,7) and (0,-7);
Vertices (0,5) and (0,-5)

Systems of Equations

Solve.

$x^2 - y^2 = -4$

$x^2 + y^2 = 4$

Vocabulary

Ellipse
Major Axis of an Ellipse
Minor Axis of an Ellipse
Vertices of an Ellipse
Foci of an Ellipse
Co-Vertices of an Ellipse
Hyperbola
Transverse Axis of a Hyperbola

__________________ A locus of points P, the difference of whose distance to the foci is constant.

__________________ The line segment between the vertices of a hyperbola.

__________________ The line segment joining the vertices of an ellipse.

__________________ A locus of points P, the sum of whose distance to the foci is constant.

Algebra 2 Builder # 80

Name:______________________________

Graph Ellipse

Write the equation in standard form, find the center, vertices, co-verticies, foci and length of the major and minor axis, then graph.

$9x^2 + 4y^2 + 36x - 8y + 4 = 0$

Equations of Ellipse

Write the equation given these conditions.

Vertices (-2,4) and (-2,-2);
Foci (-2,3) and (-2,-1)

Graph Hyperbolas

Write the equation in standard form, find the center, the vertices, slope of the asymptotes, foci, length of transverse axis, then graph.

$16x^2 - 25y^2 - 64x - 50y - 361 = 0$

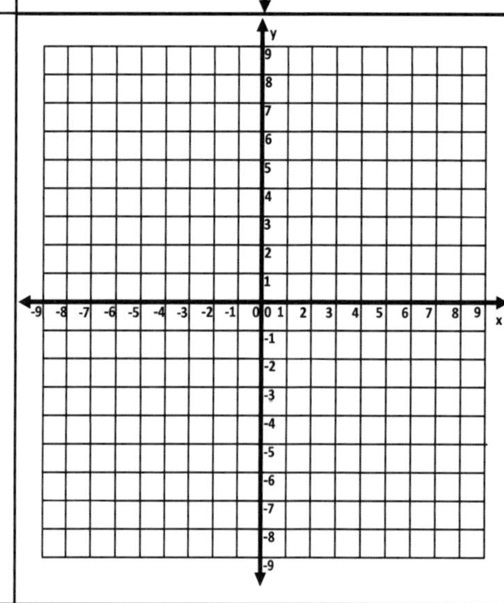

Equations of Hyperbolas

Write the equation given these conditions.

Vertices (5,-2) and (5,4);
Foci (5,-4) and (5,6)

Systems of Equations

Solve.

$6x^2 + y^2 = 10$

$2x^2 + 4y^2 = 18$

Vocabulary

- Ellipse
- Major Axis of an Ellipse
- Minor Axis of an Ellipse
- Vertices of an Ellipse
- Foci of an Ellipse
- Co-Vertices of an Ellipse
- Hyperbola
- Transverse Axis of a Hyperbola

________________ The line segment between the co-vertices of an ellipse.

________________ Where the major axis intersects the ellipse.

________________ Where the minor axis intersects the ellipse.

________________ Two fixed points inside the ellipse on the major axis.

KEYS

ALGEBRA READINESS

BUILDERS

ALGEBRA 2

Algebra 2 Builder # 1

Name:______________________

Solve Equations

$4 - 3(2x - 5) = 6x - 7$

$4 - 6x + 15 = 6x - 7$

$-6x + 19 = 6x - 7$

$+6x \quad +7 \quad +6x + 7$

$\frac{26}{12} = \frac{12x}{12}$

$\frac{13}{6} = x$

Solve Inequalities

Solve, show your answer graphically, with set builder and interval notation.

$4x + 5 < 6x - 7$

$-6x - 5 \quad -6x - 5$

$\frac{-2x}{-2} < \frac{-12}{-2}$

$x > 6$

6

$\{x | x > 6\}$

$(6, \infty)$

Evaluate Expressions

$3x - 2(3 - 4x)$ when $x = 4$

$3(4) - 2(3 - 4(4))$

$3(4) - 2(3 - 16)$

$3(4) - 2(-13)$

$12 + 26$

38

Literal Equations

$PV = nRT$ Solve for T

$\frac{PV}{nR} = \frac{nRT}{nR}$

$\frac{PV}{nR} = T$

Word Problems

Footballs cost $22.00 each. The Athletic Director has $277.00 in his budget to spend on footballs. There is a $13.00 shipping fee per order. How many footballs can the Athletic Director order?

x = number of footballs

$22x + 13 = 277$

$-13 \quad -13$

$\frac{22x}{22} = \frac{264}{22}$

$x = 12$

The atheletic director can order 12 footballs.

Relations/Functions

Determine if the relation is a function. Find the domain and range.

Function: Yes **No** (circled)

Domain: $\{-1, 0, 1\}$

Range: $\{-2, -1, 0, 1\}$

x	y
-1 → -2	
0 → -1, 0	
1 → 1	

Vocabulary

Domain
Range
Function
Solution
Equation
Inequality

Domain is the set of first elements in ordered pair or table.

Solution a value for the variable or an ordered pair that makes an equation true.

Inequality is a type of problem that often has a set of answers and can be written in interval notation.

Function a relation in which every input has exactly one output.

Representing Functions as Graphs

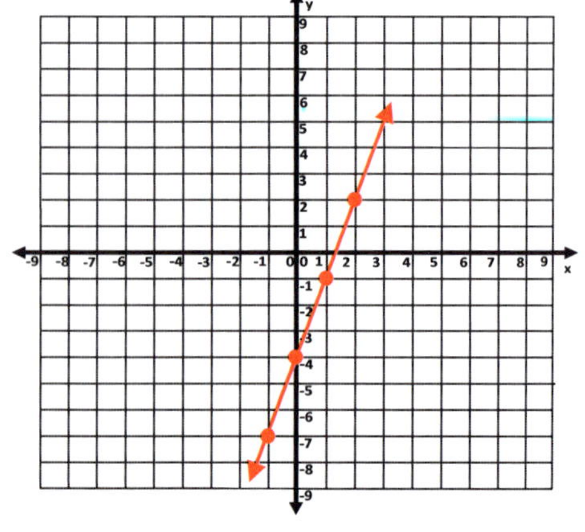

Change to slope intercept form $y = mx + b$, find the slope. Use {-2, -1, 0, 1, 2} for the x values. Make a table, plot the points and graph. Find the y-intercept by setting x to 0; then find the x-intercept by setting y to 0. $3x - y = 4$

x	y
-2	-10
-1	-7
0	-4
1	-1
2	2

x-int=(4/3,0)

y-int=(0,-4) m= 3

$3x - y = 4$
$-3x \quad -3x$
$-y = -3x + 4$
$-1 \quad -1$
$y = 3x - 4$

$y = 3x - 4$
$y = 3(-2) - 4$
$y = -6 - 4$
$y = -10$

$y = 3x - 4$
$y = 3(-1) - 4$
$y = -3 - 4$
$y = -7$

$y = 3x - 4$
$y = 3(0) - 4$
$y = 0 - 4$
$y = -4$

$y = 3x - 4$
$y = 3(1) - 4$
$y = 3 - 4$
$y = -1$

$y = 3x - 4$
$y = 3(2) - 4$
$y = 6 - 4$
$y = 2$

y-int
$3x - y = 4$
$3(0) - y = 4$
$\frac{-y}{-1} = \frac{4}{-1}$
$y = -4$

x-int
$3x - y = 4$
$3x - 0 = 4$
$\frac{3x}{3} = \frac{4}{3}$
$x = 4/3$

Distributive Property

$-6k^3 - 3k - 8k(2k^2 + 5)$

$-6k^3 - 3k - 16k^3 - 40k$

$-22k^3 - 43k$

$(x - 2y)(7x - 2y)$

$7x^2 - 2xy - 14xy + 4y^2$

$7x^2 - 16xy + 4y^2$

Algebra 2 Builder # 2

Name:______________________

Solve Equations

$5x - \frac{1}{5} = 2x - \frac{3}{5}$

$-2x + \frac{1}{5} \quad -2x + \frac{1}{5}$

$(\frac{1}{3})3x = \frac{-2}{5}(\frac{1}{3})$

$x = \frac{-2}{15}$

Solve Inequalities

Solve, show your answer graphically, with set builder and interval notation.

$2 - (4x + 3) \geq 7$

$2 - 4x - 3 \geq 7$

$-4x - 1 \geq 7$

$+1 \quad +1$

$\frac{-4x}{-4} \geq \frac{8}{-4}$

$x \leq -2$

-2

$\{x|x \leq -2\}$

$(-\infty, -2]$

Evaluate Expressions

$x^2 - 3x + 5$ when $x = -2$

$(-2)^2 - 3(-2) + 5$

$4 - 3(-2) + 5$

$4 + 6 + 5$

$10 + 5$

15

Literal Equations

$(L)\ M = \frac{Mol}{L}\ (L)$ Solve for Mol

$LM = Mol$

Relations/Functions

Determine if the relation is a function. Find the domain and range.

Function: (Yes) No

Domain: {-6,-5,-3,2,4,5}

Range: {-5, 0, 2,3,4}

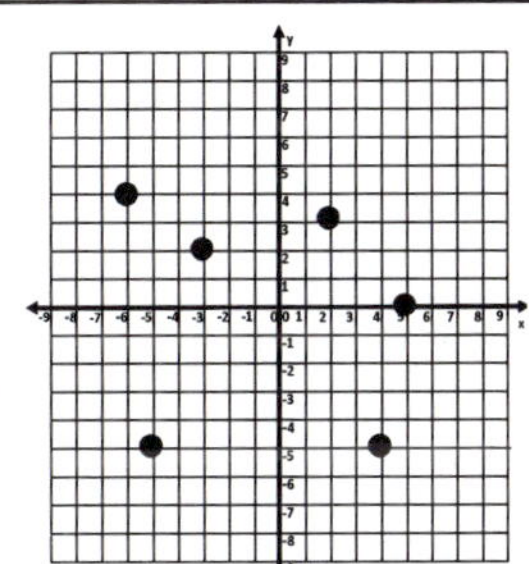

Word Problems

Harry works for a major sporting goods distributor. He earns a base salary of $30,000 per year and 5% commission on his sales. How much will Harry need to sell to earn $50,000 by the end of the year?

x = amount Harry sells

$30000 + 0.05x = 50000$

$-30000 \qquad -30000$

$\frac{0.05x}{0.05} = \frac{20000}{0.05}$

$x = 400{,}000$

Harry needs to sell $400,000 by the end of the year.

Vocabulary

Domain
Range
Function
Solution
Equation
Inequality

Range: is the set of second elements in ordered pair or table.

Equation: a mathematical statement that shows two expressions are equivalent.

Solution: a value for the variable or an ordered pair that makes an equation true.

Function: a relation in which every input has exactly one output.

Representing Functions as Graphs

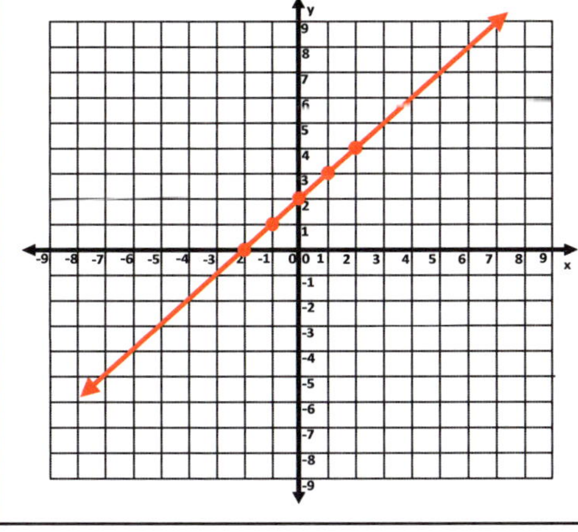

Change to slope intercept form y = mx + b, find the slope. Use {-2, -1, 0, 1, 2} for the x values. Make a table, plot the points and graph. Find the y-intercept by setting x to 0; then find the x-intercept by setting y to 0. $-3x + 3y = 6$

x	y
-2	0
-1	1
0	2
1	3
2	4

$-3x + 3y = 6$
$+3x \quad +3x$
$\frac{3y}{3} = \frac{3x + 6}{3}$
$y = x + 2$

$y = x + 2$, $y = -2 + 2$, $y = 0$

$y = x + 2$, $y = -1 + 2$, $y = 1$

$y = x + 2$, $y = 0 + 2$, $y = 2$

$y = x + 2$, $y = 1 + 2$, $y = 3$

$y = x + 2$, $y = 2 + 2$, $y = 4$

y-int: $-3x + 3y = 6$, $-3(0) + 3y = 6$, $\frac{3y}{3} = \frac{6}{3}$, $y = 2$

x-int: $-3x + 3y = 6$, $-3x + 3(0) = 6$, $\frac{-3x}{-3} = \frac{6}{-3}$, $x = -2$

x-int=(-2,0)

y-int=(0,2) m=1

Distributive Property

$-3k^3 + 8k - 8k(6k^2 - 4)$

$-3k^3 + 8k - 48k^3 + 32k$

$-51k^3 + 40k$

$(3x - 5)(2x + 7)$

$6x^2 + 21x - 10x - 35$

$6x^2 + 11x - 35$

Algebra 2 Builder # 3

Name:____________________

Solve Equations

$3(2x - 5) - x = 5(x - 3)$

$6x - 15 - x = 5x - 15$

$5x - 15 = 5x - 15$

$-5x + 15 \quad -5x + 15$

$0 = 0$

All real numbers.

Solve Inequalities

Solve, show your answer graphically, with set builder and interval notation.

$-2(3x + 4) \leq 5(x - 3)$

$-6x - 8 \leq 5x - 15$

$-5x + 8 \quad -5x + 8$

$\frac{-11x}{-11} \leq \frac{-7}{-11}$

$x \geq \frac{7}{11}$

$\frac{7}{11}$

$\{x \mid x \geq \frac{7}{11}\}$

$[\frac{7}{11}, \infty)$

Evaluate Expressions

$3x^2 + 4y^2$ when $x = -2$ and $y = 3$

$3(-2)^2 + 4(3)^2$

$3(4) + 4(9)$

$12 + 36$

48

Literal Equations

$(d^2)F_g = G\left(\frac{m_1 m_2}{d^2}\right)(d^2)$ Solve for m_2

$\frac{d^2 F_g}{G m_1} = \frac{G m_1 m_2}{G m_1}$

$\frac{d^2 F_g}{G m_1} = m_2$

Relations/Functions

Determine if the relation is a function. Find the domain and range.

Function: Yes (No) — No circled

Domain: {-3,-1,0,2}

Range: {-2,-1,3,4,7}

X	Y
-3	4
-1	-2
0	3
2	7
2	-1

Word Problems

Paul's age is 8 years less than 5 times Sarah's age. The sum of their ages is 64. Find Paul's age.

x = Sarah's age

5x – 8 = Paul's age

$x + (5x - 8) = 64$

$6x - 8 = 64$

$+8 \quad +8$

$\frac{6x}{6} = \frac{72}{6}$

$x = 12$

5x – 8 = Paul's age

$5(12) - 8 = P$

$60 - 8 = P$

$52 = P$

Paul's age is 52.

Vocabulary

Domain
Range
Function
Solution
Equation
Inequality

Function ____ a relation in which every input has exactly one output.

Domain ____ is the set of first elements in ordered pair or table.

Inequality ____ is a type of problem that often has a set of answers and can be written in interval notation.

Solution ____ a value for the variable or an ordered pair that makes an equation true.

Representing Functions as Graphs

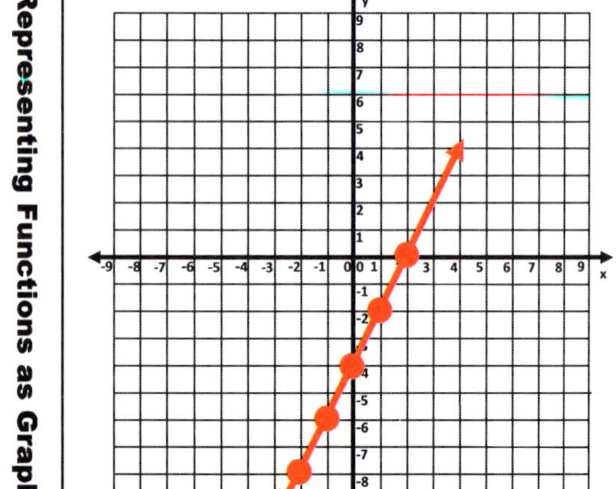

Change to slope intercept form $y = mx + b$ find the slope. Use {-2, -1, 0, 1, 2} for the x values. Make a table, plot the points and graph. Find the y-intercept by setting x to 0; then find the x-intercept by setting y to 0. $2x - y = 4$

x	y
-2	-8
-1	-6
0	-4
1	-2
2	0

x-int=(2,0)

y-int=(0,-4) m= 2

$2x - y = 4$
$-2x \quad -2x$
$\frac{-y}{-1} = \frac{-2x + 4}{-1}$
$y = 2x - 4$

$y = 2x - 4$
$y = 2(-2) - 4$
$y = -4 - 4$
$y = -8$

$y = 2x - 4$
$y = 2(-1) - 4$
$y = -2 - 4$
$y = -6$

$y = 2x - 4$
$y = 2(0) - 4$
$y = 0 - 4$
$y = -4$

$y = 2x - 4$
$y = 2(1) - 4$
$y = 2 - 4$
$y = -2$

$y = 2x - 4$
$y = 2(2) - 4$
$y = 4 - 4$
$y = 0$

y-int
$2x - y = 4$
$2(0) - y = 4$
$\frac{-y}{-1} = \frac{4}{-1}$
$y = -4$

x-int
$2x - y = 4$
$2x - 0 = 4$
$\frac{2x}{2} = \frac{4}{2}$
$x = 2$

Distributive Property

$-3m^3 - m - 2m(5m^2 + 4)$

$-3m^3 - m - 10m^3 - 8m$

$-13m^3 - 9m$

$(5 - x)(7 + 3x)$

$35 + 15x - 7x - 3x^2$

$-3x^2 + 8x + 35$

Algebra 2 Builder # 4

Name:_________________________

Solve Equations

$5(2x - 3) = 3(x - 4) + 5x$

$10x - 15 = 3x - 12 + 5x$

$10x - 15 = 8x - 12$

$-8x \quad +15 \quad -8x \quad +15$

$\frac{2x}{2} = \frac{3}{2}$

$x = \frac{3}{2}$

Solve Inequalities

Solve, show your answer graphically, with set builder and interval notation.

$3(2x - 4) + 5 \le 2 - 3(3 - 2x)$

$6x - 12 + 5 \le 2 - 9 + 6x$

$6x - 7 \le -7 + 6x$

$-6x + 7 \quad -6x + 7$

$0 \le 0$

0

$\{x \mid x \text{ is all real numbers}\}$

$(-\infty, \infty)$

Evaluate Expressions

$\frac{2x+3y+4}{3x-y}$ when x = 2 and y = -3

$\frac{2(2)+3(-3)+4}{3(2)-(-3)}$

$\frac{4-9+4}{6+3}$

$\frac{-5+4}{9} = \frac{-1}{9}$

Literal Equations

$V_1M_1 = V_2M_2$ Solve for M_2

$\frac{V_1M_1}{V_2} = \frac{V_2M_2}{V_2}$

$\frac{V_1M_1}{V_2} = M_2$

Relations/Functions

Determine if the relation is a function. Find the domain and range.

Function: (Yes) No

Domain: {-2,3,4,6}

Range: {-3,9.12}

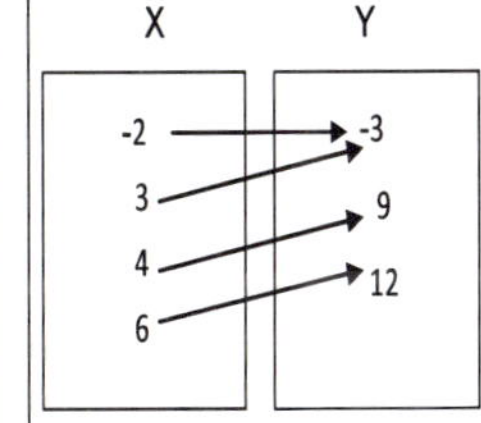

Word Problems

The smaller of two numbers is 2 less than 3/4 the larger. The sum of the two numbers is 47. Find the value of the numbers.

x = larger number

$\frac{3}{4}x - 2$ smaller number

$\frac{3}{4}x - 2 + x = 47$

$\frac{7}{4}x - 2 = 47$

$+2 \quad +2$

$\left(\frac{4}{7}\right)\frac{7}{4}x = 49\left(\frac{4}{7}\right)$

x = 28

$\frac{3}{4}(28) - 2$

21 – 2

19

The larger number is 28 and the smaller is 19.

Vocabulary

Domain
Range
Function
Solution
Equation
Inequality

Solution a value for the variable or an ordered pair that makes an equation true.

Inequality is a type of problem that often has a set of answers and can be written in interval notation.

Equation a mathematical statement that shows two expressions are equivalent.

Range is the set of second elements in ordered pair or table.

Representing Functions as Graphs

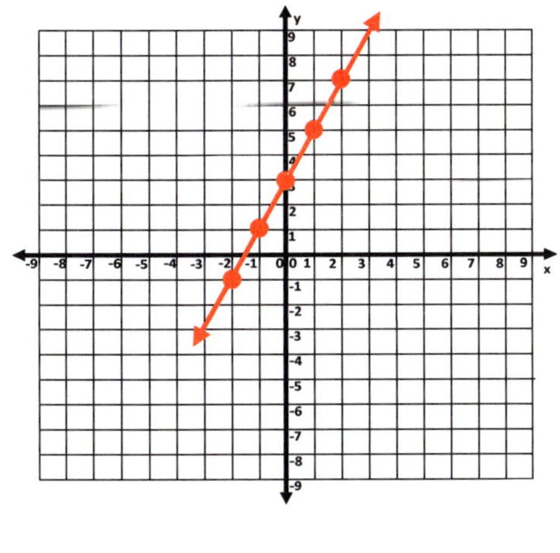

Change to slope intercept form y = mx + b, find the slope. Use {-2, -1, 0, 1, 2} for the x values. Make a table, plot the points and graph. Find the y-intercept by setting x to 0; then find the x-intercept by setting y to 0. $-4x + 2y = 6$

x	y
-2	-1
-1	1
0	3
1	5
2	7

x-int= (-3/2, 0)

y-int= (0,3) m= 2

$-4x + 2y = 6$
$+4x \quad +4x$
$\frac{2y}{2} = \frac{4x + 6}{2}$
$y = 2x + 3$

$y = 2x + 3$
$y = 2(-2) + 3$
$y = -4 + 3$
$y = -1$

$y = 2x + 3$
$y = 2(-1) + 3$
$y = -2 + 3$
$y = 1$

$y = 2x + 3$
$y = 2(0) + 3$
$y = 0 + 3$
$y = 3$

$y = 2x + 3$
$y = 2(1) + 3$
$y = 2 + 3$
$y = 5$

$y = 2x + 3$
$y = 2(2) + 3$
$y = 4 + 3$
$y = 7$

y-int
$-4x + 2y = 6$
$-4(0) + 2y = 6$
$\frac{2y}{2} = \frac{6}{2}$
$y = 3$

x-int
$-4x + 2y = 6$
$-4x + 2(0) = 6$
$\frac{-4x}{-4} = \frac{6}{-4}$
$x = -3/2$

Distributive Property

$4k(-5m - 2k) + 5k(-2m - 3k)$

$-20km - 8k^2 - 10km - 15k^2$

$-23k^2 - 30km$

$5x(3x^2 + 3x - 4)$

$15x^3 + 15x^2 - 20x$

Algebra 2 Builder # 5

Name:________________________

Solve Equations

$5(2x - 3) - x = 3(3x - 4)$

$10x - 15 - x = 9x - 12$

$9x - 15 = 9x - 12$

$-9x + 15 \quad -9x + 15$

$0 = 3$

No Solution.

Solve Inequalities

Solve, show your answer graphically, with set builder and interval notation.

$\frac{3x}{3} > \frac{-15}{3}$ and $\frac{4x}{4} < \frac{16}{4}$

$x > -5$ and $x < 4$

$\{x \mid -5 < x < 4\}$

$(-5, 4)$

Evaluate Expressions

$\frac{3x-2y-1}{x-3y}$ when x = -2 and y = 3

$\frac{3(-2) - 2(3) - 1}{-2 - 3(3)}$

$\frac{-6 - 6 - 1}{-2 - 9}$

$\frac{-13}{-11} = \frac{13}{11}$

Literal Equations

$\frac{V_1}{T_1} = \frac{V_2}{T_2}$ Solve for V_2

$\frac{T_2V_1}{T_1} = \frac{T_1V_2}{T_1}$

$\frac{T_2V_1}{T_1} = V_2$

Relations/Functions

Determine if the relation is a function. Use set builder and interval notation for the domain and range.

Function: (Yes) No

Domain: $\{x \mid x \in \mathbb{R}\}$ $(-\infty, \infty)$

Range: $\{y \mid y \in \mathbb{R}\}$ $(-\infty, \infty)$

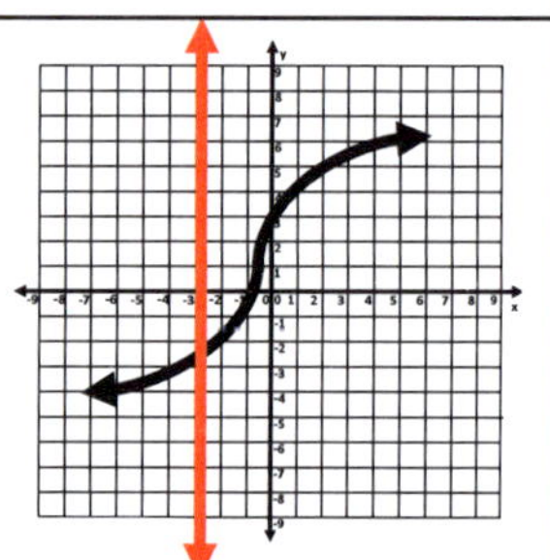

Word Problems

A large candy bar costs 35 cents more than a small candy bar. Marianne wants to write an equation for the approximate cost of 5 small candy bars and 3 large candy bars. If the total cost of the candy is around $5.50, solve for the approximate cost of a large candy bar and a small candy bar.

x= small candy bar

x + 0.35 = large candy bar

$5(x) + 3(x + 0.35) = 5.50$

$5x + 3x + 1.05 = 5.50$

$8x + 1.05 = 5.50$

$\frac{8x}{8} = \frac{4.45}{8}$

$x \approx 0.55625$

$x + 0.35$

$0.56 + 0.35$

≈ 0.91

The small candy bar cost approximately 56 cents and the large candy bar cost approximatley 91 cents.

Vocabulary

Domain
Range
Function
Solution
Equation
Inequality

Range ______ is the set of second elements in ordered pair or table.

Function ______ a relation in which every input has exactly one output.

Solution ______ a value for the variable or an ordered pair that makes an equation true.

Domain ______ is the set of first elements in ordered pair or table.

Representing Functions as Graphs

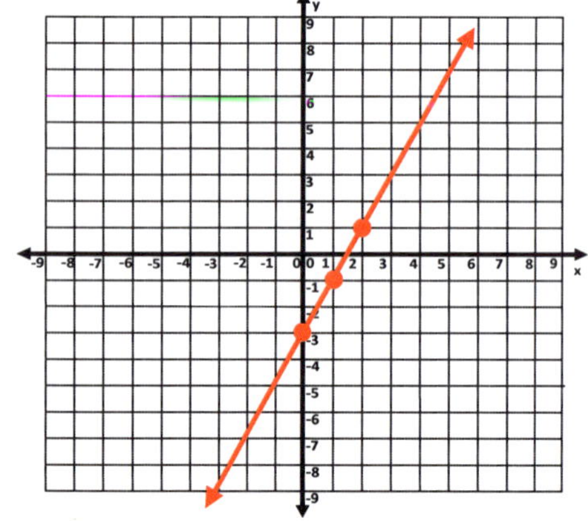

Change to slope intercept form. Find the y-intercept and the slope. Graph the function. Then find the x-intercept by setting y to 0. $6x - 3y = 9$

$6x - 3y = 9$

$-6x \quad -6x$

$\frac{-3y}{-3} = \frac{-6x + 9}{-3}$

$y = 2x - 3$

$y = mx + b$

$m = 2 \quad b = -3$

x-intercept

$6x - 3y = 9$

$6x - 3(0) = 9$

$\frac{6x}{6} = \frac{9}{6}$

$x = \frac{3}{2}$

x-int= (3/2 , 0) y-int = (0,-3) m = 2

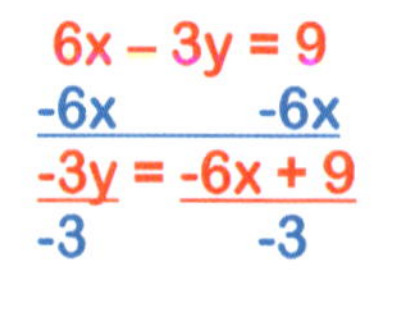

Distributive Property

$(2x^2 - 5y)(3x + 4y^2)$

$6x^3 + 8x^2y^2 - 15xy - 20y^3$

$(x - 3)(2x^2 - 4x + 5)$

$2x^3 - 4x^2 + 5x - 6x^2 + 12x - 15$

$2x^3 - 10x^2 + 17x - 15$

Algebra 2 Builder # 6

Name:________________________

Solve Equations

$\frac{1}{2}(10x + 14) = \frac{2}{3}(21 - 3x)$

$5x + 7 = 14 - 2x$

$+2x - 7 \quad -7 \quad +2x$

$\frac{7x}{7} = \frac{7}{7}$

$x = 1$

Solve Inequalities

Solve, show your answer graphically, with set builder and interval notation.

$4x > -16$ and $5x + 2 \le 7$

$\frac{4x}{4} > \frac{-16}{4}$

$x > -4$

$-2 \quad -2$

$\frac{5x}{5} \le \frac{5}{5}$

$x \le 1$

-4 1

-4 1

$\{x \mid -4 < x \le 1\}$

$(-4,1]$

Evaluate Expressions

$(2x)^2 - xy^2$ when $x = -4$ and $y = 5$

$(2(-4))^2 - (-4)(5)^2$

$(-8)^2 - (-4)(5)^2$

$64 - (-4)(25)$

$64 + 100$

164

Literal Equations

$E = mc^2$ Solve for c

$\frac{E}{m} = \frac{mc^2}{m}$

$\sqrt{\frac{E}{m}} = \sqrt{c^2}$ $\quad \sqrt{\frac{E}{m}} = c$

Word Problems

The product of 15 and a number n is at most 45. What is the largest possible number?

$\frac{15n}{15} \le \frac{45}{15}$

$n \le 3$

The largest possible number is 3.

Relations/Functions

Determine if the relation is a function. Use set builder and interval notation for the domain and range.

Function: Yes  No

Domain: $\{x \mid 2 \le x \le 8\}$ $[2, 8]$

Range: $\{y \mid -7 \le y \le -1\}$ $[-7, -1]$

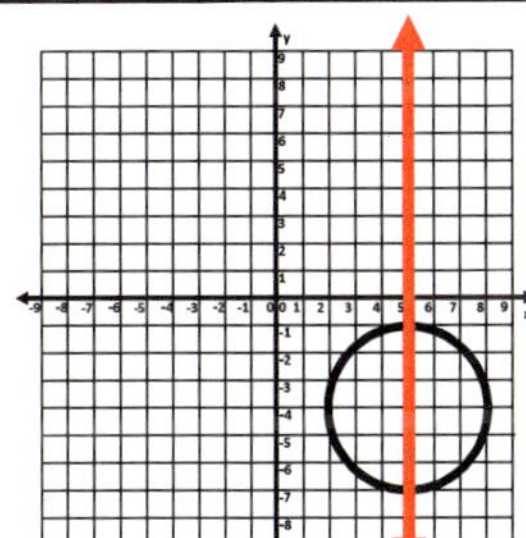

Vocabulary

Domain
Range
Function
Solution
Equation
Inequality

Equation ________ a mathematical statement that shows two expressions are equivalent.

Range ________ is the set of second elements in ordered pair or table.

Inequality ________ is a type of problem that often has a set of answers and can be written in interval notation.

Domain ________ is the set of first elements in ordered pair or table.

Representing Functions as Graphs

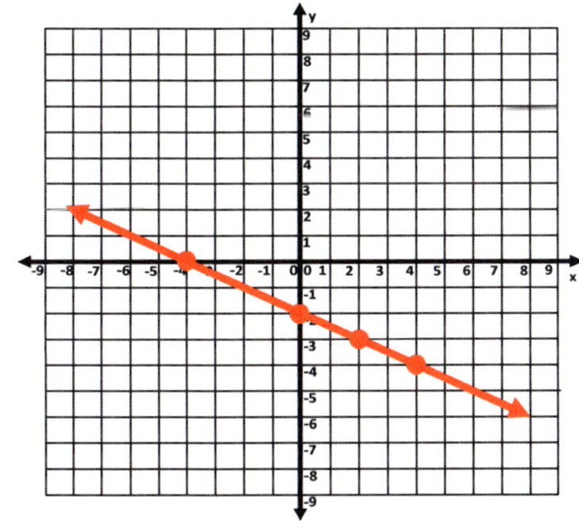

Change to slope intercept form. Find the y-intercept and the slope. Graph the function. Then find the x-intercept by setting y to 0. $4x + 8y = -16$

$4x + 8y = -16$

$-4x \quad\quad -4x$

$\frac{8y}{8} = \frac{-4x - 16}{8}$

$y = -\frac{1}{2}x - 2$

$m = -\frac{1}{2}$ $\quad b = -2$

x-intercept

$4x + 8y = -16$

$4x + 8(0) = -16$

$\frac{4x}{4} = \frac{-16}{4}$

$x = -4$

x-int= $(-4,0)$ y-int = $(0,-2)$ $m = -\frac{1}{2}$

Distributive Property

$(3x - 4)(3x + 4)$

$9x^2 + 12x - 12x - 16$

$9x^2 - 16$

$(x - 4)(3x^2 + 2x - 1)$

$3x^3 + 2x^2 - x - 12x^2 - 8x + 4$

$3x^3 - 10x^2 - 9x + 4$

Algebra 2 Builder # 7

Name:______________________________

Solve Equations

$4.3w + 3.1 = 3.2(w + 2)$

$4.3w + 3.1 = 3.2w + 6.4$

$-3.2w - 3.1 \quad -3.2w - 3.1$

$\frac{1.1w}{1.1} = \frac{3.3}{1.1}$

$w = 3$

Solve Inequalities

Solve, show your answer graphically, with set builder and interval notation.

$\frac{5x}{5} \le \frac{-15}{5}$ or $\frac{3x}{3} > \frac{12}{3}$

$x \le -3$ or $x > 4$

$\{x \mid x \le -3 \text{ or } x > 4\}$

$(-\infty, -3] \cup (4, \infty)$

Evaluate Expressions

$\frac{a^2 - 2ab + 2}{3a^2b}$ a = -2 and b= 3

$\frac{(-2)^2 - 2(-2)(3) + 2}{3(-2)^2(3)}$

$\frac{4 + 12 + 2}{3(4)(3)}$

$\frac{18}{36} = \frac{1}{2}$

Literal Equations

$d_0d_1f\left(\frac{1}{f} = \frac{1}{d_1} + \frac{1}{d_0}\right)$ Solve for f

$d_0d_1 = d_0f + d_1f$

$\frac{d_0d_1}{d_0 + d_1} = \frac{f(d_0 + d_1)}{d_0 + d_1}$ $\quad \frac{d_0d_1}{d_0 + d_1} = f$

Relations/Functions

Determine if the relation is a function. Use set builder and interval notation for the domain and range.

Function: (Yes) No

Domain: $\{x \mid x > 0\}$ $(0, \infty)$

Range: $\{y \mid y > 0\}$ $(0, \infty)$

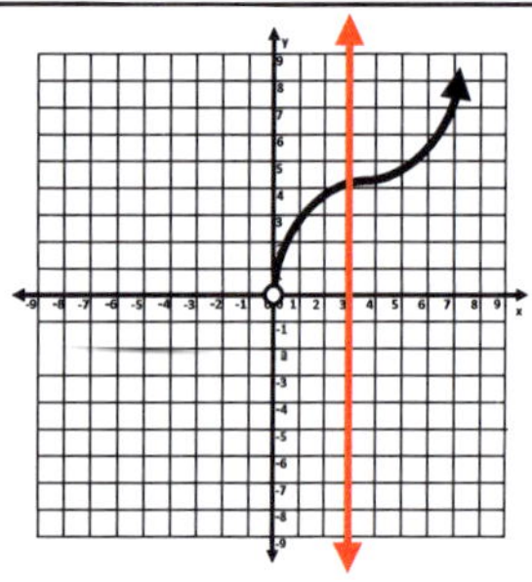

Word Problems

Ann bowled 115,121,125,118 and 122 in five games. What must Ann bowl in the sixth game so that she will have an average score of 120 for the six games?

Score on sixth game = x

$\frac{115 + 121 + 125 + 118 + 122 + x}{6} = 120$

$(6)\left(\frac{601 + x}{6}\right) = 120\,(6)$

$601 + x = 720$

$-601 \quad -601$

$x = 119$

Ann needs to bowl a 119 on her sixth game to have an average of 120.

Vocabulary

Domain
Range
Function
Solution
Equation
Inequality

Solution _____ a value for the variable or an ordered pair that makes an equation true.

Equation _____ a mathematical statement that shows two expressions are equivalent.

Domain _____ is the set of first elements in ordered pair or table.

Range _____ is the set of second elements in ordered pair or table.

Representing Functions as Graphs

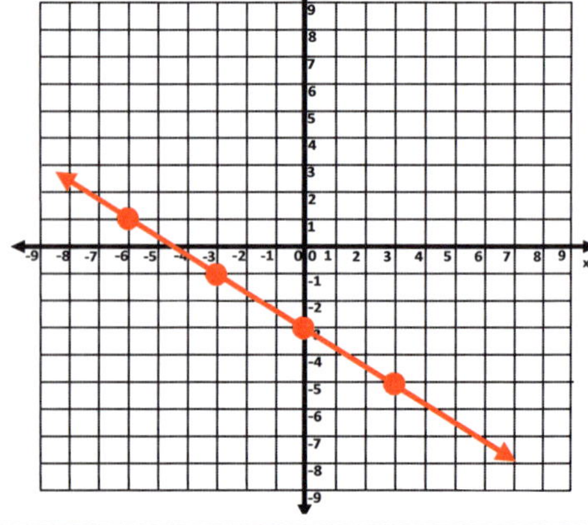

Change to slope intercept form. Find the y-intercept and the slope. Graph the function. Then find the x-intercept by setting y to 0. $2x + 3y = -9$

$2x + 3y = -9$

$-2x \quad -2x$

$\frac{3y}{3} = \frac{-2x - 9}{3}$

$y = -\frac{2}{3}x - 3$

$m = -\frac{2}{3} \quad b = -3$

x-intercept

$2x + 3y = -9$

$2x + 3(0) = -9$

$\frac{2x}{2} = \frac{-9}{2}$

$x = -\frac{9}{2}$

x-int= $(-\frac{9}{2}, 0)$ y-int = $(0, -3)$ m = $-\frac{2}{3}$

Distributive Property

$(2x + 5y)(2x - 5y)$

$4x^2 - 10xy + 10xy - 25y^2$

$4x^2 - 25y^2$

$(x - 2)[(x + 3)(x - 1)]$

$(x - 2)(x^2 - x + 3x - 3)$

$(x - 2)(x^2 + 2x - 3)$

$x^3 + 2x^2 - 3x - 2x^2 - 4x + 6$

$x^3 - 7x + 6$

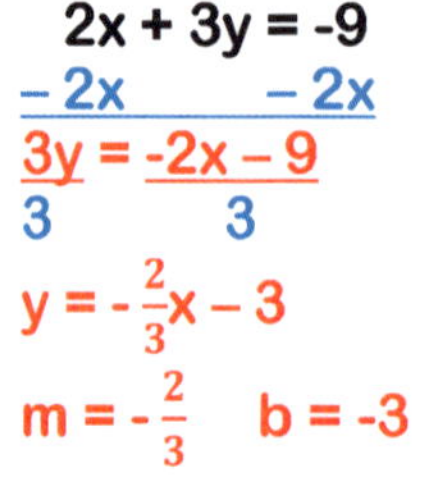

Algebra 2 Builder # 8

Name:______________________

Solve Equations

$3(4x - 3) - x = -5(2x - 4)$

$12x - 9 - x = -10x + 20$

$11x - 9 = -10x + 20$

$+10x + 9 \quad +10x + 9$

$\frac{21x}{21} = \frac{29}{21}$

$x = \frac{29}{21}$

Solve Inequalities

Solve, show your answer graphically, with set builder and interval notation.

$7x < -7$ or $-3x \geq 12$

$x < -1$ or $x \leq -4$

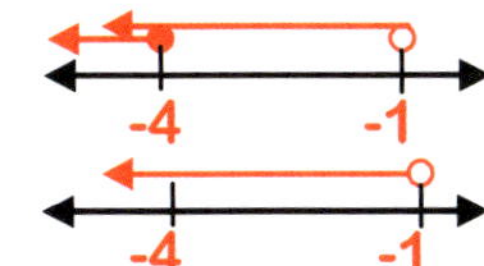

$\{x \mid x < -1\}$

$(-\infty, -1)$

Evaluate Expressions

$2x^2 \div (6 + 2x) + 4$ when $x = -4$

$2(-4)^2 \div (6 + 2(-4)) + 4$

$2(-4)^2 \div (6 - 8) + 4$

$2(-4)^2 \div (-2) + 4$

$2(16) \div (-2) + 4$

$32 \div (-2) + 4$

$-16 + 4$

-12

Literal Equations

$2(KE = \frac{1}{2}mv^2)2$ Solve for v

$\frac{2KE}{m} = \frac{mv^2}{m}$

$\sqrt{\frac{2KE}{m}} = \sqrt{v^2}$

$\sqrt{\frac{2KE}{m}} = v$

Relations/Functions

Determine if the relation is a function. Use set builder and interval notation for the domain and range.

Function: Yes (No)

Domain: $\{x: -7 \leq x \leq -1\}$ $[-7,-1]$

Range: $\{y: 1 \leq y \leq 7\}$ $[1,7]$

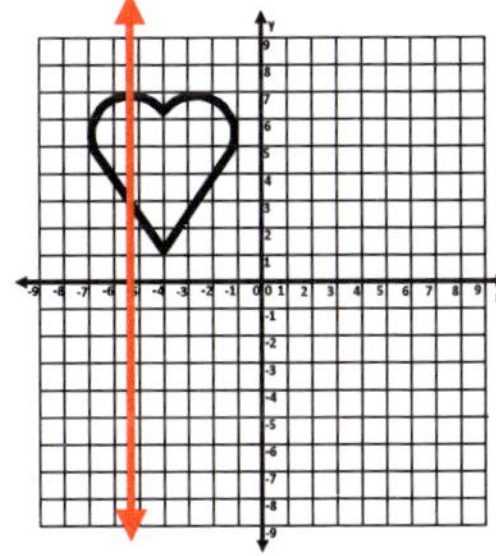

Word Problems

A rectangular tablecloth is 15 inches longer than it is wide. If Lisa has at most 242 inches of lace to sew around the tablecloth. What is the greatest possible width of the tablecloth?

width = w

length = w + 15

$2(w + 15) + 2(w) \leq 242$

$2w + 30 + 2w \leq 242$

$4w + 30 \leq 242$

$-30 \quad -30$

$\frac{4w}{4} \leq \frac{212}{4}$

$w \leq 53$

The greatest possible width of the tablecloth is 53 inches.

Vocabulary

Domain
Range
Function
Solution
Equation
Inequality

Inequality is a type of problem that often has a set of answers and can be written in interval notation.

Function a relation in which every input has exactly one output.

Range is the set of second elements in ordered pair or table.

Equation mathematical statement that two expressions are equivalent.

Representing Functions as Graphs

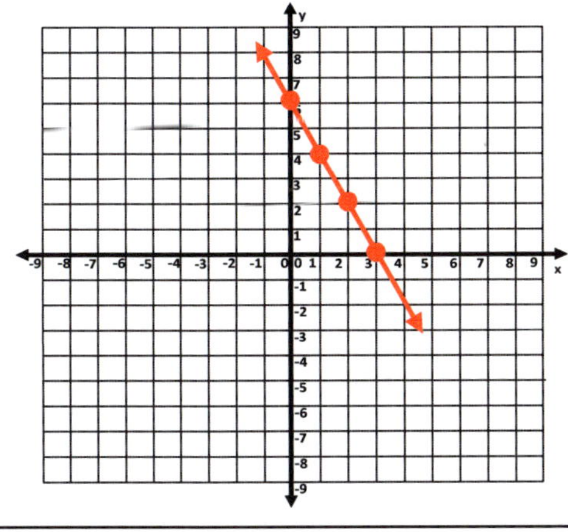

Change to slope intercept form. Find the y-intercept and the slope. Graph the function. Then find the x-intercept by setting y to 0.

$\frac{2}{3}x + \frac{1}{3}y = 2$

$-\frac{2}{3}x \quad -\frac{2}{3}x$

$(3)\left(\frac{1}{3}y\right) = \left(-\frac{2}{3}x + 2\right)(3)$

$y = -2x + 6$

$m = -2 \quad b = 6$

x- intercept

$\frac{2}{3}x + \frac{1}{3}(0) = 2$

$\left(\frac{3}{2}\right)\left(\frac{2}{3}x\right) = 2\left(\frac{3}{2}\right)$

$x = 3$

x-int = (3,0) y-int = (0,6) m = -2

Distributive Property

$(4x - 1)^2$

$(4x - 1)(4x - 1)$

$16x^2 - 4x - 4x + 1$

$16x^2 - 8x + 1$

$[(2x + 3)(3x + 2)](4x - 1)$

$(6x^2 + 4x + 9x + 6)(4x - 1)$

$(6x^2 + 13x + 6)(4x - 1)$

$24x^3 - 6x^2 + 52x^2 - 13x + 24x - 6$

$24x^3 + 46x^2 + 11x - 6$

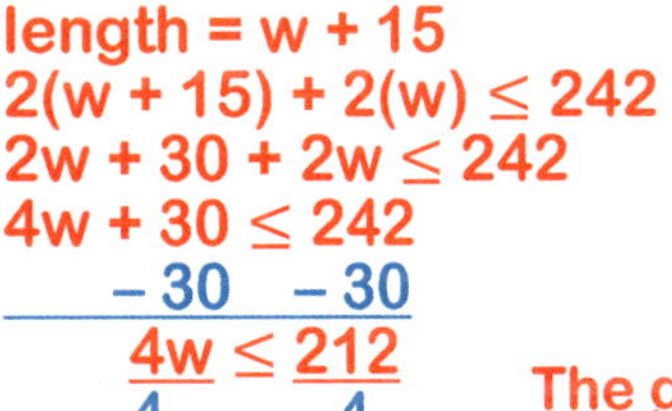

Algebra 2 Builder # 9

Name:_______________________

Transformations

The graph of y = f(x) is on the coordinate grid, use the graph to perform the transformation below.

A. Graph g(x) = f(x) + 3

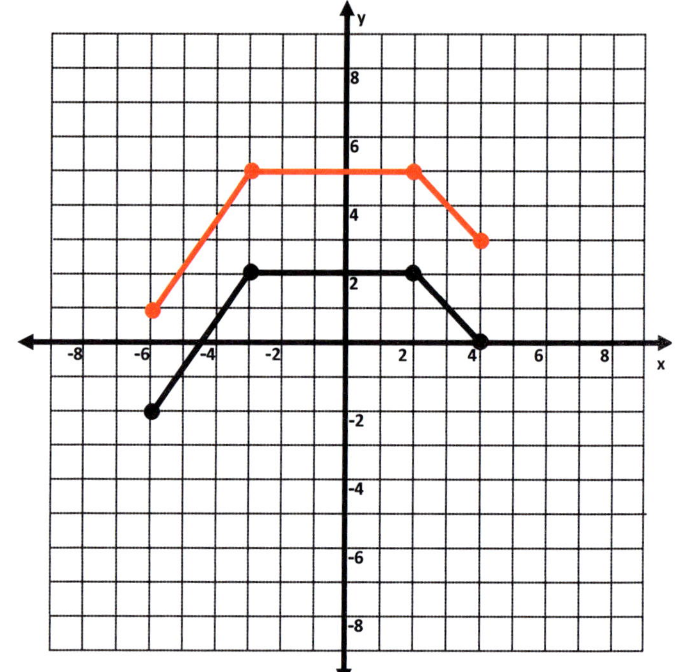

B. Explain the transformation in words.

A vertical shift 3 units up.

Vocabulary

Commutative Property
Associative Property
Distributive Property
Additive Inverse Property
Multiplicative Inverse Property
Continuous Function
Discrete Function
Inverse Function

Inverse Function	A function that results from interchanging the domain and range values of a one to one function.
Commutative Property	For all real numbers a and b, a + b = b + a or ab = ba.
Discrete Function	A function whose graph consist of separate points.
Associative Property	For all real numbers a, b, and c, (a + b) + c = a + (b + c) or (ab)c = a(bc)

Parent Functions

Write the equation and graph the parent linear function. f(x) = x

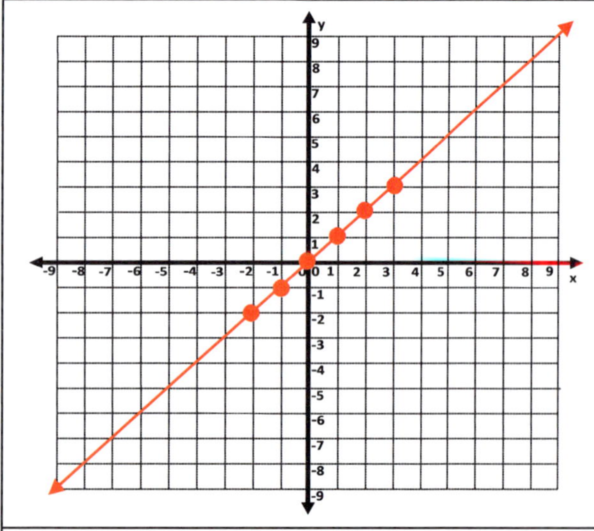

Express the domain and range in set builder and interval notation for the parent function above.

Domain:	Range:
$\{x \mid x \in \mathbb{R}\}$	$\{f(x) \mid f(x) \in \mathbb{R}\}$
$(-\infty, \infty)$	$(-\infty, \infty)$

Graphing Inequalities

Graph y > -2x + 3

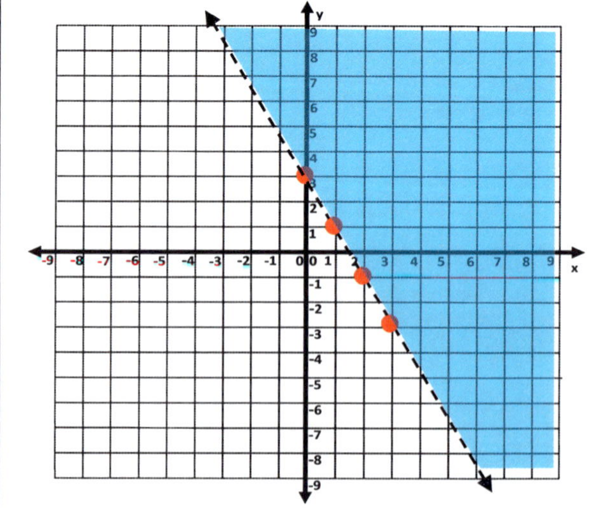

Function Notation

If f(x) = 3x + 5, find f(2).

f(2) = 3(2) + 5

f(2) = 6 + 5

f(2) = 11

Algebra 2 Builder # 10

Name: 

Transformations

The graph of $y = f(x)$ is on the coordinate grid, use the graph to perform the transformation below.

A. Graph $g(x) = f(x - 2)$

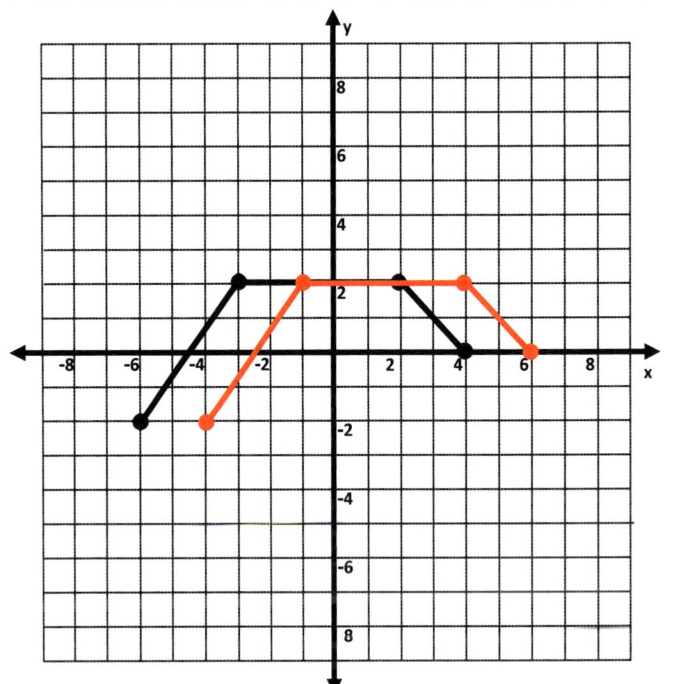

B. Explain the transformation in words.

A horizontal shift 2 units to the right.

Vocabulary

Commutative Property
Associative Property
Distributive Property
Additive Inverse Property
Multiplicative Inverse Property
Continuous Function
Discrete Function
Inverse Function

Distributive Property ______ For all real numbers a, b and c, $a(b + c) = ab + ac$.

Continuous Function ______ A function whose graph has no gaps or breaks.

Multiplicative Inverse Property For all real number a, $a \cdot \frac{1}{a} = 1$, $a \neq 0$.

Additive Inverse Property ______ For all real numbers a, $a + (-a) = 0$.

Parent Functions

Write the equation and graph the parent quadratic function. $f(x) = x^2$

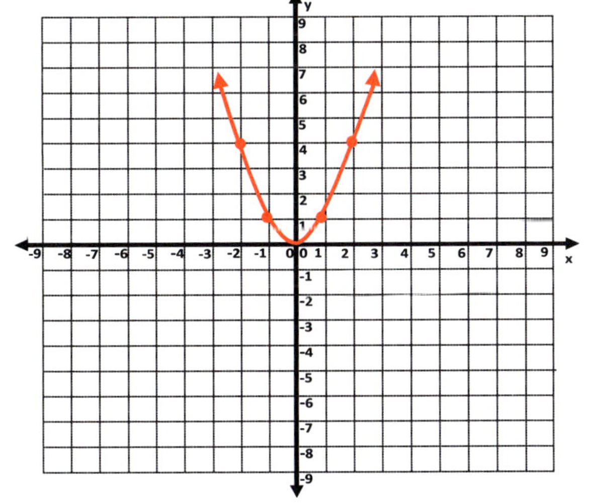

Express the domain and range in set builder and interval notation for the parent function above.

Domain:	Range:
$\{x \mid x \in \mathbb{R}\}$	$\{f(x) \mid f(x) \geq 0\}$
$(-\infty, \infty)$	$[0, \infty)$

Graphing Inequalities

Graph $y \leq 3x - 5$

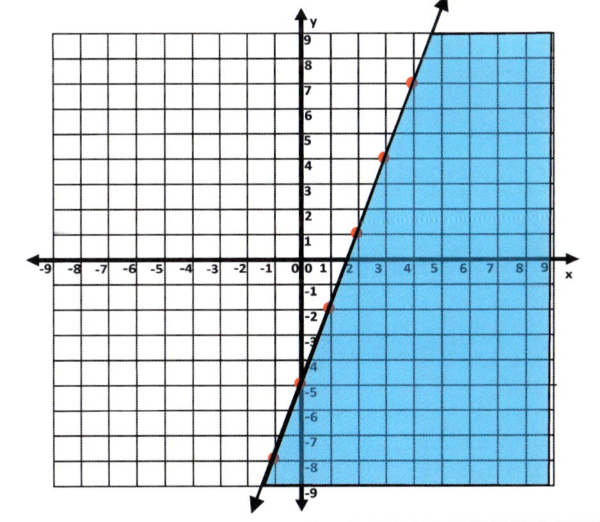

Function Notation

If $f(x) = 2x^2 + 3x + 7$, find $f(-1)$.

$f(-1) = 2(-1)^2 + 3(-1) + 7$
$f(-1) = 2(1) + 3(-1) + 7$
$f(-1) = 2 - 3 + 7$
$f(-1) = -1 + 7$
$f(-1) = 6$

Algebra 2 Builder # 11

Name:_______________________

Transformations

The graph of y = f(x) is on the coordinate grid, use the graph to perform the transformation below.

A. Graph g(x) = -f(x)

B. Explain the transformation in words.

The graph is reflected over the x-axis.

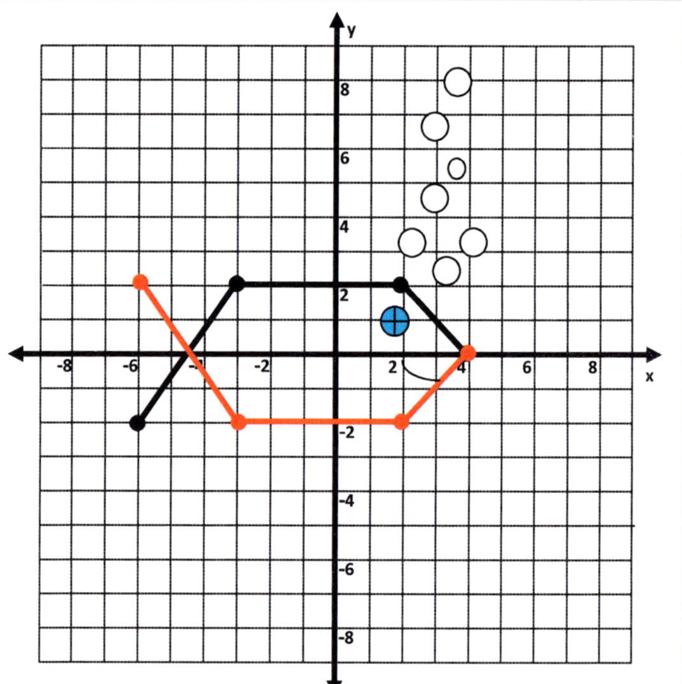

Vocabulary

Commutative Property
Associative Property
Distributive Property
Additive Inverse Property
Multiplicative Inverse Property
Continuous Function
Discrete Function
Inverse Function

Additive Inverse Property For all real numbers a, a + (-a) = 0.

Inverse Function A function that results from interchanging the domain and range values of a one to one function.

Multiplicative Inverse Property For all real number a, $a \cdot \frac{1}{a} = 1, \quad a \neq 0.$

Associative Property For all real numbers a, b, and c, (a + b) + c = a + (b + c) or (ab)c = a(bc)

Parent Functions

Write the equation and graph the parent absolute value function. $f(x) = |x|$

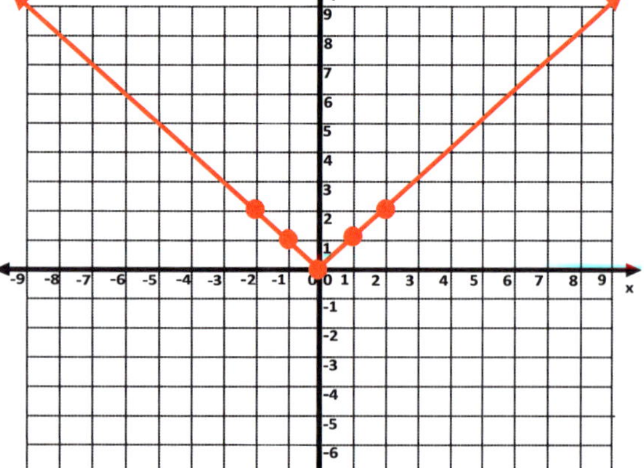

Express the domain and range in set builder and interval notation for the parent function above.

Domain:

$\{x | x \in \mathbb{R}\}$

$(-\infty, \infty)$

Range:

$\{f(x) | f(x) \geq 0\}$

$[0, \infty)$

Graphing Inequalities

Graph $4x + 2y > 3$ $\quad y > -2x + \frac{3}{2}$

Function Notation

If $f(x) = 2|4x - 5| + 7$, find f(1/2).

$f\left(\frac{1}{2}\right) = 2\left|4\left(\frac{1}{2}\right) - 5\right| + 7$

$f\left(\frac{1}{2}\right) = 2|2 - 5| + 7$

$f\left(\frac{1}{2}\right) = 2|-3| + 7$

$f\left(\frac{1}{2}\right) = 2(3) + 7$

$f\left(\frac{1}{2}\right) = 6 + 7$

$f\left(\frac{1}{2}\right) = 13$

Algebra 2 Builder # 12

Name:_______________________

Transformations

The graph of y = f(x) is on the coordinate grid, use the graph to perform the transformation below.

A. Graph g(x) = f(-x)

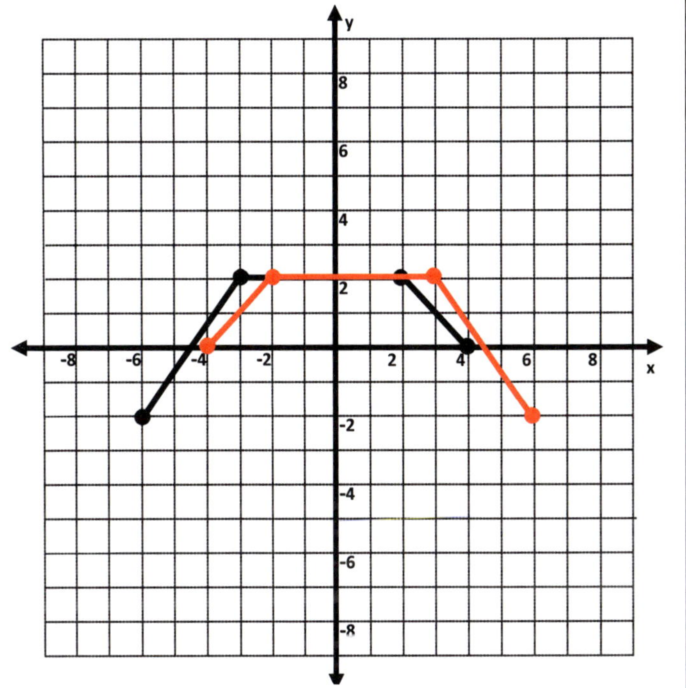

B. Explain the transformation in words.

The graph is reflected over the y-axis.

Vocabulary

Commutative Property
Associative Property
Distributive Property
Additive Inverse Property
Multiplicative Inverse Property
Continuous Function
Discrete Function
Inverse Function

Commutative Property For all real numbers a and b, a + b = b + a or ab = ba.

Continuous Function A function whose graph has no gaps or breaks.

Discrete Function A function whose graph consist of separate points.

Distributive Property For all real numbers a, b and c. a(b + c) = ab + ac.

Parent Functions

Write the equation and graph the parent square root function. $f(x) = \sqrt{x}$

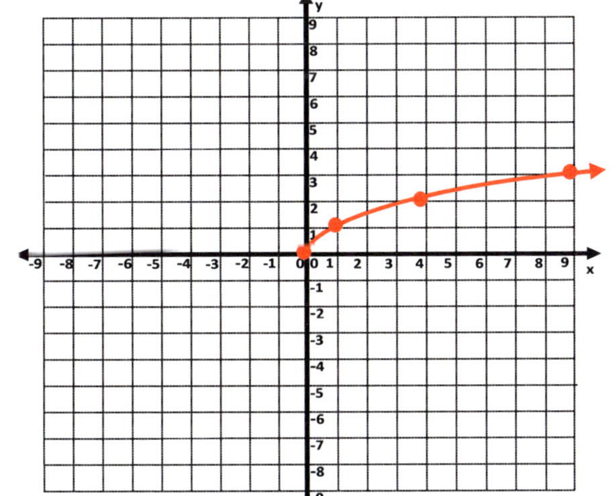

Express the domain and range in set builder and interval notation for the parent function above.

Domain:

$\{x | x \geq 0\}$

$[0, \infty)$

Range:

$\{f(x) | f(x) \geq 0\}$

$[0, \infty)$

Graphing Inequalities

Graph $3x - 6y \leq 12$ $-6y \leq -3x + 12$ $y \geq \frac{1}{2}x - 2$

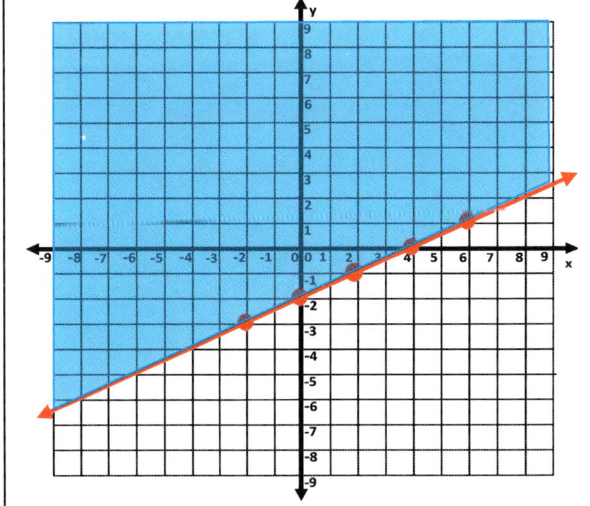

Function Notation

If $f(x) = -|2x + 3|$, find f(-5).

$f(-5) = -|2(-5) + 3|$

$f(-5) = -|-10 + 3|$

$f(-5) = -|-7|$

$f(-5) = -7$

Algebra 2 Builder # 13 Name:___________________________

Transformations

The graph of y = f(x) is on the coordinate grid, use the graph to perform the transformation below.

A. Graph g(x) = f(2x)

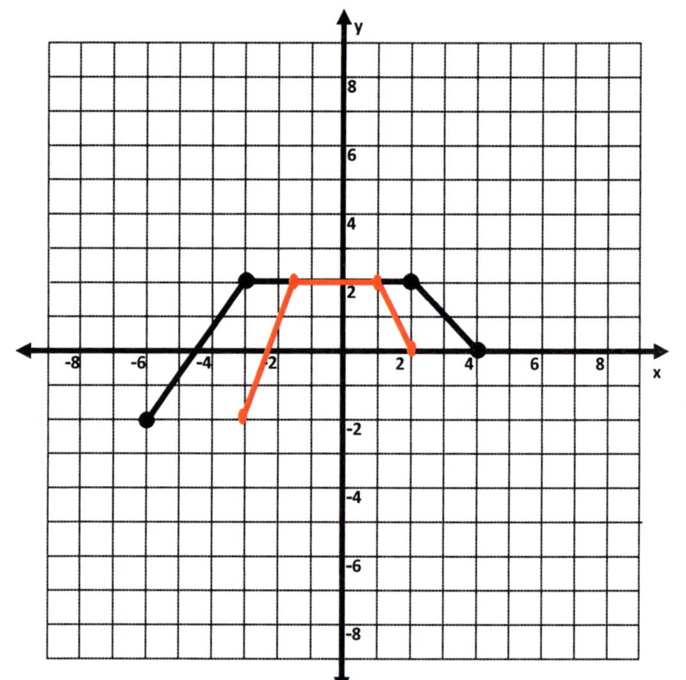

B. Explain the transformation in words.

The graph is a horizontally compressed by a factor of $\frac{1}{2}$.

Vocabulary

Commutative Property
Associative Property
Distributive Property
Additive Inverse Property
Multiplicative Inverse Property
Continuous Function
Discrete Function
Inverse Function

Associative Property For all real numbers a, b, and c, (a + b) + c = a + (b + c) or (ab)c = a(bc)

Distributive Property For all real numbers a, b and c, a(b + c) = ab + ac.

Continuous Function A function whose graph has no gaps or breaks.

Discrete Function A function whose graph consist of separate points.

Parent Functions

Write the equation and graph the parent rational function. $f(x) = \frac{1}{x}$

Express the domain and range in set builder and interval notation for the parent function above.

Domain:

$\{x | x \neq 0\}$

$(-\infty, 0) \cup (0, \infty)$

Range:

$\{f(x) | f(x) \neq 0\}$

$(-\infty, 0) \cup (0, \infty)$

Graphing Inequalities

Graph $y > |x|$

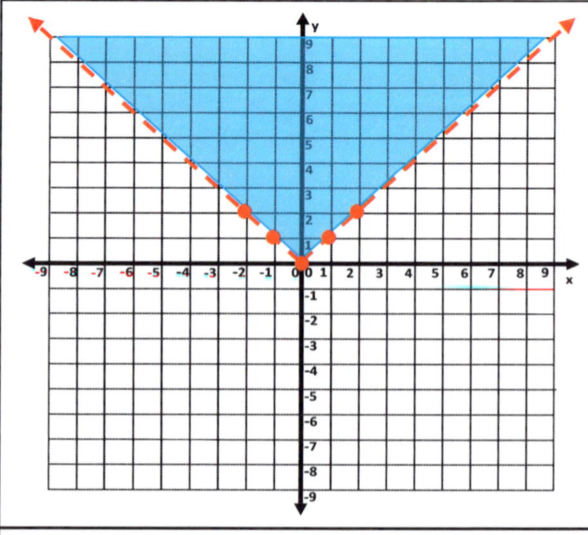

Function Notation

If $f(x) = \frac{x+3}{2x-5}$, find f(3).

$f(3) = \frac{(3)+3}{2(3)-5}$

$f(3) = \frac{6}{6-5}$

$f(3) = \frac{6}{1}$

$f(3) = 6$

Algebra 2 Builder # 14

Name:______________________________

Transformations

The graph of y = f(x) is on the coordinate grid, use the graph to perform the transformation below.

A. Graph g(x) = 2f(x)

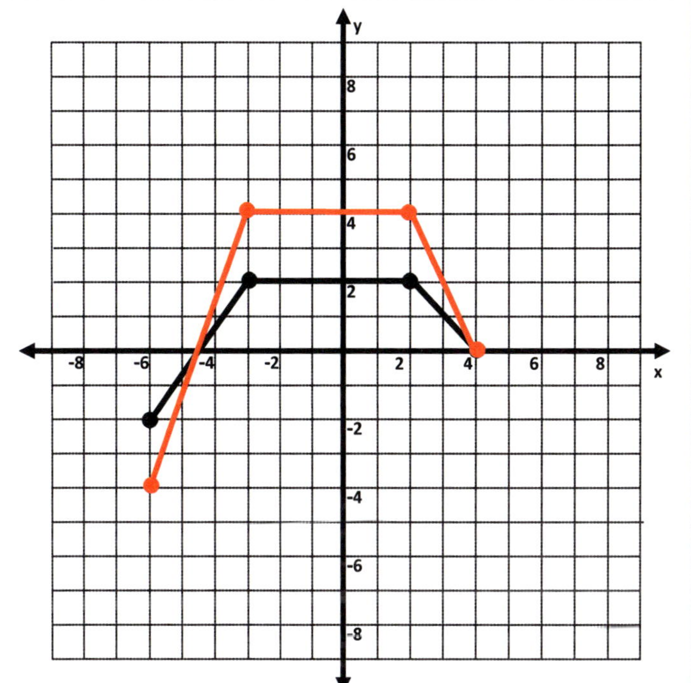

B. Explain the transformation in words.

The graph is stretched vertically by a factor of 2 units.

Vocabulary

Commutative Property
Associative Property
Distributive Property
Additive Inverse Property
Multiplicative Inverse Property
Continuous Function
Discrete Function
Inverse Function

Commutative Property ____ For all real numbers a and b, a + b = b + a or ab = ba.

Additive Inverse Property ____ For all real numbers a, a + (-a) = 0.

Inverse Function ____ A function that results from interchanging the domain and range values of a one to one function.

Multiplicative Inverse Property ____ For all real number a, $a \cdot \frac{1}{a} = 1$, $a \neq 0$.

Parent Functions

Write the equation and graph the parent cube root function. $f(x) = \sqrt[3]{x}$

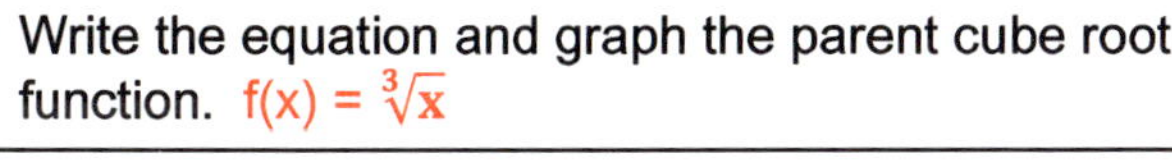

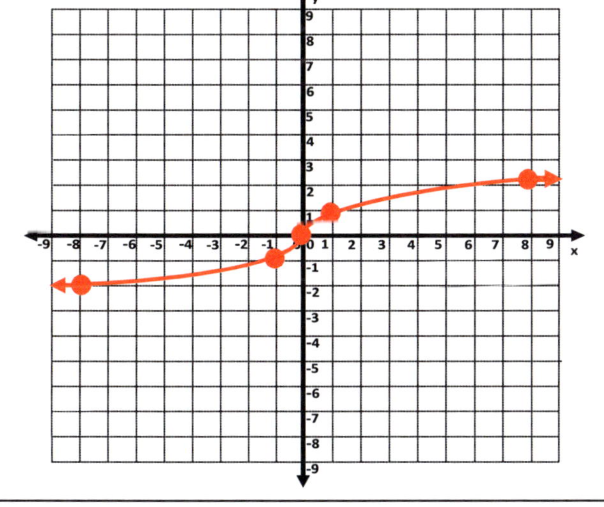

Express the domain and range in set builder and interval notation for the parent function above.

Domain:	Range:
$\{x \mid x \in \mathbb{R}\}$	$\{f(x) \mid f(x) \in \mathbb{R}\}$
$(-\infty, \infty)$	$(-\infty, \infty)$

Graphing Inequalities

Graph $y \leq |x| - 4$

Function Notation

If $f(x) = \frac{x+4}{3x-2}$, find $f(\frac{1}{2})$.

$f\left(\frac{1}{2}\right) = \frac{\frac{1}{2}+4}{3\left(\frac{1}{2}\right)-2}$

$f\left(\frac{1}{2}\right) = \frac{\frac{9}{2}}{\frac{3}{2}-2}$ $\quad f\left(\frac{1}{2}\right) = \frac{\frac{9}{2}}{-\frac{1}{2}}$ $\quad f\left(\frac{1}{2}\right) = -9$

Algebra 2 Builder # 15

Name:____________________________

Transformations

The graph of y = f(x) is on the coordinate grid, use the graph to perform the transformation below.

A. Graph g(x) = f(x – 3) + 2

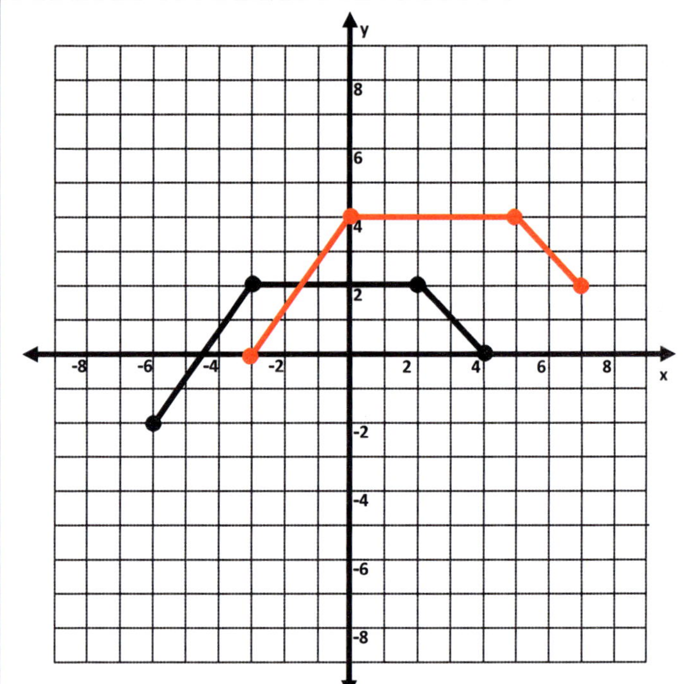

B. Explain the transformation in words.

The graph is a horizontal shift 3 units to the right and a vertical shift 2 units up.

Vocabulary

Commutative Property
Associative Property
Distributive Property
Additive Inverse Property
Multiplicative Inverse Property
Continuous Function
Discrete Function
Inverse Function

Inverse Function: A function that results from interchanging the domain and range values of a one to one function.

Commutative Property: For all real numbers a and b, a + b = b + a or ab = ba.

Discrete Function: A function whose graph consist of separate points.

Associative Property: For all real numbers a, b, and c, (a + b) + c = a + (b + c) or (ab)c = a(bc)

Parent Functions

Write the equation and graph the parent quadratic function. $f(x) = x^2$

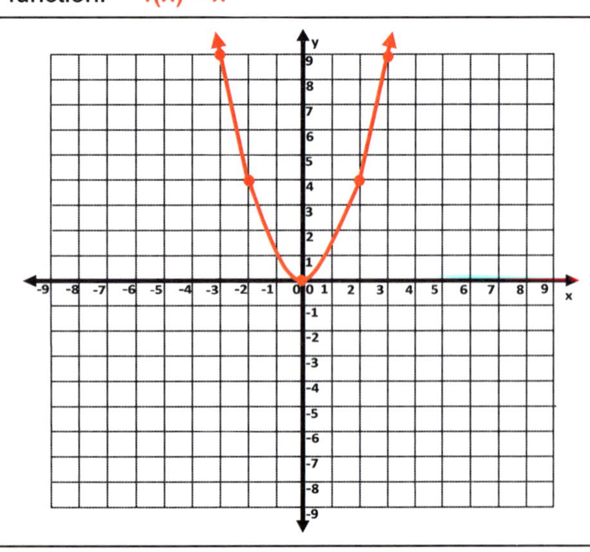

Express the domain and range in set builder and interval notation for the parent function above.

Domain:

$\{x: x \in \mathbb{R}\}$

$(-\infty, \infty)$

Range:

$\{f(x) \mid f(x) \geq 0\}$

$[0, \infty)$

Graphing Inequalities

Graph $y > |x| + 2$

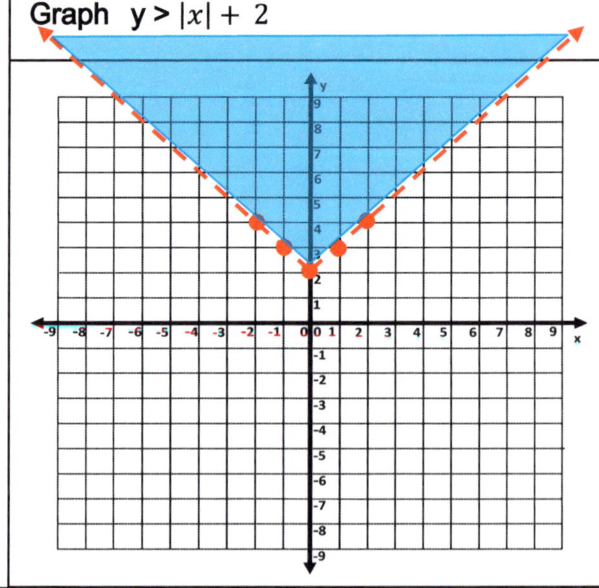

Function Notation

If $f(x) = \frac{x^2 + 5x - 4}{x + 2}$, find f(-2).

$f(-2) = \frac{(-2)^2 + 5(-2) - 4}{(-2) + 2}$

$f(-2) = \frac{4 - 10 - 4}{0}$ $f(-2) = \frac{-10}{0}$ f(-2) = **undefined**

Algebra 2 Builder # 16

Name:______________________________

Transformations

The graph of y = f(x) is on the coordinate grid, use the graph to perform the transformation below.

A. Graph g(x) = ½ f(x)

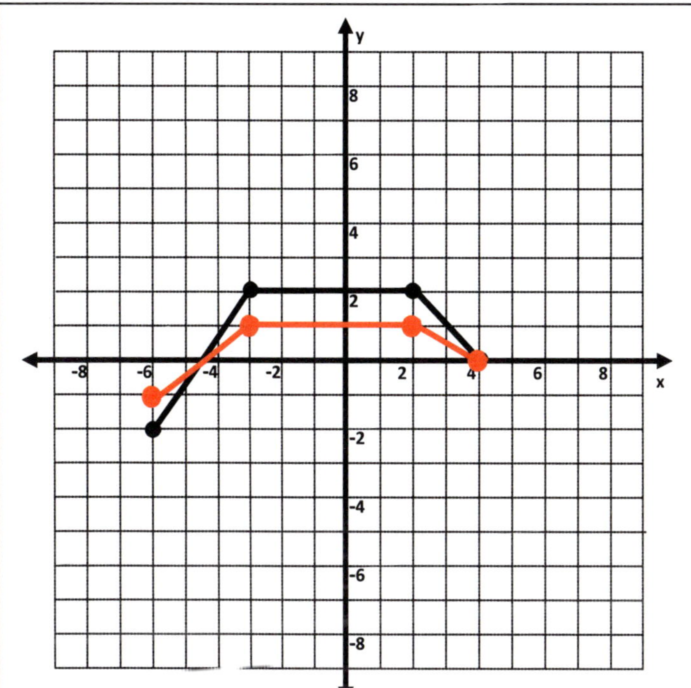

B. Explain the transformation in words.

The graph is compressed vertically by a factor of $\frac{1}{2}$.

Vocabulary

Commutative Property
Associative Property
Distributive Property
Additive Inverse Property
Multiplicative Inverse Property
Continuous Function
Discrete Function
Inverse Function

Distributive Property ______ For all real numbers a, b and c. a(b + c) = ab + ac.

Continuous Function ______ A function whose graph has no gaps or breaks.

Multiplicative Inverse Property For all real number a, $a \cdot \frac{1}{a} = 1$, $a \neq 0$.

Additive Inverse Property ______ For all real numbers a, a + (-a) = 0.

Parent Functions

Write the equation and graph the parent cubic function. $f(x) = x^3$

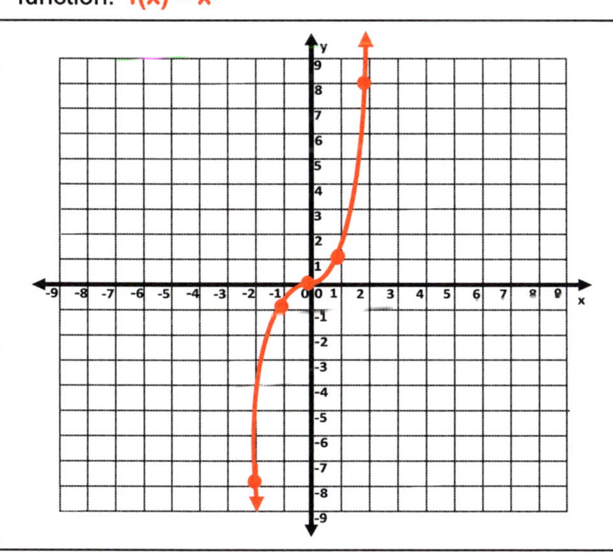

Express the domain and range in set builder and interval notation for the parent function above.

Domain:

$\{x \mid x \in \mathbb{R}\}$

$(-\infty, \infty)$

Range:

$\{f(x) \mid f(x) \in \mathbb{R}\}$

$(-\infty, \infty)$

Graphing Inequalities

Graph $y \leq -|x|$

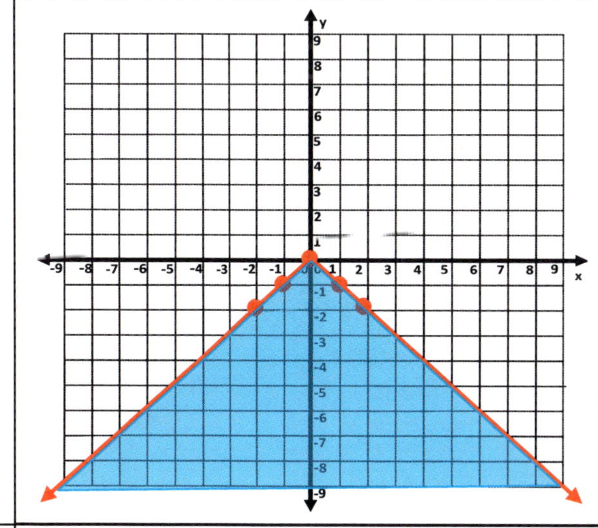

Function Notation

If $f(x) = \frac{x^2 - 9}{x^2 - 4}$, find f(3).

$f(3) = \frac{(3)^2 - 9}{(3)^2 - 4}$

$f(3) = \frac{9 - 9}{9 - 4}$

$f(3) = \frac{0}{5}$ $f(3) = 0$

Algebra 2 Builder # 17

Name:

Scatter Plots

x	1	5	7	-2	4	3
y	6	3	1	9	4	5

A. Make a scatterplot of the data.
B. Find the correlation coefficient r and the line of best fit.

$y = -0.86x + 7.25$
$r = -0.995$

C. Predict the value of y when x = 10. -1.35

$y = -0.86(10) + 7.25$
$y = -8.60 + 7.25$
$y = -1.35$

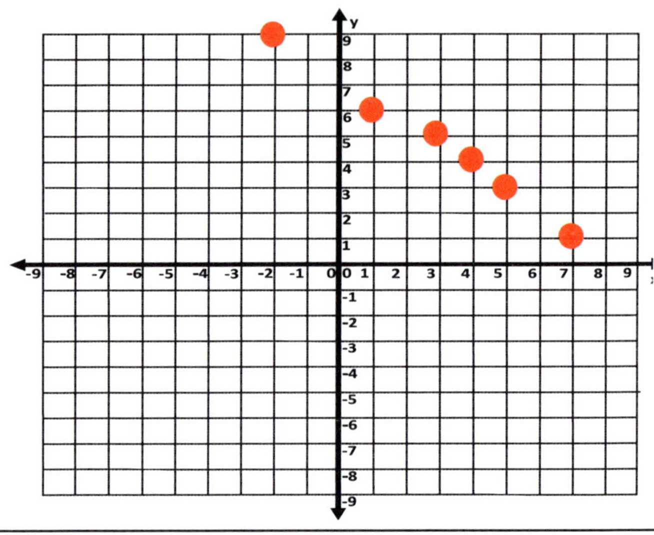

Transformations

Graph: $y = x^2 + 1$

Name the parent function: Quadratic

Explain the transformation in words:

The graph is a vertical shift 1 unit up of the parent quadratic function.

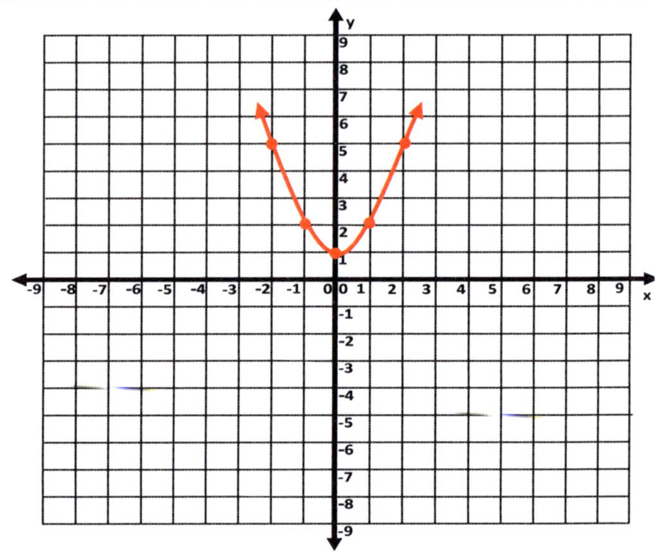

Inverse Functions

Given the table, find the inverse.

Original

x	y
2	8
3	9
4	10
5	11
6	12

Inverse

x	y
8	2
9	3
10	4
11	5
12	6

Writing Equations of Lines

Write an equation of a line in slope intercept form, that passes through the points (2 , 1) and (3 , 5).

$m = \frac{5-1}{3-2}$

$m = \frac{4}{1}$

$m = 4$

m = 4 (2,1)

$y = mx + b$
$1 = 4(2) + b$
$1 = 8 + b$
$-8 \quad -8$
$-7 = b$

$y = 4x - 7$

Vocabulary

Parallel Lines
Perpendicular Lines
Scatter Plot
Parent Function
Transformations
Representations
Slope
Discrete Function
Continuous Function

Slope: The ratio of the vertical change (rise) to the horizontal change (run).

Parallel Lines: Lines that have the same slope.

Scatter Plot: A graph with points plotted to find the relationship between two sets of data.

Discrete Function: A function whose graph consist of separate points.

Algebra 2 Builder # 18

Name:______________________

Scatter Plots

x	-2	-1	0	1	2
y	9	0	-5	-6	-3

A. Make a scatterplot of the data.
B. Find the quadratic regression equation.

$y = 2x^2 - 3x - 5$

C. Predict the value of x when y = 49. 6

$49 = 2x^2 - 3x - 5$
Use table on the graphing calculator.
x = 6

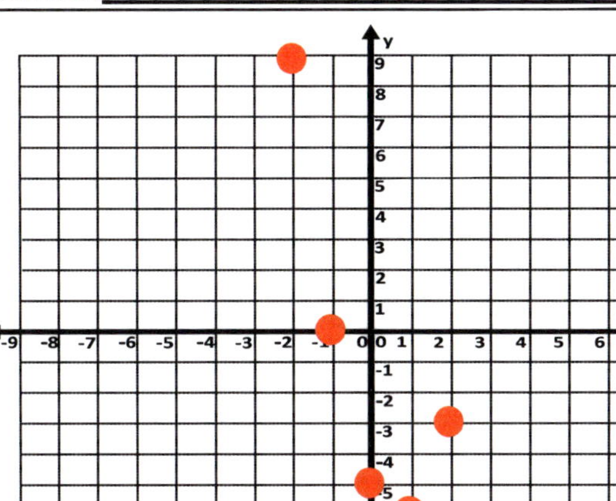

Transformations

Graph: $f(x) = \sqrt{x - 4}$

Name the parent function:

Square root

Explain the transformation in words:

The graph is a horizontal shift 4 units to the right.

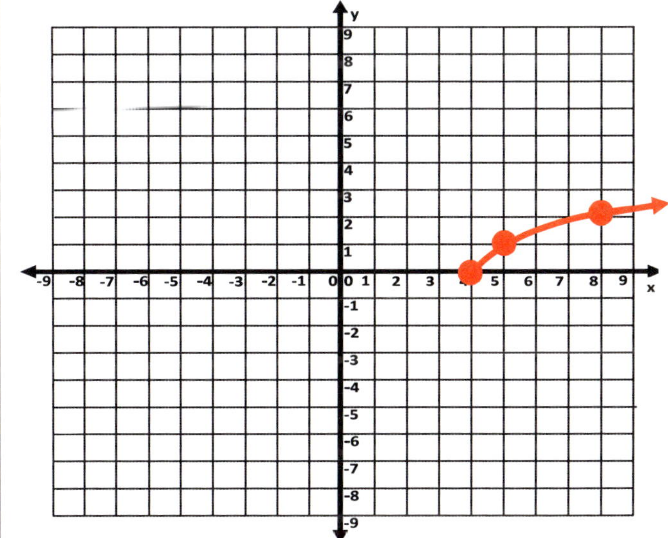

Inverse Functions

Given the equation below, find the inverse.

2x + 3y = 6

$2y + 3x = 6$
$\quad - 3x \quad - 3x$

$\frac{2y}{2} = \frac{-3x + 6}{2}$

$y = -\frac{3}{2}x + 3$ ← inverse

Writing Equations of Lines

Write an equation of a line in standard form that passes through the point (3,1) and is parrallel to the line **y = 3x + 4.**

(3,1) m = 3

$y = mx + b$
$1 = 3(3) + b$
$1 = 9 + b$
$-9 \quad -9$
$-8 = b$
$y = 3x - 8$
$-3x \quad -3x$
$\frac{-3x + y}{-1} = \frac{-8}{-1}$
$3x - y = 8$ ← Standard form

Vocabulary

Parallel Lines
Perpendicular Lines
Scatter Plot
Parent Function
Transformations
Representations
Slope
Discrete Function
Continuous Function

Perpendicular Lines — Lines whose slopes are negative reciprocals.

Parent Function — The most basic function in a family of functions.

Transformations — Ways to manipulate a graphs, size, shape, position or orientation.

Representations — Models, graphs, equations, tables and verbal descriptions of data.

Algebra 2 Builder # 19

Name:______________________________

Scatter Plots

x	-4	-2	0	1	-3	-1
y	-6.6	5	-5	1.4	5.8	-1.2

A. Make a scatterplot of the data.
B. Find the cubic regression equation.
$y = 1.3x^3 + 5.1x^2 - 5$

C. Predict the value of y when x = -7. -201

$y = 1.3(-7)^3 + 5.1(-7)^2 - 5$
$y = -201$

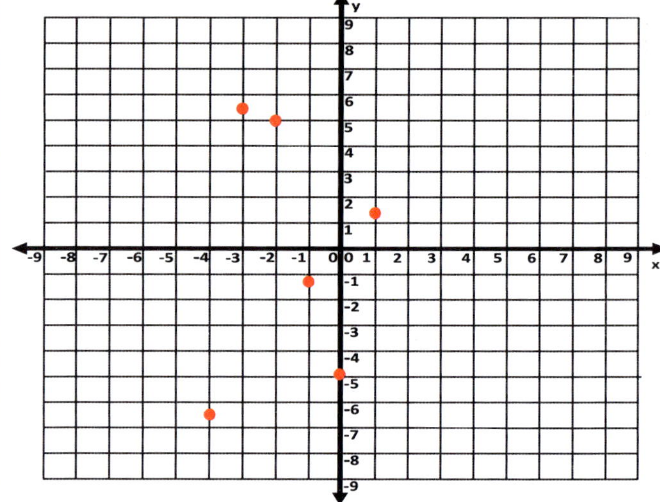

Transformations

Graph: y = |x – 4| + 2

Name the parent function:

Absolute value

Explain the transformation in words:

The graph is a horizontal shift 4 units to the right and a vertical shift 2 units up.

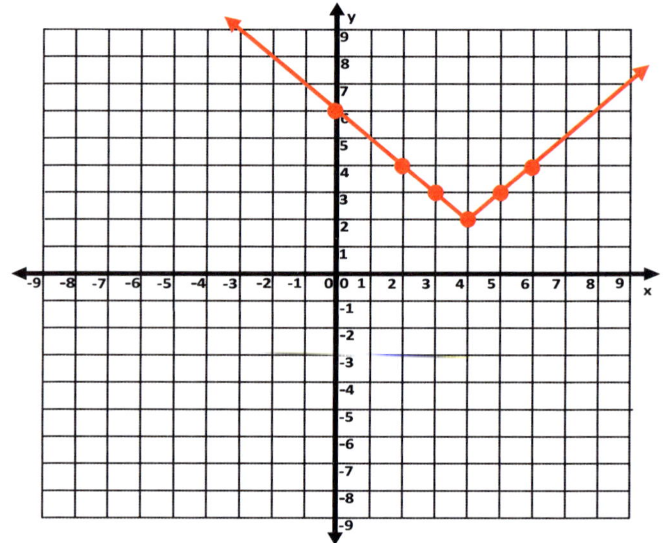

Inverse Functions

Given the graph, graph the inverse.

Graph	Inverse
(-2,-1)	(-1,-2)
(-1,2)	(2,-1)
(0,0)	(0,0)
(1,-4)	(-4,1)
(2,3)	(3,2)
(3,5)	(5,3)

Writing Equations of Lines

Write an equation of a line in slope intercept form that passes through the point (-1,2) and is perpendicular to the line **2x + 4y = 8**

$2x + 4y = 8$
$-2x \quad -2x$
$4y = -2x + 8$
$\frac{4y}{4} = \frac{-2x + 8}{4}$

$y = -\frac{1}{2}x + 2$

$m = -\frac{1}{2}$

$\perp m = 2 \quad (-1,2)$
$y = mx + b$
$2 = 2(-1) + b$
$2 = -2 + b$
$+2 \quad +2$

$4 = b$

$y = 2x + 4$

Vocabulary

Parallel Lines
Perpendicular Lines
Scatter Plot
Parent Function
Transformations
Representations
Slope
Discrete Function
Continuous Function

Slope The ratio of the vertical change (rise) to the horizontal change (run).

Parallel Lines Lines that have the same slope.

Scatter Plot A graph with points plotted to find the relationship between two sets of data.

Continuous Function A funtion whose graph has no gaps or breaks.

Algebra 2 Builder # 20

Name:______________________________

Scatter Plots

x	-6	-3	1	0
y	0.01	0.17	7.74	3

A. Make a scatterplot of the data.

B. Find the exponential regression equation.

$y = 2.99(2.59)^x$

C. Predict the value of y when x = 3.2 62.84

$y = 2.99(2.59)^{3.2}$

$y = 62.84$

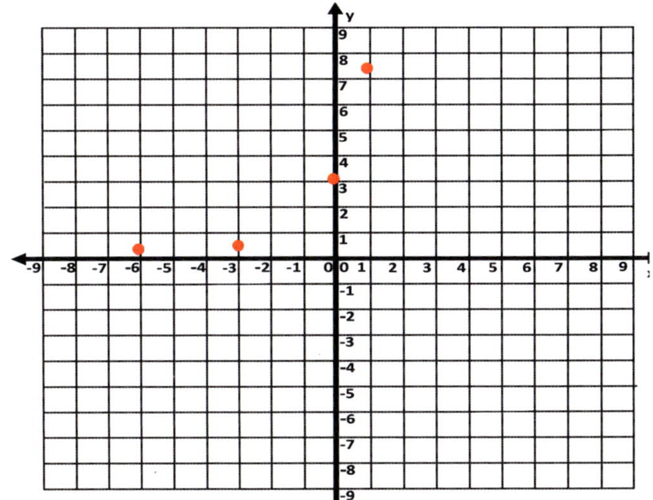

Transformations

Graph: $f(x) = 2x^3$

Name the parent function:

Cubic

Explain the transformation in words:

The graph is streched vertically by a factor of 2 units.

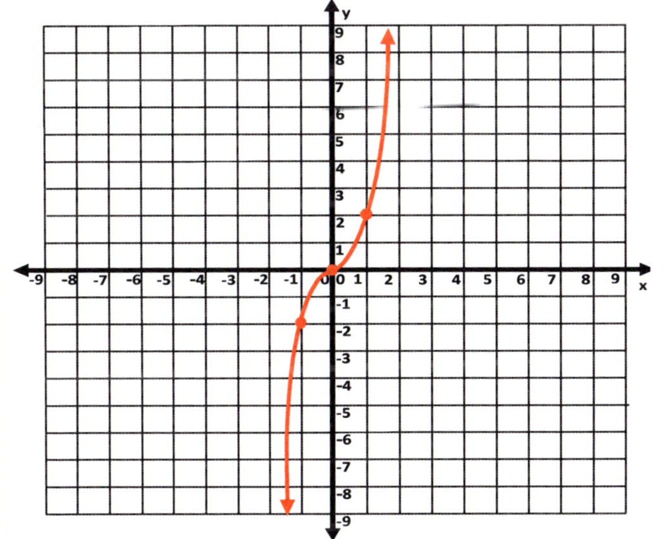

Inverse Functions

Given the equation $y = \sqrt{x} + 2$ find the inverse.

$y = \sqrt{x} + 2$

$x = \sqrt{y} + 2$

$-2 \qquad -2$

$(x-2)^2 = (\sqrt{y})^2$

$(x-2)(x-2) = y$

$x^2 - 2x - 2x + 4 = y$

$x^2 - 4x + 4 = y$

$y = x^2 - 4x + 4$ Inverse

Writing Equations of Lines

Write the equation of the line shown in the graph in slope intercept form.

(-2,1)(2,3)

$m = \frac{3-1}{2-(-2)}$

$m = \frac{2}{4}$ or $\frac{1}{2}$

$m = \frac{1}{2}$ (-2,1)

$y = mx + b$

$1 = \frac{1}{2}(-2) + b$

$1 = -1 + b$

$+1 \quad +1$

$2 = b$

$y = \frac{1}{2}x + 2$

Vocabulary

Parallel Lines
Perpendicular Lines
Scatter Plot
Parent Function
Transformations
Representations
Slope
Discrete Function
Continuous Function

Perpendicular Lines — Lines whose slopes are negative reciprocals.

Transformations — Ways to manipulate a graphs, size, shape, position or orientation.

Representations — Models, graphs, equations, tables and verbal descriptions of data.

Parent Function — The most basic function in a family of functions.

Algebra 2 Builder # 21

Name:____________________________

Discrete/Continuous Functions

Write and graph the functions described. Express the domain and range in set builder notation. State if the function is discrete or continuous.

A dog trots at an average speed of 4.5 mph. The function d(x) gives the distance in miles the dog trots in x hours.

Funciton: $d(x) = 4.5x$

Domain: $\{ x \mid x \geq 0 \}$

Range: $\{ d(x) \mid d(x) \geq 0 \}$

Discrete or Continuous: Continuous

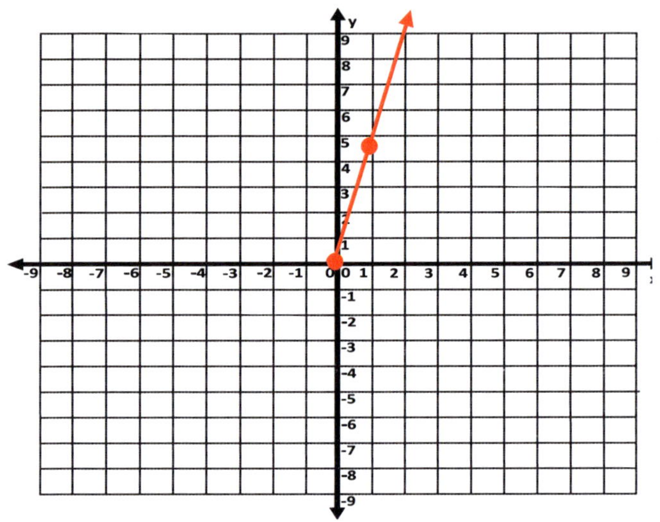

Transformations

Graph: $y = \sqrt[3]{2x}$

Name the parent function:

Cube Root

Explain the transformation in words:

The graph is compressed horizontally by a factor of $\frac{1}{2}$ unit.

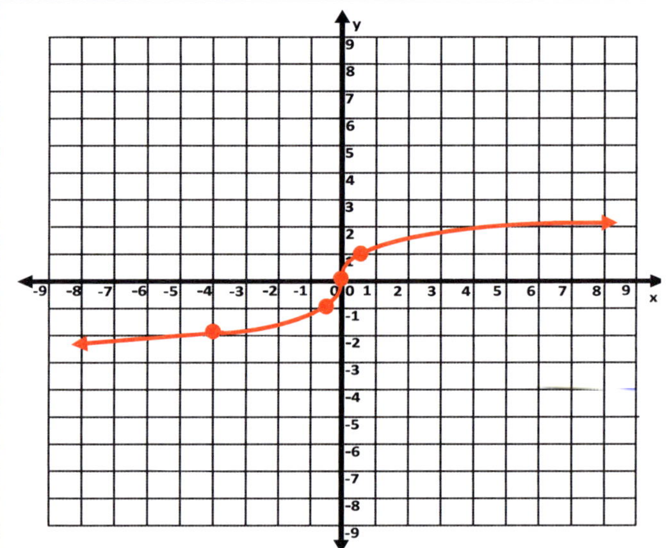

Inverse Functions

Given the graph, graph the inverse.

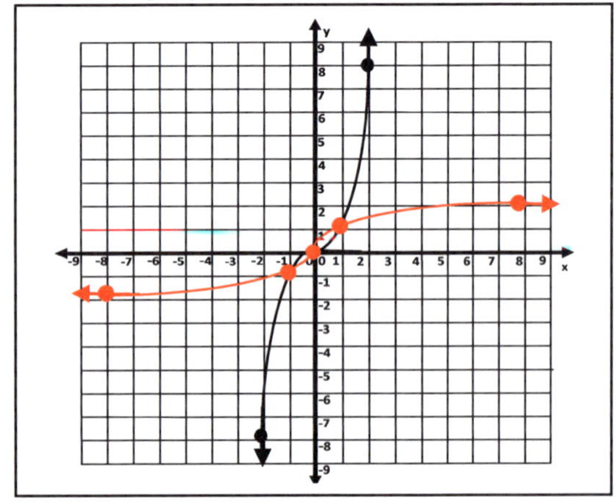

Writing Equations of Lines

Write an equation of a line in standard form that passes through the point (-1,3) and is perpendicular to the line that passes through (3,7) and (4,7).

$m = \frac{7-7}{4-3}$

$m = \frac{0}{1}$

$m = 0$

horizontal line

⊥ line is a vertical line

$x = -1$

$x + 0y = -1$

Vocabulary

Parallel Lines
Perpendicular Lines
Scatter Plot
Parent Function
Transformations
Representations
Slope
Discrete Function
Continuous Function

Parallel Lines — Lines that have the same slope.

Slope — The ratio of the vertical change (rise) to the horizontal change (run).

Scatter Plot — A graph with points plotted to find the relationship between two sets of data.

Discrete Function — A function whose graph consist of separate points.

Algebra 2 Builder # 22

Name:______________________

Discrete/Continuous Functions

Write and graph the functions described. Express the domain and range in set builder notation. State if the function is discrete or continuous.

An ice cream cone cost $2.50. The functions C(x) gives the cost of purchasing x number of cones.

Function: $c(x) = 2.50x$

Domain: $\{ x \mid x \in \text{whole numbers}\}$

Range: { c(x)| c(x) = positive multiples of 2.5 }

Discrete or Continuous: Discrete

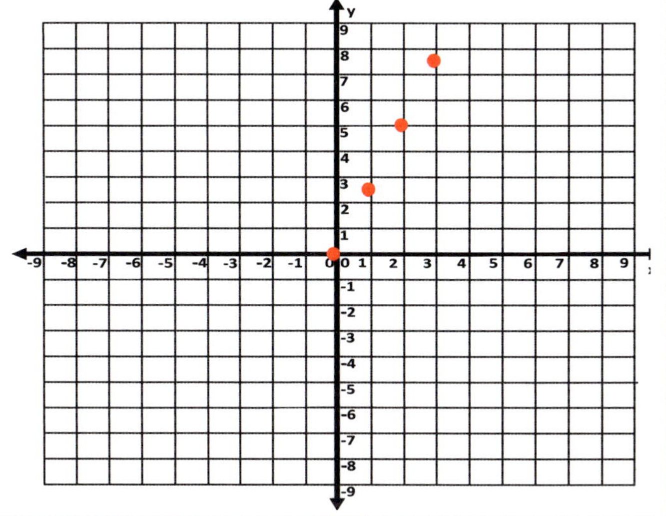

Transformations

Graph: $f(x) = 3x + 4$

Name the parent function: Linear

Explain the transformation in words:

The graph is streched vertically by a factor of 3 and vertically shifted 4 units up.

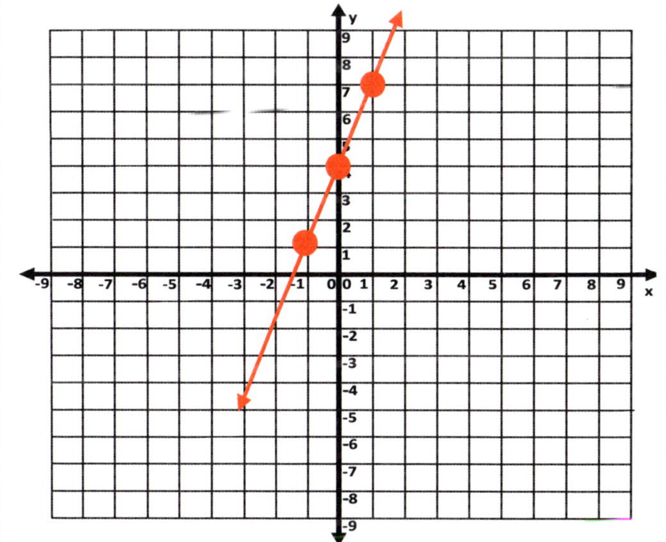

Inverse Functions

Given the equation below, find the inverse.

$f(x) = x^2 + 3$ for $x \geq 0$

$y = x^2 + 3$

$x = y^2 + 3$

$-3 \quad -3$

$\sqrt{x-3} = \sqrt{y^2}$

$\sqrt{x-3} = y$

$f^{-1}(x) = \sqrt{x-3}$ inverse

Writing Equations of Lines

Write the equation of the line in slope intercept form with the given properties.

x	-5	-2	1
y	9	4	-1

pick any 2 points

(-2,4) (1,-1)

$m = \frac{-1-4}{1-(-2)}$

$m = \frac{-5}{3}$

$m = \frac{-5}{3}$ (1,-1)

$y = mx + b$

$-1 = \frac{-5}{3}(1) + b$

$+\frac{5}{3} \quad +\frac{5}{3}$

$b = \frac{2}{3}$

$y = -\frac{5}{3}x + \frac{2}{3}$

Vocabulary

Parallel Lines
Perpendicular Lines
Scatter Plot
Parent Function
Transformations
Representations
Slope
Discrete Function
Continuous Function

Representations ______ Models, graphs, equations, tables and verbal descriptions of data.

Perpendicular Lines ______ Lines whose slopes are negative reciprocals.

Parent Function ______ The most basic function in a family of functions.

Transformations ______ Ways to manipulate a graphs, size, shape, position or orientation.

Algebra 2 Builder # 23

Name:________________________

Discrete/Continuous Functions

Write and graph the functions described. Express the domain and range in set builder notation. State if the function is discrete or continuous.

Chris drops $3 into his piggy bank every week. The function p(x) gives the total amount of money in the piggy bank after x weeks.

Function: $p(x) = 3x$

Domain: $\{ x \mid x \in \text{whole numbers}\}$

Range: $\{ p(x) \mid p(x) = \text{is a positive multiple of } 3 \}$

Discrete or Continuous: Discrete

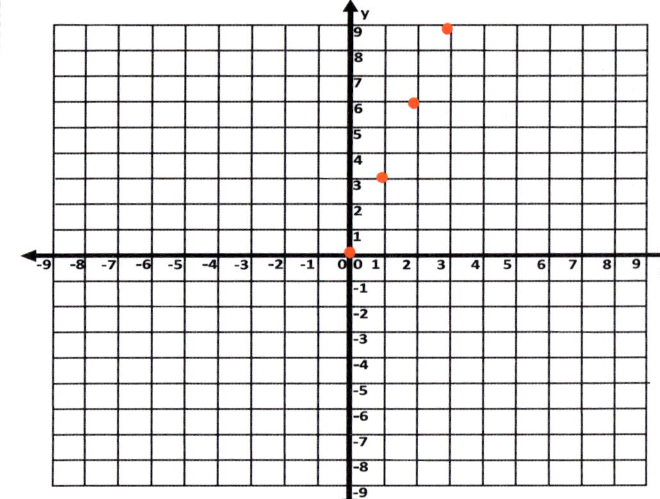

Transformations

Graph: $y = 2^x + 1$

Name the parent function:

Exponential

Explain the transformation in words:

The graph is a vertically shift 1 unit up.

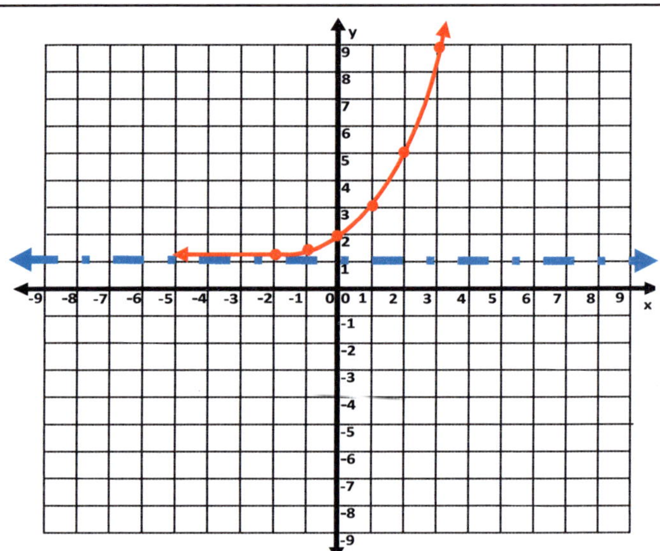

Inverse Functions

Given the equation below find the inverse.

$f(x) = (x-2)^2 + 1$ for $x \le 0$

$y = (x-2)^2 + 1$

$x = (y-2)^2 + 1$

$-1 \qquad -1$

$\sqrt{x-1} = \sqrt{(y-2)^2}$

$-\sqrt{x-1} = y - 2$

$+2 \qquad +2$

$-\sqrt{x-1} + 2 = y$

$f^{-1}(x) = -\sqrt{x-1} + 2$ inverse

Writing Equations of Lines

A mechanic charges $20.00 an hour, h for labor plus parts. If the parts cost $217.00, write a linear equation that will find the total cost, c.

$c = 20h + 217$

Vocabulary

Parallel Lines
Perpendicular Lines
Scatter Plot
Parent Function
Transformations
Representations
Slope
Discrete Function
Continuous Function

Slope — The ratio of the vertical change (rise) to the horizontal change (run).

Scatter Plot — A graph with points plotted to find the relationship between two sets of data.

Parallel Lines — Lines that have the same slope.

Continuous Function — A funtion whose graph has no gaps or breaks.

Algebra 2 Builder # 24

Name:

Discrete/Continuous Functions

Write and graph the functions described. Express the domain and range in set builder notation. State if the function is discrete or continuous.

The open bathroom faucet uses 3 gallons per minute. The function f(x) gives the volume of water used after x minutes.

Function: $f(x) = 3x$

Domain: $\{ x : x \geq 0 \}$

Range: $\{ f(x) : f(x) \geq 0 \}$

Discrete or Continuous: Continuous

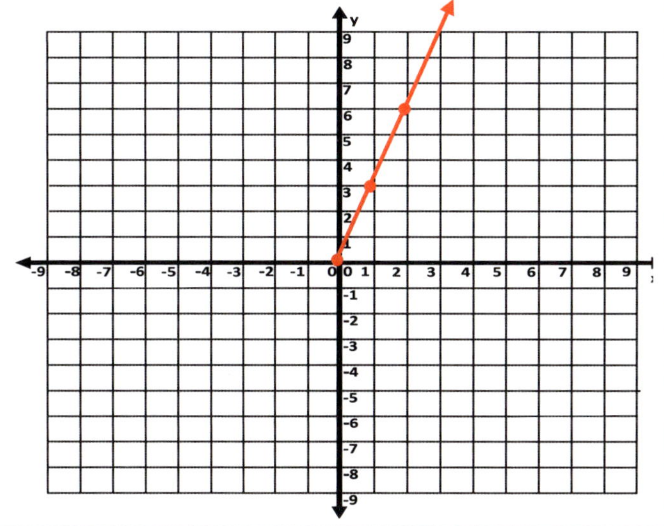

Transformations

Graph: $f(x) = \frac{1}{x-2}$

Name the parent function:

Rational

Explain the transformation in words:

The graph is a horizontal shift 2 units to the right.

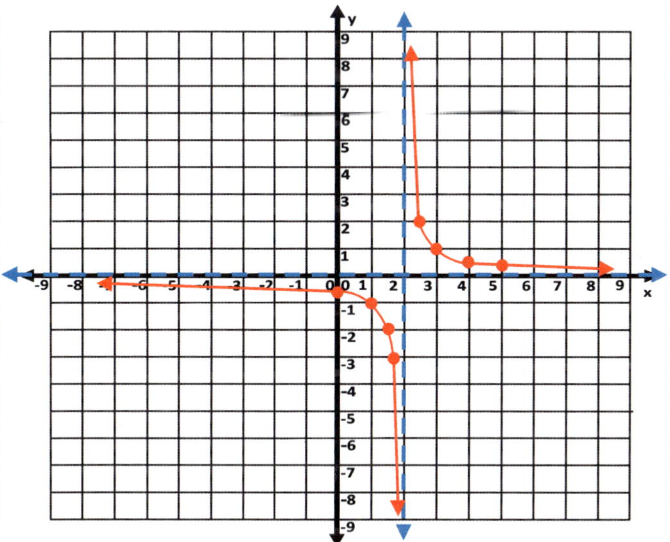

Inverse Functions

Given the graph below, graph the inverse.

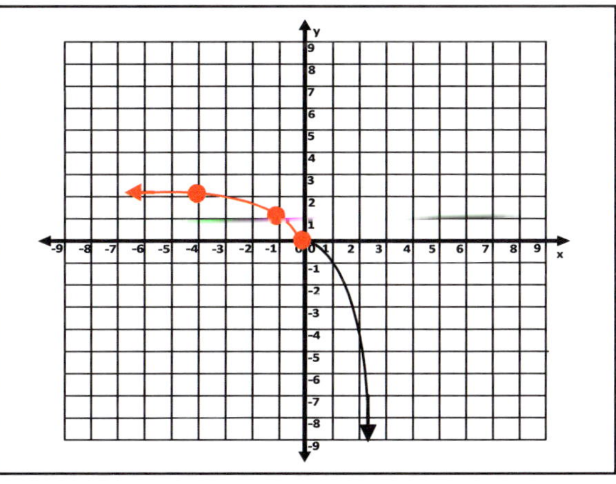

Writing Equations of Lines

The river is rising at a constant rate. On day 5, the river is at 6 feet, and on day 10 the river is at 8 feet. Write a linear equation to find the height of the river, h after d, days.

(5,6) (10,8)

$m = \frac{8-6}{10-5}$

$m = \frac{2}{5}$

$m = \frac{2}{5}$ (5,6)

$y = mx + b$

$6 = \frac{2}{5}(5) + b$

$6 = 2 + b$

$b = 4$

$h = \frac{2}{5}d + 4$

Vocabulary

Parallel Lines
Perpendicular Lines
Scatter Plot
Parent Function
Transformations
Representations
Slope
Discrete Function
Continuous Function

Perpendicular Lines — Lines whose slopes are negative reciprocals.

Parent Function — The most basic function in a family of functions.

Representations — Models, graphs, equations, tables and verbal descriptions of data.

Transformations — Ways to manipulate a graphs, size, shape, position or orientation.

Algebra 2 Builder # 25 Name:______________________________

System of Equations

Solve the system of equations by graphing, then classify the system as consistent and independent, consistent and dependent, or inconsistent.

$3x + 2y = 6$
$2x - 4y = 20$

$3x + 2y = 6$
$-3x \quad -3x$
$2y = -3x + 6$
$2 \quad 2 \quad 2$

$y = -\frac{3}{2}x + 3$

$2x - 4y = 20$
$-2x \quad -2x$
$-4y = -2x + 20$
$-4 \quad -4 \quad -4$

$y = \frac{1}{2}x - 5$

(4, -3)
Consistent and Independent

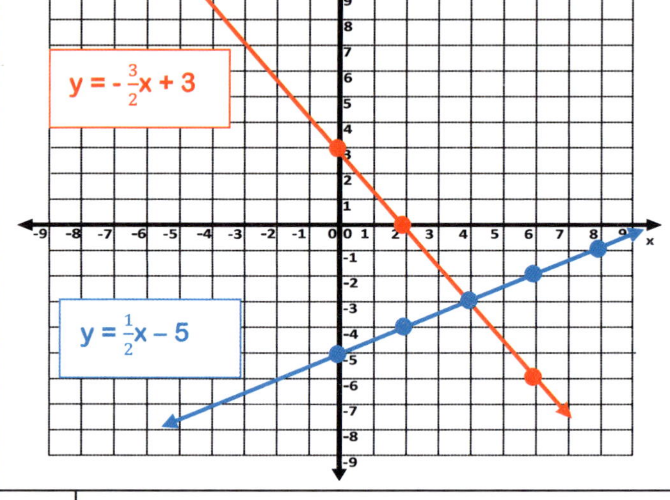

Factoring

Factor completely.

$3x^2 + 6x$

$3x(x + 2)$

$x^2 - 16$

$(x - 4)(x + 4)$

Simplify Radicals

Simplify the radical.

$\sqrt{8}$

$2\sqrt{2}$

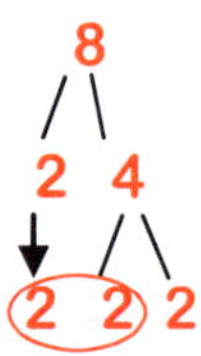

8
2 4
2 2 2

$2\sqrt{40}$

$4\sqrt{10}$

40
4 10
2 2 2 5

Vocabulary

Vertex form of a quadratic function
System of Equations
Linear programming
Discriminant
Radical
Standard form of a quadratic function
Complex Number
Polynomial

Discriminant: a part of the quadratic formula that is used to determine the number and type of roots of a quadratic equation.

Linear Programming: a method of finding a minimum or maximum value of a linear function, that satisfies a given set of constraints.

Radical: an expression in the form $\sqrt{b}$ or the $\sqrt[n]{b}$ where b is a number or an expression, and n is an integer greater than 2.

Systems of Equations: a set of two or more equations that have two or more variables.

Graphing System of Inequalities

Graph the system of inequalitites.

$x > 4$
$y \leq 2$

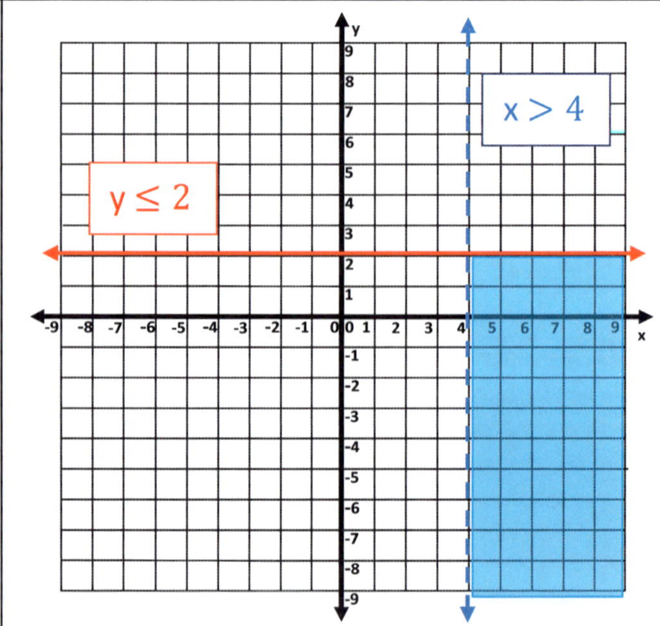

Algebra 2 Builder # 26

Name:_______________________

System of Equations

Solve the system of equations by substitution, then classify the system as consistent and independent, consistent and dependent, or inconsistent.

$5x + y = 4$
$6x - y = 7$

$5x + y = 4$
$-5x \quad -5x$
$y = -5x + 4$

$6x - y = 7$
$6x - (-5x + 4) = 7$
$6x + 5x - 4 = 7$
$11x - 4 = 7$
$+4 \quad +4$
$11x = 11$
$\frac{11x}{11} = \frac{11}{11}$
$X = 1$

$y = -5(1) + 4$
$y = -5 + 4$
$y = -1$

consistent and independent (1, -1)

Solve the system of equations by elimination, then classify the system as consistent and independent, consistent and dependent, or inconsistent.

$-1(x + y = -4)$
$3x + y = 6$

$-x - y = 4$
$3x + y = 6$
$2x = 10$
$\frac{2x}{2} = \frac{10}{2}$
$x = 5$

$x + y = -4$
$5 + y = -4$
$-5 \quad -5$
$y = -9$

(5, -9)

consistent and independent

Factoring

Factor completely.

$x^2 - 25$

$(x - 5)(x + 5)$

$x^2 - 5x - 6$

$(x + 1)(x - 6)$

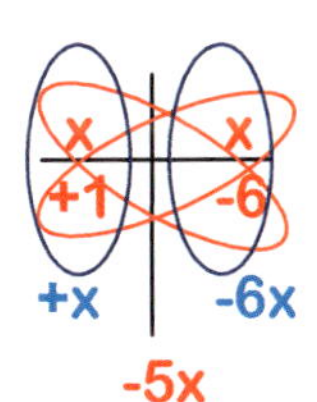

Simplify Radicals

Simplify the radical.

$\sqrt{32}$

$4\sqrt{2}$

$4\sqrt{27}$

$12\sqrt{3}$

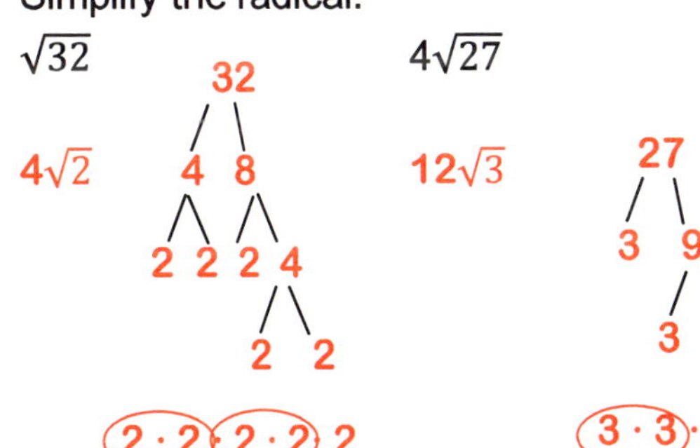

Vocabulary

Vertex form of a quadratic function
System of Equations
Linear programming
Discriminant
Radical
Standard form of a quadratic function
Complex Number
Polynomial

Polynomial_______ a monomial or a sum of monomials.

Complex Number_______ a number written in the form a + bi where a and b are real numbers and $i = \sqrt{-1}$.

Vertex Form of a Quadratic Function a quadratic function written in the form $f(x) = a(x - h)^2 + k$.

Standard Form of a Quadratic Function a quadratic function written in the form $f(x) = ax^2 + bx + c$

Graphing System of Inequalities

Graph the system of inequalitites.

$y > |x|$
$y - 5x \leq 5$

$y - 5x \leq 5$
$+5x \quad +5x$
$y \leq 5x + 5$

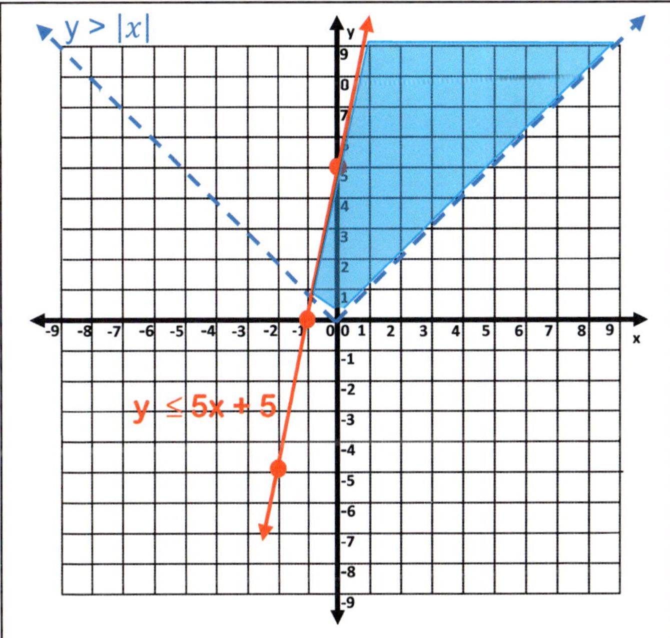

Algebra 2 Builder # 27

Name:______________________________

System of Equations

Solve the system of equations by substitution, then classify the system as consistent and independent, consistent and dependent, or inconsistent.

$2x - 4y = -8$
$2y = x + 4$

$2y = x + 4$
$-4 \quad\quad -4$

$2y - 4 = x$

$2x - 4y = -8$
$2(2y - 4) - 4y = -8$
$4y - 8 - 4y = -8$
$-8 = -8$

$\{(x,y) \mid 2x - 4y = -8\}$

Consistent and Dependent

Solve the system of equations by elimination, then classify the system as consistent and independent, consistent and dependent, or inconsistent.

$-2(3x + 4y = 7)$
$6x - 8y = -18$

$-6x - 8y = -14$
$6x - 8y = -18$
$-16y = -32$
$-16 \quad\quad -16$

$y = 2$

$3x + 4y = 7$
$3x + 4(2) = 7$
$3x + 8 = 7$
$-8 \quad -8$
$3x = -1$
$3 \quad\quad 3$

$x = -\frac{1}{3}$

$(-\frac{1}{3}, 2)$ **Consistent and Independent**

Factoring

Factor completely.

$5x^3 + 7x^2 + x$

$x(5x^2 + 7x + 1)$

$x^4 - 16$

$(x^2 - 4)(x^2 + 4)$

$(x - 2)(x + 2)(x^2 + 4)$

Simplify Radicals

Simplify the radical.

$\frac{\sqrt{6}}{\sqrt{5}} \cdot \frac{\sqrt{5}}{\sqrt{5}}$

$\frac{\sqrt{30}}{\sqrt{25}}$

$\frac{\sqrt{30}}{5}$

$\frac{\sqrt{18}}{\sqrt{4}}$

$\frac{3\sqrt{2}}{2}$

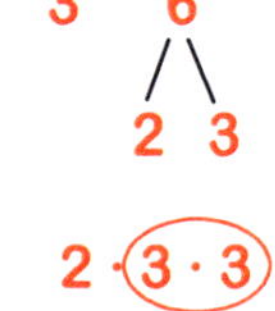

Vocabulary

Vertex form of a quadratic function
System of Equations
Linear programming
Discriminant
Radical
Standard form of a quadratic function
Complex Number
Polynomial

Discriminant a part of the quadratic formula that is used to determine the number and type of roots of a quadratic equation.

Linear Programming a method of finding a minimum or maximum value of a linear function, that satisfies a given set of constraints.

Radical an expression in the form $\sqrt{b}$ or the $\sqrt[n]{b}$ where b is a number or an expression, and n is an integer greater than 2.

Systems of Equations a set of two or more equations that have two or more variables.

Graphing System of Inequalities

Graph the system of inequalitites.

$y - 2x < 7$
$y + 2x > -1$

$y - 2x < 7$
$+2x \quad +2x$

$y < 2x + 7$

$y + 2x > -1$
$-2x \quad -2x$

$y > -2x - 1$

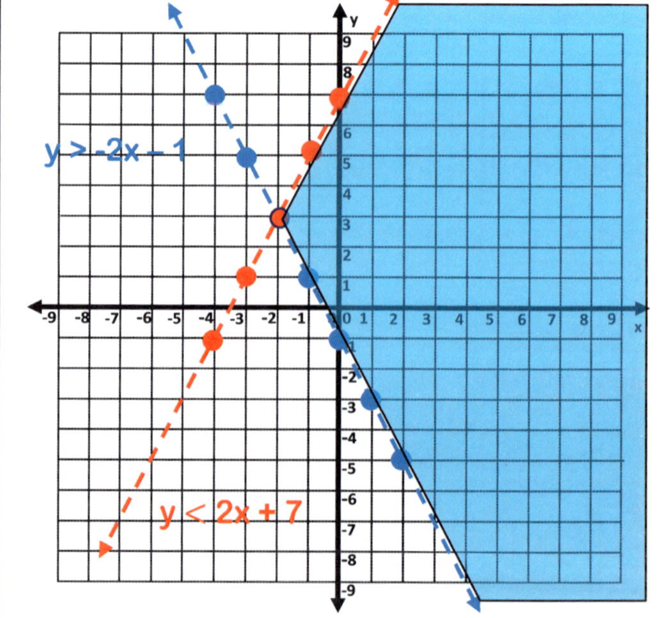

Algebra 2 Builder # 28

Name:________________________

System of Equations

Show the augmented matrix you would put into your calculator. What is the solution when you use **rref** on your calculator?

$7x - 5y = 20$
$-8x - 3y = 12$

$$\left[\begin{array}{cc|c} 7 & -5 & 20 \\ -8 & -3 & 12 \end{array}\right]$$

$$\left[\begin{array}{cc|c} 1 & 0 & 0 \\ 0 & 1 & -4 \end{array}\right]$$

(0,-4)

Write the matrix equation for the system then use the inverse matrix to solve the system.

$y = 2x - 6$
$5x = y + 9$

$y = 2x - 6$
$-2x \quad -2x$
$-2x + y = -6$

$5x = y + 9$
$-y \quad -y$
$5x - y = 9$

Coefficient Matrix · Matrix of Variables = Matrix of Constants

$$\begin{bmatrix} -2 & 1 \\ 5 & -1 \end{bmatrix} \cdot \begin{bmatrix} x \\ y \end{bmatrix} = \begin{bmatrix} -6 \\ 9 \end{bmatrix}$$

$$\begin{bmatrix} x \\ y \end{bmatrix} = \begin{bmatrix} -2 & 1 \\ 5 & -1 \end{bmatrix}^{-1} \cdot \begin{bmatrix} -6 \\ 9 \end{bmatrix}$$

$$\begin{bmatrix} x \\ y \end{bmatrix} = \begin{bmatrix} 1 \\ -4 \end{bmatrix}$$

(1,-4)

Factoring

Factor completely.

$6x^2 + 17x + 12$

$(2x + 3)(3x + 4)$

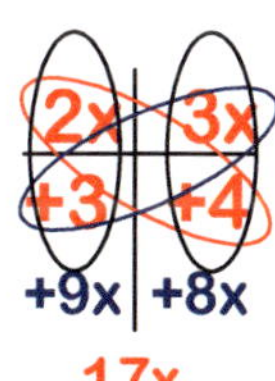

$x^4 - 4x^2$

$x^2(x^2 - 4)$

$x^2(x - 2)(x + 2)$

Simplify Radicals

Simplify the radical.

$$\frac{(2+\sqrt{5})}{(3-\sqrt{5})} \cdot \frac{(3+\sqrt{5})}{(3+\sqrt{5})}$$

$$\frac{6 + 2\sqrt{5} + 3\sqrt{5} + \sqrt{25}}{9 + 3\sqrt{5} - 3\sqrt{5} - \sqrt{25}}$$

($\sqrt{25}$ crossed out and replaced with 5 in numerator and denominator)

$$\frac{11 + 5\sqrt{5}}{4}$$

Vocabulary

Vertex form of a quadratic function
System of Equations
Linear programming
Discriminant
Radical
Standard form of a quadratic function
Complex Number
Polynomial

Polynomial a monomial or a sum of monomials.

Standard Form of a Quadratic Function a quadratic function written in the form $f(x) = ax^2 + bx + c$

Complex Number a number written in the form $a + bi$ where a and b are real numbers and $i = \sqrt{-1}$.

Vertex Form of a Quadratic Function a quadratic function written in the form $f(x) = a(x - h)^2 + k$.

Graphing System of Inequalities

Graph the system of inequalitites.

$y < -|x - 2|$
$x - 2y \leq 4$

$x - 2y \leq 4$
$-x \qquad -x$
$\frac{-2y}{-2} \leq \frac{-x + 4}{-2}$

$y \geq \frac{1}{2}x - 2$

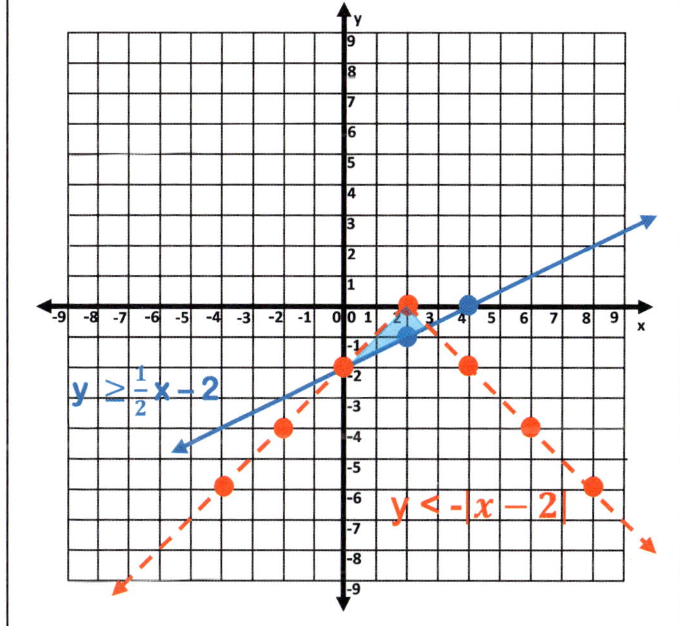

Algebra 2 Builder # 29

Name:____________________________

System of Equations

Lyndalyn and Amanda are going to the movies with friends. Lyndalyn bought 3 bags of popcorn and 5 candy bars for $21.00. Amanda bought 5 bags of popcorn and 5 candy bars for $32.50. How much does each bag of popcorn and each candy bar cost? Solve using the elimination method.

Cost of a bag of popcorn = P Cost of a candy bar = C

$-1(3P + 5C = 21)$
$5P + 5C = 32.50$
$-3P - 5C = -21$
$5P + 5C = 32.50$
$2P = 11.50$
$\frac{2P}{2} = \frac{11.50}{2}$

$P = 5.75$

$3P + 5C = 21$
$3(5.75) + 5C = 21$
$17.25 + 5C = 21$
$-17.25 \quad -17.25$
$\frac{5C}{5} = \frac{3.75}{5}$

$C = 0.75$

A bag of popcorn cost $5.75 and a candy bar cost $0.75

Factoring

Factor completely.

$x^2 - 6x + 9$

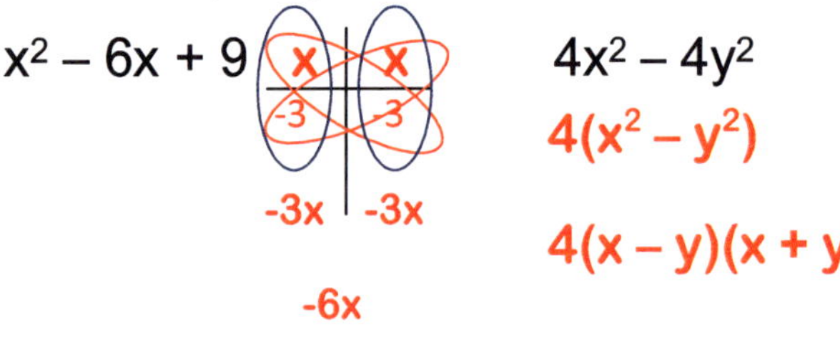

$-3x \quad -3x$

$-6x$

$(x - 3)^2$

$4x^2 - 4y^2$

$4(x^2 - y^2)$

$4(x - y)(x + y)$

Simplify Radicals

Simplify the radical.

$$\frac{(4 - \sqrt{3})}{(-2 + \sqrt{3})} \cdot \frac{(-2 - \sqrt{3})}{(-2 - \sqrt{3})}$$

$$\frac{-8 - 4\sqrt{3} + 2\sqrt{3} + \sqrt{9}}{4 + 2\sqrt{3} - 2\sqrt{3} - \sqrt{9}} \quad (\sqrt{9} = 3)$$

$-5 - 2\sqrt{3}$

Vocabulary

Vertex form of a quadratic function
System of Equations
Linear programming
Discriminant
Radical
Standard form of a quadratic function
Complex Number
Polynomial

Linear Programming — a method of finding a minimum or maximum value of a linear function, that satisfies a given set of constraints.

Discriminant — a part of the quadratic formula that is used to determine the number and type of roots of a quadratic equation.

Radical — an expression in the form $\sqrt{b}$ or the $\sqrt[n]{b}$ where b is a number or an expression, and n is an integer greater than 2.

Systems of Equations — a set of two or more equations that have two or more variables.

Linear Programming

Find the minimum value of the objective function subject to the the given constraints.

Objective Function: $C = 2x + 5y$

Constraints: $x \geq 0$ $y \leq 0$
$x \leq 6$ $y \geq \frac{1}{2}x - 4$

(x,y)	2x + 5y	C
(0,0)	2(0) + 5(0)	0
(6,0)	2(6) + 5(0)	12
(6,-1)	2(6) + 5(-1)	7
(0,-4)	2(0) + 5(-4)	-20

The minimum value is -20 and occurs at (0,-4).

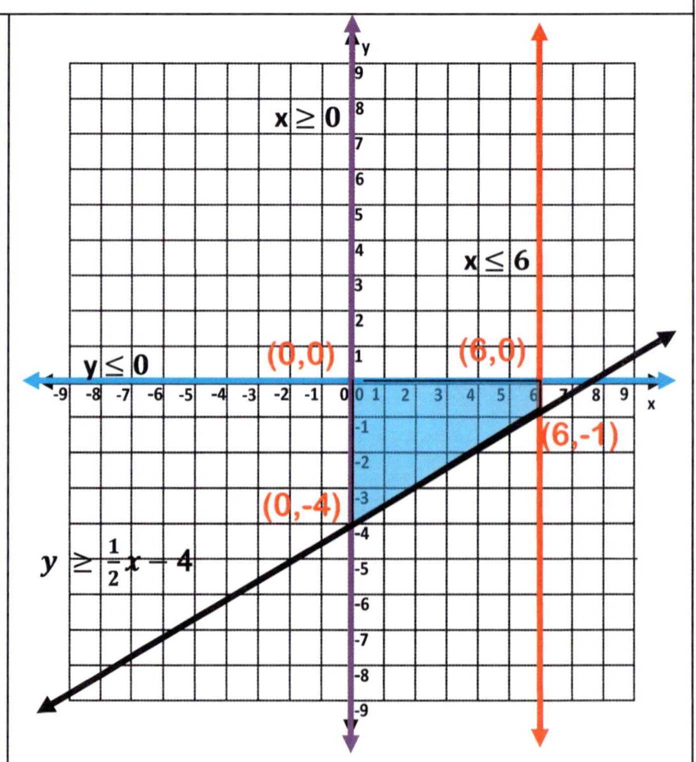

Algebra 2 Builder # 30 Name:______________________________

System of Equations

At the theater, orchestra seats cost $20.00 more than balcony seats. If a company buys 25 orchestra seats and 30 balcony seats, the total cost would be $1875.00. What would be the price for one orchestra seat and one balcony seat? Solve using the substitution method.

Cost of orchestra seats = x Cost of balcony seats = y

x = y + 20
25x + 30y = 1875

25(y + 20) + 30y = 1875
25y + 500 + 30y = 1875
55y + 500 = 1875
-500 -500
$\frac{55y}{55} = \frac{1375}{55}$
y = 25

x = y + 20
x = 25 + 20
x = 45

The price of one orchestra seat is $45, and the price of one balcony seat is $25.

Factoring

Factor completely.

$x^3 - 8$

$a^3 - b^3 = (a - b)(a^2 + ab + b^2)$

$(x - 2)(x^2 + 2x + 4)$

$x^3 + 8$

$a^3 + b^3 = (a + b)(a^2 - ab + b^2)$

$(x + 2)(x - 2x + 4)$

Simplify Radicals

Simplify the radical.

$$\frac{(-2 - 4\sqrt{7})}{(-5 - 2\sqrt{7})} \cdot \frac{(-5 + 2\sqrt{7})}{(-5 + 2\sqrt{7})}$$

$$\frac{10 - 4\sqrt{7} + 20\sqrt{7} - 8\sqrt{49}}{25 - 10\sqrt{7} + 10\sqrt{7} - 4\sqrt{49}} \quad \frac{56}{28}$$

$$\frac{-46 + 16\sqrt{7}}{-3} = \frac{46 - 16\sqrt{7}}{3}$$

Vocabulary

Vertex form of a quadratic function
System of Equations
Linear programming
Discriminant
Radical
Standard form of a quadratic function
Complex Number
Polynomial

Vertex Form of a Quadratic Function: a quadratic function written in the form $f(x) = a(x - h)^2 + k$.

Polynomial: a monomial or a sum of monomials.

Complex Number: a number written in the form a + bi where a and b are real numbers and $i = \sqrt{-1}$.

Standard Form of a Quadratic Function: a quadratic function written in the form $f(x) = ax^2 + bx + c$

Linear Programming

Find the maximum value of the objective function subject to the the given constraints.

Objective Function: P = 2x + 3y

Constraints: $x \geq 2$ $y \geq 3$ $y \leq -\frac{1}{2}x + 7$

(x,y)	2x + 3y	P
(2,3)	2(2) + 3(3)	13
(2,6)	2(2) + 3(6)	22
(8,3)	2(8) + 3(3)	25

The maximum value is 25 and occurs at (8,3).

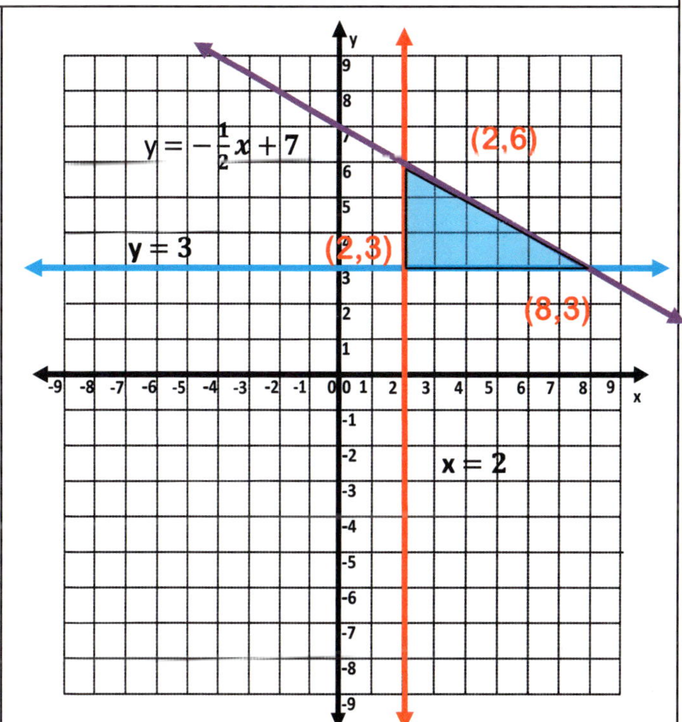

Algebra 2 Builder # 31

Name:______________________

System of Equations

Mrs. West invested $6000.00 into 2 accounts. One account earns 1.5% simple interest and the other account earns 2% simple interest. How much did she invest in each account if in 1 year she earned in $110.00 in interest? Solve using an augmented matrix.

Amount of money in the 1.5% account = x. Amount of money in the 2% account = y.

$x + y = 6000$
$0.015x + 0.02y = 110$

$$\left[\begin{array}{cc|c} 1 & 1 & 6000 \\ 0.015 & 0.02 & 110 \end{array}\right] = \left[\begin{array}{cc|c} 1 & 0 & 2000 \\ 0 & 1 & 4000 \end{array}\right]$$

Mrs. West invested $2000 at 1.5% simple interest and $4000 at 2% simple interest.

Factoring

Factor completely.

$2x^3 + 54$

$2(x^3 + 27)$

$2(x + 3)(x^2 - 3x + 9)$

$-3x^3 + 24$

$-3(x^3 - 8)$

$-3(x - 2)(x^2 + 2x + 4)$

Simplify Radicals

Simplify the radical.

$\sqrt{-25}$

$5i$

$2\sqrt{-8}$

$4i\sqrt{2}$

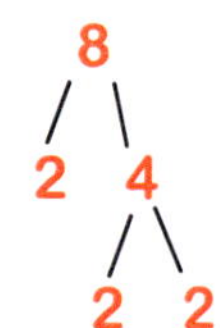

Vocabulary

Vertex form of a quadratic function
System of Equations
Linear programming
Discriminant
Radical
Standard form of a quadratic function
Complex Number
Polynomial

Discriminant a part of the quadratic formula that is used to determine the number and type of roots of a quadratic equation.

Radical an expression in the form $\sqrt{b}$ or the $\sqrt[n]{b}$ where b is a number or an expression, and n is an integer greater than 2.

Systems of Equations a set of two or more equations that have two or more variables.

Linear Programming a method of finding a minimum or maximum value of a linear function, that satisfies a given set of constraints.

Linear Programming

Zach is the manager at a seafood restaurant. Zach orders at most 100 fish every day. He needs at least 40 but no more than 70 catfish and at least 30 tilapia. Catfish cost $5 each and tilapia cost $4 each. How many of each fish should he order to minimize his daily cost?

x = number of catfish y = number of tilapia

Constraints: $x + y \le 100$ $x \le 70$
$y \le -x + 100$ $x \ge 40$ $y \ge 30$

Objective Function: $C = 5x + 4y$

(x,y)	5x + 4y	C
(40,60)	5(40) + 4(60)	440
(70,30)	5(70) + 4(30)	470
(40,30)	5(40) + 4(30)	320

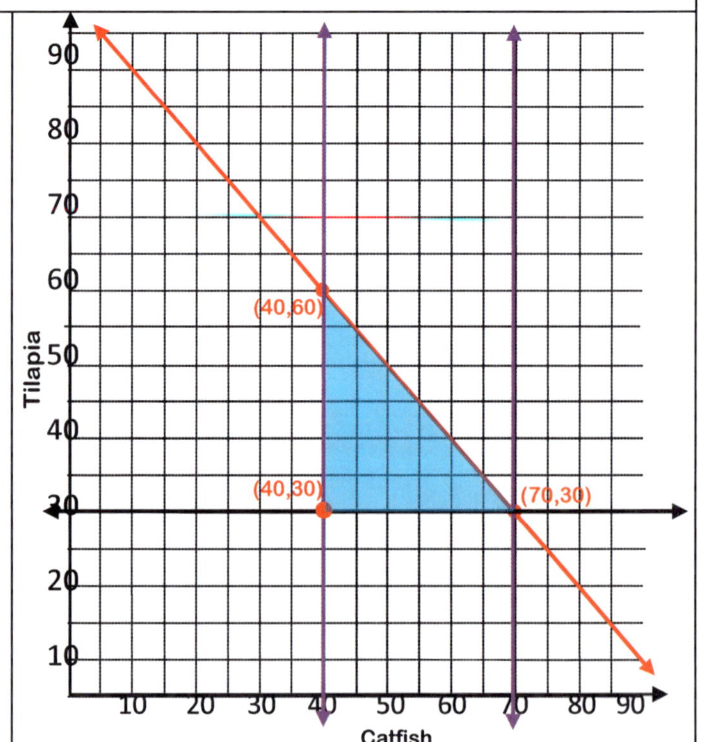

To minimize Zach's daily cost, he should buy 40 catfish and 30 tilapia each day.

Algebra 2 Builder # 32 Name:______________________________

System of Equations

Mrs. McDonald has a farm with ducks and pigs. There are 27 heads and 84 legs. How many ducks and pigs are on Mrs. McDonalds farm? Solve using an inverse matrix.

Number of ducks = d **Number of pigs = p**

d + p = 27
2d + 4p = 84

$$\begin{bmatrix}1 & 1\\2 & 4\end{bmatrix} \cdot \begin{bmatrix}x\\y\end{bmatrix} = \begin{bmatrix}27\\84\end{bmatrix}$$

$$\begin{bmatrix}x\\y\end{bmatrix} = \begin{bmatrix}1 & 1\\2 & 4\end{bmatrix}^{-1} \cdot \begin{bmatrix}27\\84\end{bmatrix}$$

$$\begin{bmatrix}x\\y\end{bmatrix} = \begin{bmatrix}12\\15\end{bmatrix}$$

Mrs. McDonald has 12 ducks and 15 pigs on her farm.

Factoring

Factor completely.

$5x^3 - 2x^2 - 20x + 8$

$x^2(5x - 2) - 4(5x - 2)$

$(5x - 2)(x^2 - 4)$

$(5x - 2)(x - 2)(x + 2)$

Simplify Radicals

Simplify the radical.

$3\sqrt{-27}$ $-4\sqrt{-54}$

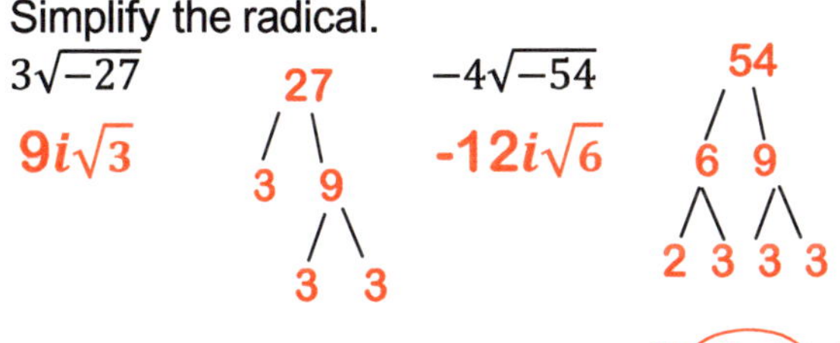

Vocabulary

Vertex form of a quadratic function
System of Equations
Linear programming
Discriminant
Radical
Standard form of a quadratic function
Complex Number
Polynomial

Vertex Form of a Quadratic Function a quadratic function written in the form $f(x) = a(x - h)^2 + k$.

Polynomial a monomial or a sum of monomials.

Standard Form of a Quadratic Function a quadratic function written in the form $f(x) = ax^2 + bx + c$

Complex Number a number written in the form a + bi where a and b are real numbers and $i = \sqrt{-1}$.

Linear Programming

Renee makes jewelry and it takes her 2 hours to make a bracelet and 4 hours to make a necklace. She can work at most 120 hours a month. It cost $2 to make a bracelet and $8 to make a necklace. Renee wants to spend no more than $160 a month on supplies. A local store buys 5 of each type of jewelry each month. If Renee makes a profit of $15 on a bracelet and $40 on a necklace, how many bracelets and necklaces should she make each month to maximize her profit?

b = number of braclets **n = number of necklaces**

Constraints: $2b + 4n \le 120$ $2b + 8n \le 160$ $b \ge 5$ $n \ge 5$

$n \le -\frac{1}{2}b + 30$ $n \le -\frac{1}{4}x + 20$

Objective Function: P = 15b + 40n

(b,n)	15b + 40n	P
(5,5)	15(5) + 40(5)	275
(5,18.75)	15(5) + 40(18.75)	825
(40,10)	15(40) + 40(10)	1000
(50,5)	15(50) + 40(5)	950

Renee should make 40 bracelets and 10 necklaces a month to have a maximum profit of $1000 per month.

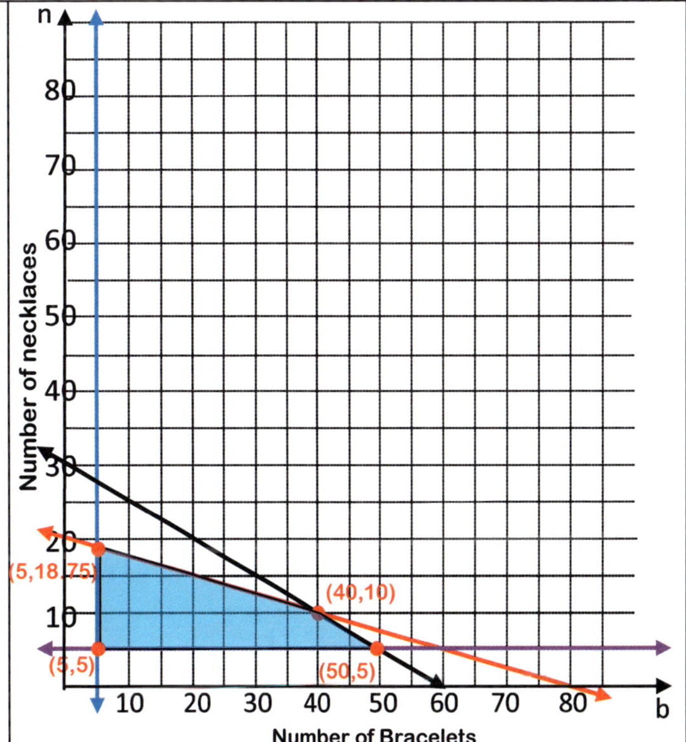

Algebra 2 Builder # 33 Name:______________________________

Simplify Radicals

$2\sqrt{3} + 3\sqrt{3}$

$5\sqrt{3}$

Complex Numbers

Write the expression as a complex number in standard form.
$(5 - 6i) - (-2 - 3i)$

$5 - 6i + 2 + 3i$

$7 - 3i$

Factoring Quadratics

Solve by factoring.
$x^2 - 4x - 5 = 0$

$(x + 1)(x - 5) = 0$

$x + 1 = 0$	$x - 5 = 0$
$-1 \quad -1$	$+5 \quad +5$
$x = -1$	$x = 5$

or

-1,5

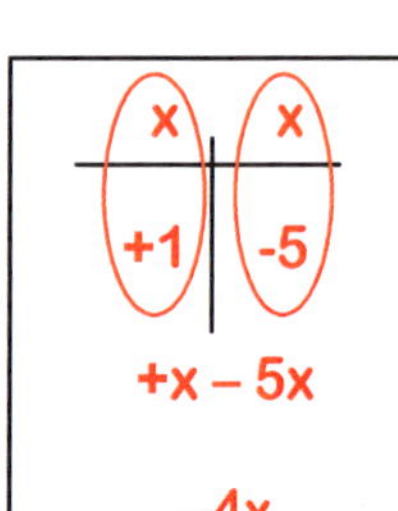

Completing the Square

Solve by completing the square
$x^2 - 4x - 5 = 0$

$x^2 - 4x - 5 = 0$
$\quad +5 \; +5$

$x^2 - 4x + 4 = 5 + 4$

$\sqrt{(x-2)^2} = \sqrt{9}$

$x - 2 = \pm 3$
$\quad +2 \; +2$

$x = 2 \pm 3$ →

$-4 \cdot \frac{1}{2}$

$(-2)^2$

4

$x = 2 - 3$	or	$x = 2 + 3$
$x = -1$		$x = 5$

-1,5

Quadratic Formula

Solve by the Quadratic Formula
$x^2 - 4x - 5 = 0$ a = 1 b = -4 c = -5

$$x = \frac{-b \pm \sqrt{b^2 - 4ac}}{2a}$$

$$x = \frac{-(-4) \pm \sqrt{(-4)^2 - 4(1)(-5)}}{2(1)}$$

$$x = \frac{4 \pm \sqrt{16 + 20}}{2}$$

$$x = \frac{4 \pm \sqrt{36}}{2}$$

$$x = \frac{4 \pm 6}{2}$$ →

$x = 2 \pm 3$

$x = 2 - 3$	or	$x = 2 + 3$
$x = -1$		$x = 5$

-1,5

Discriminant

Find the discriminant, then determine the nature of the roots.
$x^2 + 4x + 4 = 0$ a = 1 b = 4 c = 4

$b^2 - 4ac$

$(4)^2 - 4(1)(4)$

$16 - 16$

0

One rational root, double.

Vocabulary

Zero(s) of a Function
Axis of Symmetry
Parabola
Discriminant
Rational Number
Irrational Number
Conjugate
Vertex of a Parabola

Discriminant: For a quadratic equation, the expression under the radical in the quadratic formula.

Parabola: The shape of the graph of a quadratic function.

Zero(s) of a Function: Value(s) of x for which f(x) = 0.

Axis of Symmentry: The line that divides the graph into equal halves.

Algebra 2 Builder # 34 Name:______________________________

Simplify Radicals

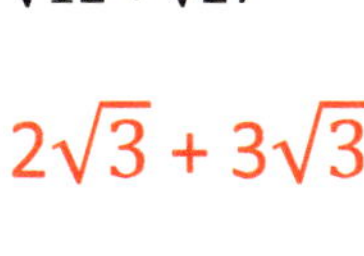

$\sqrt{12} + \sqrt{27}$

$2\sqrt{3} + 3\sqrt{3}$

$5\sqrt{3}$

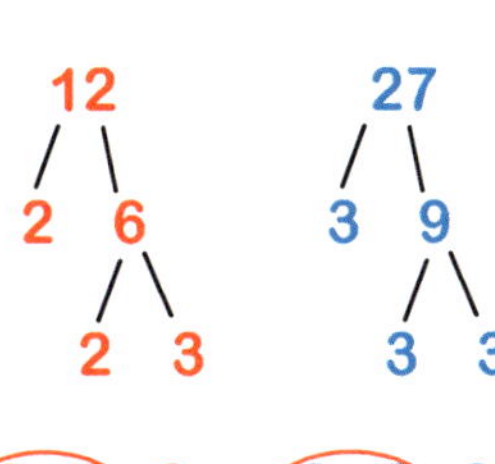

Complex Numbers

Write the expression as a complex number in standard form.
$3(2 - 4i) - 2(3 + 5i)$

$6 - 12i - 6 - 10i$

$-22i$ or

$0 - 22i$

Factoring Quadratics

Solve by factoring.
$x^2 - 4x - 21 = 0$

$(x - 7)(x + 3) = 0$

$x - 7 = 0$	$x + 3 = 0$
$+7 \quad +7$	$-3 \quad -3$
$x = 7$	$x = -3$

or

$-3, 7$

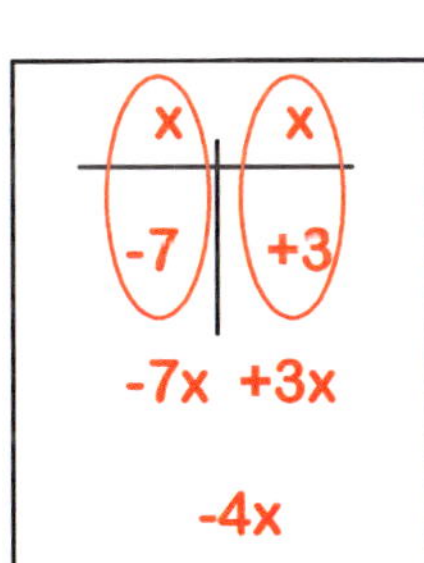

Completing the Square

Solve by completing the square.
$x^2 - 4x - 21 = 0$

$x^2 - 4x - 21 = 0$
$+21 \quad +21$

$-4 \cdot \frac{1}{2}$

$x^2 - 4x + 4 = 21 + 4$

$(-2)^2$

4

$\sqrt{(x-2)^2} = \sqrt{25}$

$x - 2 = \pm 5$
$+2 \quad +2$

$x = 2 \pm 5$ →

$x = 2 - 5$ or $x = 2 + 5$
$x = -3 \qquad x = 7$

$-3, 7$

Quadratic Formula

Solve by the Quadratic Formula.
$x^2 - 4x - 21 = 0$ $a = 1$ $b = -4$ $c = -21$

$$x = \frac{-b \pm \sqrt{b^2 - 4ac}}{2a}$$

$$x = \frac{-(-4) \pm \sqrt{(-4)^2 - 4(1)(-21)}}{2(1)}$$

$$x = \frac{4 \pm \sqrt{16 + 84}}{2}$$

$$x = \frac{4 \pm \sqrt{100}}{2}$$

$$x = \frac{4 \pm 10}{2}$$

$x = 2 \pm 5$

$x = 2 - 5$ or $x = 2 + 5$
$x = -3 \qquad x = 7$

$-3, 7$

Discriminant

Find the discriminant, then determine the nature of the roots.
$3x^2 + 7x + 8 = 0$ $a = 3$ $b = 7$ $c = 8$

$b^2 - 4ac$

$(7)^2 - 4(3)(8)$

$49 - 96$

-47

Two imaginary roots, conjugates.

Vocabulary

Zero(s) of a Function
Axis of Symmetry
Parabola
Discriminant
Rational Number
Irrational Number
Conjugate
Vertex of a Parabola

Rational Number A number that can be expressed as the ratio of two integers and the denominator cannot equal zero.

Conjugate Two binomials that are the same except the middle signs are opposite.

Irrational Number A number that neither repeats or terminates.

Vertex of the Parabola The maximum or minimum point on a parabola.

Algebra 2 Builder # 35

Name:______________________________

Simplify Radicals

$\sqrt{16x^2y} - x\sqrt{25y}$

$4x\sqrt{y} - 5x\sqrt{y}$

$-x\sqrt{y}$

Complex Numbers

Write the expression as a complex number in standard form.

$(2 - 3i)^2$

$(2 - 3i)(2 - 3i)$

$4 - 6i - 6i + 9i^2$ (with $9i^2$ crossed out and -9 written above)

$-5 - 12i$

$i^2 = -1$

$9i^2$

$9(-1)$

-9

Factoring Quadratics

Solve by factoring.

$2x^2 + 5x - 12 = 0$

$(2x - 3)(x + 4) = 0$

$2x - 3 = 0 \quad x + 4 = 0$

$+3 \quad +3 \qquad -4 \quad -4$

$\frac{2x}{2} = \frac{3}{2} \qquad x = -4$

$x = 3/2 \quad x = -4$

$-4, \frac{3}{2}$

2x	x
-3	+4

$-3x \quad +8x$

$5x$

Completing the Square

Solve by completing the square.

$x^2 - 6x = 7$

$x^2 - 6x + 9 = 7 + 9$

$x^2 - 6x + 9 = 16$

$\sqrt{(x-3)^2} = \sqrt{16}$

$x - 3 = \pm 4$

$+3 \quad +3$

$x = 3 \pm 4$

$-6 \cdot \frac{1}{2}$

$(-3)^2$

9

$x = 3 - 4$ or $x = 3 + 4$

$x = -1 \qquad x = 7$

$-1, 7$

Quadratic Formula

Solve by the Quadratic Formula.

$3x^2 - 4x + 1 = 0$ $a = 3 \quad b = -4 \quad c = 1$

$$x = \frac{-b \pm \sqrt{b^2 - 4ac}}{2a}$$

$$x = \frac{-(-4) \pm \sqrt{(-4)^2 - 4(3)(1)}}{2(3)}$$

$$x = \frac{4 \pm \sqrt{16 - 12}}{6}$$

$$x = \frac{4 \pm \sqrt{4}}{6}$$

$$x = \frac{4 \pm 2}{6}$$

$$x = \frac{2 \pm 1}{3}$$

$$x = \frac{2 + 1}{3} \qquad x = \frac{2 - 1}{3}$$

$$x = \frac{3}{3} = 1 \qquad x = \frac{1}{3}$$

$\frac{1}{3}, 1$

Discriminant

Find the discriminant, then determine the nature of the roots.

$2x^2 - 5x - 3 = 0$ $a = 2 \quad b = -5 \quad c = -3$

$b^2 - 4ac$

$(-5)^2 - 4(2)(-3)$

$25 + 24$

49

Two rational roots.

Vocabulary

Zero(s) of a Function
Axis of Symmetry
Parabola
Discriminant
Rational Number
Irrational Number
Conjugate
Vertex of a Parabola

Parabola ______ The shape of the graph of a quadratic function.

Discriminant ______ For a quadratic equation, the expression under the radical in the quadratic formula.

Axis of Symmentry ______ The line that divides the graph into equal halves.

Zero(s) of a Function ______ Value(s) of x for which f(x) = 0

Algebra 2 Builder # 36

Name:______________________________

Simplify Radicals

$2\sqrt{27x^3y^5} - 4xy\sqrt{3xy^3}$

$6xy^2\sqrt{3xy} - 4xy^2\sqrt{3xy}$

$2xy^2\sqrt{3xy}$

27 → 3, 9; 9 → 3, 3

$(3 \cdot 3) \cdot 3$

$(x \cdot x) \cdot x$

$(y \cdot y)(y \cdot y) \cdot y$

$(y \cdot y) \cdot y$

Complex Numbers

Write the expression as a complex number in standard form.

$\frac{(3-2i)\ (1-i)}{(1+i)\ (1-i)}$

$\frac{3-3i-2i+2i^2}{1-i+i-i^2}$ (with i^2 replaced: -2, 1)

$\frac{3-3i-2i-2}{1-i+i+1} = \frac{1-5i}{2} = \frac{1}{2} - \frac{5}{2}i$

Factoring Quadratics

Solve by factoring.

$15x^2 + 34x + 15 = 0$

$(3x + 5)(5x + 3) = 0$

$3x + 5 = 0$	$5x + 3 = 0$
$-5 \quad -5$	$-3 \quad -3$
$\frac{3x}{3} = \frac{-5}{3}$	$\frac{5x}{5} = \frac{-3}{5}$
$x = -5/3$	$x = -3/5$

$-5/3$, $-3/5$

3x	5x
+5	+3

+25x +9x

34x

Completing the Square

Solve by completing the square.

$x^2 - 6x + 3 = 0$

$x^2 - 6x + 9 = -3 + 9$ $\qquad -6 \cdot \frac{1}{2}$

$x^2 - 6x + 9 = 6$ $\qquad (-3)^2$

$\sqrt{(x-3)^2} = \sqrt{6}$ $\qquad 9$

$x - 3 = \pm\sqrt{6}$

$+3 \quad +3$

$x = 3 \pm \sqrt{6}$ →

$x = 3 - \sqrt{6}$ or $x = 3 + \sqrt{6}$

$3 - \sqrt{6}, 3 + \sqrt{6}$

Quadratic Formula

Solve by the Quadratic Formula.

$x^2 + 2x + 3 = 0$ a = 1 b = 2 c = 3

$x = \frac{-b \pm \sqrt{b^2 - 4ac}}{2a}$

$x = \frac{-(2) \pm \sqrt{(2)^2 - 4(1)(3)}}{2(1)}$

$x = \frac{-2 \pm \sqrt{-8}}{2}$

$x = \frac{-2 \pm 2i\sqrt{2}}{2}$

$x = -1 \pm i\sqrt{2}$

$x = -1 + i\sqrt{2}$ or $x = -1 - i\sqrt{2}$

8 → 2, 4; 4 → 2, 2

$(2 \cdot 2) \cdot 2$

Discriminant

Find the discriminant, then determine the nature of the roots.

$2x^2 - 3x - 4 = 0$ a = 2 b = -3 c = -4

$b^2 - 4ac$

$(-3)^2 - 4(2)(-4)$

$9 + 32$

41

Two Irrational roots.

Vocabulary

Zero(s) of a Function
Axis of Symmetry
Parabola
Discriminant
Rational Number
Irrational Number
Conjugate
Vertex of a Parabola

Vertex of the Parabola The maximum or minimum point on a parabola.

Conjugate Two binomials that are the same except the middle signs are opposite.

Rational Number A number that can be expressed as the ratio of two integers and the denominator cannot equal zero.

Irrational Number A number that neither repeats or terminates.

Algebra 2 Builder # 37

Name:______________________________

Simplify Radicals

$\sqrt[3]{18}\cdot\sqrt[3]{6}$

$\sqrt[3]{108}$

$3\sqrt[3]{4}$

Factor tree: 108 → 6, 18; 6 → 2, 3; 18 → 2, 9; 9 → 3, 3

$2\cdot 2\cdot(3\cdot 3\cdot 3)$

Complex Numbers

Write the expression as a complex number in standard form.

$$\frac{(4-3i)(-2-i)}{(-2+i)(-2-i)}$$

$$\frac{-8-4i+6i+3i^2}{4+2i-2i-i^2}$$

($3i^2 \to -3$, $-i^2 \to +1$)

$$\frac{-11+2i}{5} = \frac{-11}{5}+\frac{2}{5}i$$

Solve by Factoring

Find the real zeros.

$x^4 - 16 = 0$

$(x^2-4)(x^2+4)=0$

$(x-2)(x+2)(x^2+4)=0$

$x-2=0$	$x+2=0$	$x^2+4=0$
$+2\ \ +2$	$-2\ \ -2$	$-4\ \ -4$
$x=2$	$x=-2$	$x^2=-4$
or	or	$\sqrt{x^2}=\sqrt{-4}$
		$x=\pm 2i$
		reject

-2,2

Completing the Square

Solve by completing the square.

$x^2 - 4x + 5 = 0$

$x^2-4x+4 = -5+4$ $\quad -4\cdot\frac{1}{2}$

$x^2-4x+4=-1$ $\quad (-2)^2$

$\sqrt{(x-2)^2}=\sqrt{-1}$ $\quad 4$

$x-2=\pm i$

$+2\quad +2$

$x = 2\pm i$

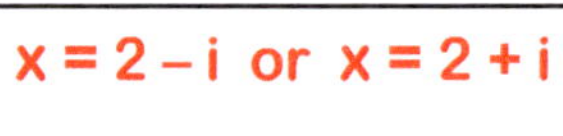

$x = 2-i$ or $x = 2+i$

$2-i,\ 2+i$

Quadratic Formula

Solve by the Quadratic Formula.

$2x^2 - 5x = -7$ $\quad a = 2\ \ b = -5\ \ c = 7$

$2x^2-5x+7=0$

$$x=\frac{-(-5)\pm\sqrt{(-5)^2-4(2)(7)}}{2(2)}$$

$$x=\frac{5\pm\sqrt{25-56}}{4}$$

$$x=\frac{5\pm\sqrt{-31}}{4}$$

$$x=\frac{5\pm i\sqrt{31}}{4}$$

$$x=\frac{5+i\sqrt{31}}{4}$$

$\frac{5}{4}+\frac{i\sqrt{31}}{4},\ \frac{5}{4}-\frac{i\sqrt{31}}{4}$

Discriminant

Find the discriminant, then determine the nature of the roots.

$\frac{1}{2}x^2 + 8x - 4 = 0$ $\quad a=\frac{1}{2}\ \ b=8\ \ c=-4$

b^2-4ac

$(8)^2-4(\frac{1}{2})(-4)$

$64+8$

72

Two Irrational roots.

Vocabulary

Zero(s) of a Function
Axis of Symmetry
Parabola
Discriminant
Rational Number
Irrational Number
Conjugate
Vertex of a Parabola

Parabola ______ The shape of the graph of a quadratic function.

Zero(s) of a Function ______ Value(s) of x for which f(x) = 0.

Axis of Symmentry ______ The line that divides the graph into equal halves.

Discriminant ______ For a quadratic equation, the expression under the radical in the quadratic formula.

Algebra 2 Builder # 38

Name:________________________________

Simplify Radicals

$\sqrt[3]{4x^2y} \cdot \sqrt[3]{6xy^4}$

$\sqrt[3]{24x^3y^5}$

$2xy\sqrt[3]{3y^2}$

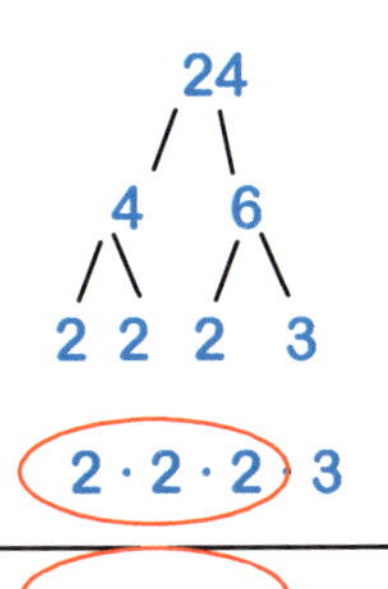

Complex Numbers

Write the expression as a complex number in standard form.

$\frac{(-3-2i)}{(1-3i)} \frac{(1+3i)}{(1+3i)}$

$\frac{-3-9i-2i-6i^2}{1+3i-3i-9i^2}$ (+6, +9)

$\frac{3-11i}{10} = \frac{3}{10} - \frac{11}{10}i$

Solve by Factoring

Find the real zeros.

$x^3 - 8 = 0$

$(x-2)(x^2+2x+4) = 0$

$x - 2 = 0$ $+2 \quad +2$ $x = 2$ or	$x^2 + 2x + 4 = 0$ $x = \frac{-2 \pm \sqrt{(2)^2 - 4(1)(4)}}{2(1)}$ $x = \frac{-2 \pm \sqrt{-12}}{2}$ $x = \frac{-2 \pm 2i\sqrt{3}}{2}$ $x = -1 \pm i\sqrt{3}$ reject

2

Completing the Square

Solve by completing the square.

$x^2 - 5x + 2 = 0$
$\quad\quad -2 \quad -2$

$-5 \cdot \frac{1}{2}$

$(-\frac{5}{2})^2$

$\frac{25}{4}$

$x^2 - 5x + \frac{25}{4} = -2 + \frac{25}{4}$

$\sqrt{(x-\frac{5}{2})^2} = \sqrt{\frac{17}{4}}$

$x - \frac{5}{2} = \pm\frac{\sqrt{17}}{2}$

$x = \frac{5}{2} \pm \frac{\sqrt{17}}{2}$ →

$x = \frac{5}{2} - \frac{\sqrt{17}}{2}$ $\quad x = \frac{5}{2} + \frac{\sqrt{17}}{2}$

$\frac{5}{2} - \frac{\sqrt{17}}{2}, \frac{5}{2} + \frac{\sqrt{17}}{2}$

Quadratic Formula

Solve by the Quadratic Formula.

$3x^2 + 6x = 5$

$3x^2 + 6x - 5 = 0 \qquad a = 3 \; b = 6 \; c = -5$

$x = \frac{-(6) \pm \sqrt{(6)^2 - 4(3)(-5)}}{2(3)}$

$x = \frac{-6 \pm \sqrt{96}}{6}$

$x = \frac{-6 \pm \sqrt{16 \cdot 6}}{6}$

$x = \frac{-6 \pm 4\sqrt{6}}{6}$

$x = \frac{-3 \pm 2\sqrt{6}}{3}$

$x = \frac{-3 - 2\sqrt{6}}{3}, \; x = \frac{-3 + 2\sqrt{6}}{3}$

Discriminant

Find the discriminant, then determine the nature of the roots.

$x^2 - 5x + 2 = 0 \qquad a = 1 \; b = -5 \quad c = 2$

$b^2 - 4ac$

$(-5)^2 - 4(1)(2)$

$25 - 8$

17

Two Irrational roots.

Vocabulary

Zero(s) of a Function
Axis of Symmetry
Parabola
Discriminant
Rational Number
Irrational Number
Conjugate
Vertex of a Parabola

Irrational Number — A number that neither repeats or terminates.

Vertex of the Parabola — The maximum or minimum point on a parabola.

Rational Number — A number that can be expressed as the ratio of two integers and the denominator cannot equal zero.

Conjugate — Two binomials that are the same except the middle signs are opposite.

Algebra 2 Builder # 39

Name:______________________

Simplify Radicals

$\sqrt[3]{\frac{2}{3}}$

$$\frac{\sqrt[3]{2}}{\sqrt[3]{3}} \cdot \frac{\sqrt[3]{9}}{\sqrt[3]{9}} = \frac{\sqrt[3]{18}}{\sqrt[3]{27}} = \frac{\sqrt[3]{18}}{3}$$

Complex Numbers

Write the expression as a complex number in standard form.

$$\frac{(3+i)-(2+3i)}{(1-3i)-(3-2i)}$$

$$\frac{3+i-2-3i}{1-3i-3+2i}$$

$$\frac{(1-2i)(-2+i)}{(-2-i)(-2+i)}$$

$$\frac{-2+i+4i-2i^2}{4-2i+2i-i^2} \quad (-2i^2 \to +2,\ -i^2 \to +1)$$

$$\frac{-2+i+4i+2}{4-2i+2i+1}$$

$\frac{5i}{5} = i$ or $0 + i$

Solve by Factoring

Find the real zeros.

$x^3 + x^2 - 4x - 4 = 0$

$x^2(x+1) - 4(x+1) = 0$

$(x+1)(x^2-4) = 0$

$(x+1)(x-2)(x+2) = 0$

$x + 1 = 0$	$x - 2 = 0$	$x + 2 = 0$
$-1 \quad -1$	$+2 \quad +2$	$-2 \quad -2$
$x = -1$	$x = 2$	$x = -2$
or	or	

-2, -1, 2

Completing the Square

Solve by completing the square.

$5x^2 + 20x = 10$

$$\frac{5x^2 + 20x = 10}{5}$$

$4 \cdot \frac{1}{2}$

$(2)^2$

4

$x^2 + 4x + 4 = 2 + 4$

$\sqrt{(x+2)^2} = \sqrt{6}$

$x + 2 = \pm\sqrt{6}$

$-2 \qquad -2$

$x = -2 \pm \sqrt{6} = -2-\sqrt{6},\ -2+\sqrt{6}$

Quadratic Formula

Solve by the Quadratic Formula.

$$\frac{x-1}{x-3} = \frac{2}{x+1}$$

$2(x-3) = (x-1)(x+1)$

$2x - 6 = x^2 - 1$

$0 = x^2 - 2x + 5$ $\quad$ a=1 b = -2 c = 5

$$x = \frac{-(-2) \pm \sqrt{(-2)^2 - 4(1)(5)}}{2(1)}$$

$$x = \frac{2 \pm \sqrt{-16}}{2}$$

$$x = \frac{2 \pm 4i}{2}$$

$x = 1 \pm 2i$

$1 - 2i,\ 1 + 2i$

Discriminant

Find the discriminant, then determine the nature of the roots.

$x^2 - 6x + 9 = 0$ $\quad$ a = 1 b = -6 c = 9

$b^2 - 4ac$

$(-6)^2 - 4(1)(9)$

$36 - 36$

0

One rational root, double.

Vocabulary

Zero(s) of a Function
Axis of Symmetry
Parabola
Discriminant
Rational Number
Irrational Number
Conjugate
Vertex of a Parabola

Parabola ______ The shape of the graph of a quadratic function.

Zero(s) of a Function ______ Value(s) of x for which f(x) = 0

Axis of Symmentry ______ The line that divides the graph into equal halves.

Discriminant ______ For a quadratic equation, the expression under the radical in the quadratic formula.

Algebra 2 Builder # 40

Name:______________________________

Simplify Radicals

$\sqrt[3]{\frac{3y^2}{4x}}$

$\frac{\sqrt[3]{3y^2}}{\sqrt[3]{4x}} \cdot \frac{\sqrt[3]{2x^2}}{\sqrt[3]{2x^2}}$

$\frac{\sqrt[3]{6x^2y^2}}{\sqrt[3]{8x^3}} = \frac{\sqrt[3]{6x^2y^2}}{2x}$

Complex Numbers

Write the expression as a complex number in standard form.

$\frac{2(1-i)-3(1+2i)}{3(2+3i)-(3+4i)}$

$\frac{2-2i-3-6i}{6+9i-3-4i}$

$\frac{(-1-8i)(3-5i)}{(3+5i)(3-5i)}$

$\frac{-3+5i-24i+40i^2}{9-15i+15i-25i^2}$

$\frac{-3+5i-24i-40}{9-15i+15i+25}$

$\frac{-43-19i}{34}$

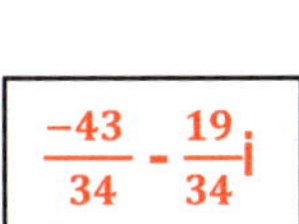

$\frac{-43}{34} - \frac{19}{34}i$

Solve by Factoring

Find the real zeros.

$2x^3 + 5x^2 + 6x + 15 = 0$

$x^2(2x+5) + 3(2x+5) = 0$

$(2x+5)(x^2+3) = 0$

$2x + 5 = 0$ $-5 \quad -5$ $\frac{2x}{2} = \frac{-5}{2}$ $x = -\frac{5}{2}$ or	$x^2 + 3 = 0$ $-3 \quad -3$ $x^2 = -3$ $\sqrt{x^2} = \sqrt{-3}$ $x = \pm i\sqrt{3}$ reject

$-\frac{5}{2}$

Completing the Square

Solve by completing the square.

$2\left(\frac{1}{2}x^2 + 4x = -2\right)$

$8 \cdot \frac{1}{2}$

$(4)^2$

16

$x^2 + 8x + 16 = -4 + 16$

$\sqrt{(x+4)^2} = \sqrt{12}$

$x + 4 = \pm\sqrt{12}$

$-4 \qquad -4$

12 → 2, 6 → 2, 3

$x = -4 \pm 2\sqrt{3}$

$2 \cdot 2 \cdot 3$

$-4 - 2\sqrt{3}, -4 + 2\sqrt{3}$

Quadratic Formula

Solve by the Quadratic Formula.

$\frac{x-2}{2x+3} = \frac{x-5}{x+3}$

$(2x+3)(x-5) = (x-2)(x+3)$

$2x^2 - 10x + 3x - 15 = x^2 + 3x - 2x - 6$

$2x^2 - 7x - 15 = x^2 + x - 6$

$-x^2 - x + 6 \quad -x^2 - x + 6$

$x^2 - 8x - 9 = 0 \qquad a = 1 \quad b = -8 \quad c = -9$

$x = \frac{-(-8) \pm \sqrt{(-8)^2 - 4(1)(-9)}}{2(1)}$

$x = \frac{8 \pm \sqrt{100}}{2}$

$x = \frac{8 \pm 10}{2}$

$x = 4 \pm 5$

$x = 4 - 5$	$x = 4 + 5$
$x = -1$	$x = 9$
$-1, 9$	

Discriminant

Find the discriminant, then determine the nature of the roots.

$5x^2 + 8x + 9 = 0 \qquad a = 5 \quad b = 8 \quad c = 9$

$b^2 - 4ac$

$(8)^2 - 4(5)(9)$

$64 - 180$

-116

Two imaginary roots, conjugates.

Vocabulary

Zero(s) of a Function
Axis of Symmetry
Parabola
Discriminant
Rational Number
Irrational Number
Conjugate
Vertex of a Parabola

Irrational Number	A number that neither repeats or terminates.
Conjugate	Two binomials that are the same except the middle signs are opposite.
Vertex of the Parabola	The maximum or minimum point on a parabola.
Rational Number	A number that can be expressed as the ratio of two integers and the denominator cannot equal zero.

Algebra 2 Builder # 41 Name:________________________

Vertex Form

Write in vertex form.

$f(x) = x^2 - 4x + 5$

$f(x) = (x^2 - 4x + 4) + 5 - 4$

$f(x) = (x - 2)^2 + 1$

$-4 \cdot \frac{1}{2}$

$(-2)^2$

4

Exponent Rules

$x^5 \cdot x^3$	$\frac{x^8}{x^2}$
x^{5+3}	x^{8-2}
x^8	x^6

Solve Quadratic Inequalities

Solve algebraically.

$x^2 - 8x < 0$

(number line with open circles at 0 and 8, segment between them)

0 8

$x(x - 8) < 0$

$x = 0$ or $x - 8 = 0$

$+8 \quad +8$

$x = 8$

$\{x | 0 < x < 8\}$

$(0,8)$

Test Points -1, 1, 9		
$x = -1$	$x = 1$	$x = 9$
$(-1)^2 - 8(-1) < 0$	$(1)^2 - 8(1) < 0$	$(9)^2 - 8(9) < 0$
$1 + 8 < 0$	$1 - 8 < 0$	$81 - 72 < 0$
$9 < 0$	$-7 < 0$	$9 < 0$
false	true	false

Vertex

Use $-\frac{b}{2a}$ to find the vertex.

$f(x) = x^2 - 2x + 3$

$a = 1 \quad b = -2$

$h = \frac{-b}{2a} = \frac{-(-2)}{2(1)} = \frac{2}{2} = 1$

$k = (1)^2 - 2(1) + 3 = 2$

Vertex = (1,2)

Graph Quadratics

$f(x) = (x - 6)(x - 2)$ intercept form $y = a(x - p)(x - q)$

$a = 1 \quad p = 6 \quad q = 2$

$h = \frac{p+q}{2} = \frac{6+2}{2} = \frac{8}{2} = 4$

$k = (4 - 6)(4 - 2) = (-2)(2) = -4$

x-intercept = (6,0)(2,0)

vertex = (4,-4)

axis of symetry x = 4

opens up

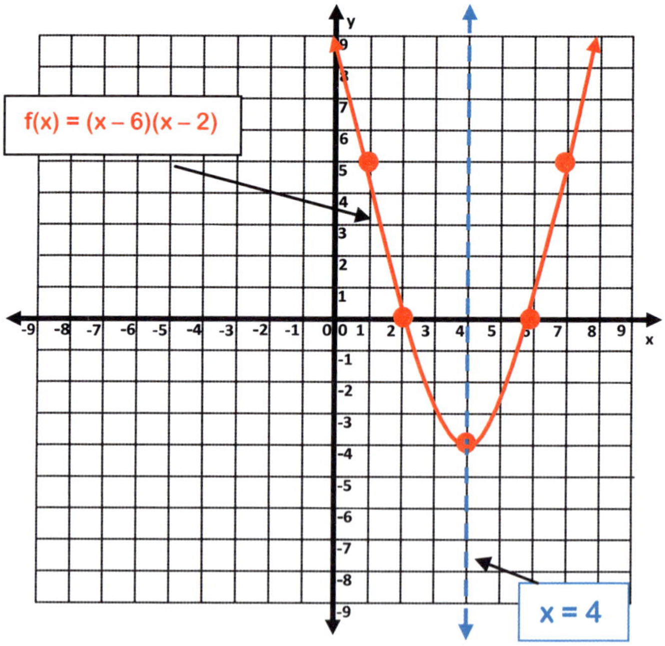

Vocabulary

Product of Powers Property

Power of a Power Property

Power of a Quotient Property

Quotient of Powers Property

Power of a Product Property

Negative Exponent Property

Zero Exponent Property

Product of Powers Property ______ $a^m a^n = a^{m+n}$

Quotient of Powers Property ______ $\frac{a^m}{a^n} = a^{m-n} \quad a \neq 0$

Power of a Product Property ______ $(ab)^m = a^m b^m$

Zero Exponent Property ______ $a^0 = 1 \quad a \neq 0$

Algebra 2 Builder # 42

Name:_______________________________

Vertex Form

Write in vertex form.

$f(x) = x^2 - 8x - 7$

$f(x) = (x^2 - 8x + 16) - 7 - 16$

$f(x) = (x - 4)^2 - 23$

$-8 \cdot \frac{1}{2}$

$(-4)^2$

16

Exponent Rules

$(x^5)^2$	$3x^0$
$x^{5(2)}$	$3(1)$
x^{10}	3

Solve Quadratic Inequalities

Solve algebraically.

$x^2 - 5x \geq 6$

$x^2 - 5x - 6 \geq 0$

$(x - 6)(x + 1) \geq 0$

$x = 6 \quad x = -1$

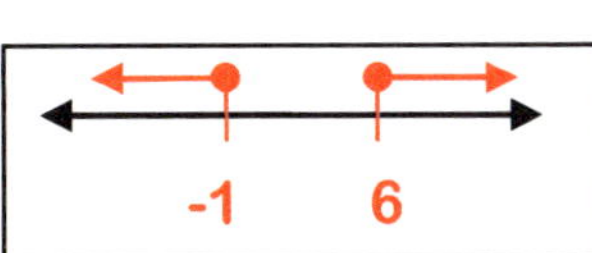

Test Points -2, 0, 7		
x = -2	x = 0	x = 7
$(-2)^2 - 5(-2) > 6$	$(0)^2 - 5(0) \geq 6$	$(7)^2 - 5(7) \geq 6$
$4 + 10 \geq 6$	$0 - 0 \geq 6$	$49 - 35 \geq 6$
$14 \geq 6$	$0 \geq 6$	$14 \geq 6$
true	false	true

$\{x \mid x \leq -1 \text{ or } x \geq 6\}$ $\quad (-\infty, -1] \cup [6, \infty)$

Vertex

Use $-\frac{b}{2a}$ to find the vertex.

$y = 2x^2 + 4x + 9$

$a = 2 \quad b = 4 \quad c = 9$

$h = \frac{-b}{2a} = \frac{-(4)}{2(2)} = \frac{-4}{4} = -1$

$k = 2(-1)^2 + 4(-1) + 9 = 7$

Vertex = (-1,7)

Graph Quadratics

$y = (x - 2)^2 - 4$ vertex form $y = a(x - h)^2 + k$

$a = 1 \quad h = 2 \quad k = -4$

Vertex = (2,-4)

Axis of Symmetry x = 2

Opens up

x	$(x - 2)^2 - 4$	y
3	$(3-2)^2 - 4$	-3
4	$(4-2)^2 - 4$	0

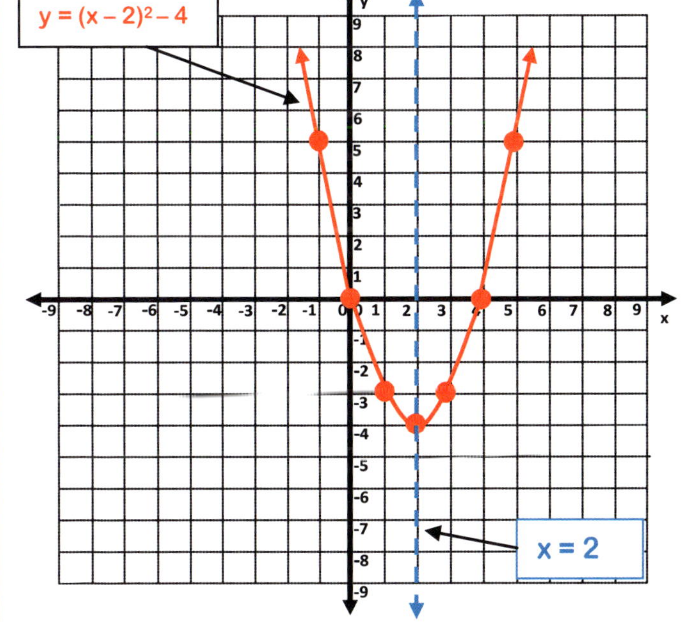

Vocabulary

Product of Powers Property
Power of a Power Property
Power of a Quotient Property
Quotient of Powers Property
Power of a Product Property
Negative Exponent Property
Zero Exponent Property

Negative Exponent Property	$a^{-n} = \frac{1}{a^n}$ or $\frac{1}{a^{-n}} = a^n \quad a \neq 0$
Power of a Quotient Property	$\left(\frac{a}{b}\right)^n = \frac{a^n}{b^n} \quad b \neq 0$
Power of a Power Property	$(a^m)^n = a^{mn}$
Quotient of Powers Property	$\frac{a^m}{a^n} = a^{m-n} \quad a \neq 0$

Algebra 2 Builder # 43

Name:______________________________

Vertex Form

Write in vertex form.

$y = 2x^2 + 8x + 5$

$y = 2(x^2 + 4x + 4) + 5 - 8$

$y = 2(x + 2)^2 - 3$

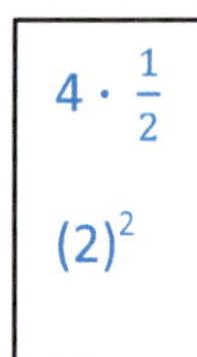

Exponent Rules

$(2xy^2)^3$

$2^3x^{1(3)}y^{2(3)}$

$8x^3y^6$

$(5x^2y)^2$

$5^2x^{2(2)}y^{1(2)}$

$25x^4y^2$

Solve Quadratic Inequalities

Solve algebraically.

$x^2 \leq 4x$

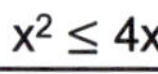

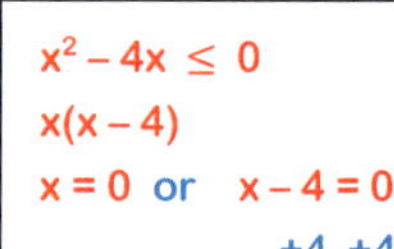

$x^2 - 4x \leq 0$

$x(x - 4)$

$x = 0$ or $x - 4 = 0$

+4 +4

$x = 4$

$\{x \mid 0 \leq x \leq 4\}$

[0,4]

Test Points -1, 1, 5

x = -1	x = 1	x = 5
$x^2 \leq 4x$	$x^2 \leq 4x$	$x^2 \leq 4x$
$(-1)^2 \leq 4(-1)$	$(1)^2 \leq 4(1)$	$(5)^2 \leq 4(5)$
$1 \leq -4$	$1 \leq 4$	$25 \leq 20$
false	true	false

Vertex

Use $-\frac{b}{2a}$ to find the vertex.

$f(x) = 3x^2 + 6x + 7$

$a = 3 \quad b = 6$

$h = \frac{-b}{2a} = \frac{-(6)}{2(3)} = \frac{-6}{6} = -1$

$k = 3(-1)^2 + 6(-1) + 7 = 4$

Vertex = (-1,4)

Graph Quadratics

$y = x^2 + 4x + 4$ standard form $y = ax^2 + bx = c$

$h = \frac{-b}{2a} = \frac{-(4)}{2(1)} = \frac{-4}{2} = -2$

$k = (-2)^2 + 4(-2) + 4 = 0$

Vertex = (-2,0)

Axis of Symmetry x = -2

Opens up

x	$x^2 + 4x + 4$	y
-1	$(-1)^2 + 4(-1) + 4$	1
0	$(0)^2 + 4(0) + 4$	4

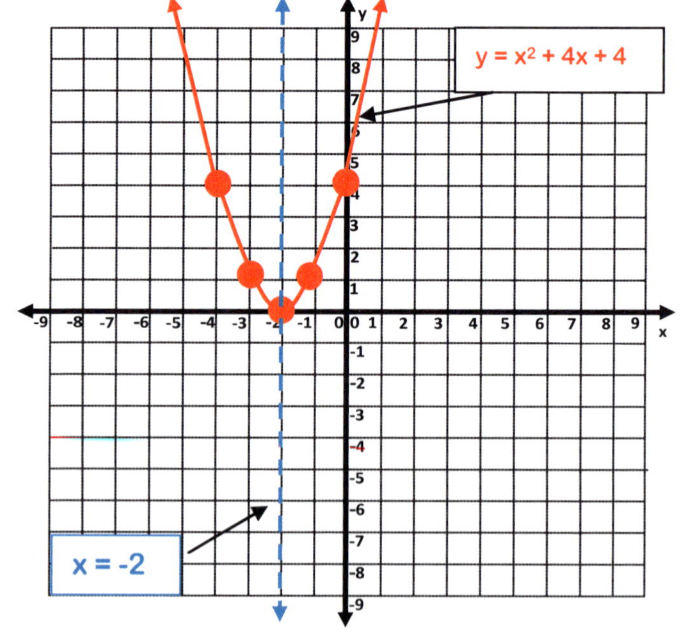

Vocabulary

Product of Powers Property
Power of a Power Property
Power of a Quotient Property
Quotient of Powers Property
Power of a Product Property
Negative Exponent Property
Zero Exponent Property

Power of a Product Property ______ $(ab)^m = a^mb^m$

Zero Exponent Property ______ $a^0 = 1 \quad a \neq 0$

Product of Powers Property ______ $a^ma^n = a^{m+n}$

Quotient of Powers Property ______ $\frac{a^m}{a^n} = a^{m-n} \quad a \neq 0$

Algebra 2 Builder # 44

Name:______________________________

Vertex Form

Write in vertex form.

f(x) = $-3x^2 - 6x - 5$

$f(x) = -3(x^2 + 2x + 1) - 5 + 3$

$f(x) = -3(x + 1)^2 - 2$

$2 \cdot \frac{1}{2}$

$(1)^2$

1

Exponent Rules

$(x^{-3}y^{-4})^{-2}$

$x^{-3(-2)}y^{-4(-2)}$

x^6y^8

$\frac{x^{-5}}{y^{-3}}$

$\frac{y^3}{x^5}$

Solve Quadratic Inequalities

Solve algebraically.

$2x^2 - 2x - 4 > 0$

-1 2

$2(x^2 - x - 2) > 0$

$2(x - 2)(x + 1) > 0$

$2 = 0$ or $x - 2 = 0$ or $x + 1 = 0$

+2 +2 -1 -1

$x = 2$ $x = -1$

$\{x \mid x < -1 \text{ or } x > 2\}$

$(-\infty, -1) \cup (2, \infty)$

Test Points -2, 0, 3

x = -2	x = 0	x = 3
$2x^2 - 2x - 4 > 0$	$2x^2 - 2x - 4 > 0$	$2x^2 - 2x - 4 > 0$
$2(-2)^2 - 2(-2) - 4 > 0$	$2(0)^2 - 2(0) - 4 > 0$	$2(3)^2 - 2(3) - 4 > 0$
$8 > 0$	$-4 > 0$	$8 > 0$
true	false	true

Vertex

Use $-\frac{b}{2a}$ to find the vertex.

$y = x^2 - 5x + 7$

a = 1 b = -5

$h = \frac{-b}{2a} = \frac{-(-5)}{2(1)} = \frac{5}{2}$

$k = \left(\frac{5}{2}\right)^2 - 5\left(\frac{5}{2}\right) + 7 = \frac{3}{4}$

Vertex = $\left(\frac{5}{2}, \frac{3}{4}\right)$

Graph Quadratics

f(x) = $-x^2 - 2x + 8$ standard form $y = ax^2 + bx = c$

a = -1 b = -2 c = 8

$h = \frac{-b}{2a} = \frac{-(-2)}{2(-1)} = \frac{2}{-2} = -1$

$k = -(-1)^2 - 2(-1) + 8 = 9$

Vertex = (-1,9)

Axis of Symmetry x = -1

Opens down

x	$-x^2 - 2x + 8$	y
0	$-(0)^2 - 2(0) + 8$	8
1	$-(1)^2 - 2(1) + 8$	5
2	$-(2)^2 - 2(2) + 8$	0

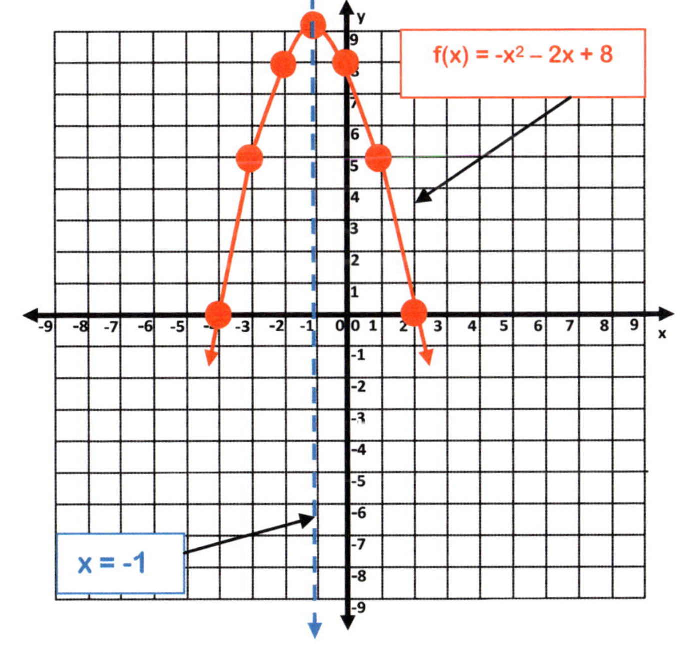

Vocabulary

Product of Powers Property
Power of a Power Property
Power of a Quotient Property
Quotient of Powers Property
Power of a Product Property
Negative Exponent Property
Zero Exponent Property

Quotient of Powers Property $\frac{a^m}{a^n} = a^{m-n}$ $a \neq 0$

Power of a Quotient Property $\left(\frac{a}{b}\right)^n = \frac{a^n}{b^n}$ $b \neq 0$

Negative Exponent Property $a^{-n} = \frac{1}{a^n}$ or $\frac{1}{a^{-n}} = a^n$ $a \neq 0$

Power of a Power Property $(a^m)^n = a^{mn}$

Algebra 2 Builder # 45

Name:______________________________

Vertex Form

Write in vertex form.

$f(x) = \frac{1}{2}x^2 + 4x + 5$

$f(x) = \frac{1}{2}(x^2 + 8x + 16) + 5 - 8$

$f(x) = \frac{1}{2}(x + 4)^2 - 3$

$8 \cdot \frac{1}{2}$

$(4)^2$

16

Exponent Rules

$\frac{2x^{-2}y^{-3}}{4x^6y^{-2}}$

$\frac{x^{-2-6}y^{-3-(-2)}}{2}$

$\frac{x^{-8}y^{-1}}{2}$

$\frac{1}{2x^8y}$

$\frac{9x^{-6}y^4}{3x^{-2}y^0}$

$\frac{3x^{-6}y^4}{x^{-2}}$

$3x^{-6-(-2)}y^4$

$3x^{-4}y^4$

$\frac{3y^4}{x^4}$

Solve Quadratic Inequalities

Solve algebraically.

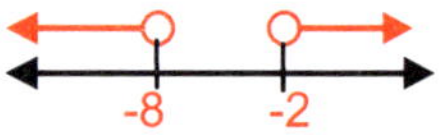

$\frac{1}{2}x^2 + 5x > -8$

$2(\frac{1}{2}x^2 + 5x + 8 > 0) = x^2 + 10x + 16 > 0$

$(x + 2)(x + 8) > 0$

$x + 2 = 0$ or $x + 8 = 0$

$\underline{\ \ -2\ \ -2}$ $\underline{\ \ -8\ \ -8}$

$x = -2$ $x = -8$

$\{x \mid x < -8 \text{ or } x > -2\}$

$(-\infty, -8) \cup (-2, \infty)$

Test Points -9, -3, 0

x = -9	x = -3	x = 0
$\frac{1}{2}(-9)^2 + 5(-9) > -8$	$\frac{1}{2}(-3)^2 + 5(-3) > -8$	$\frac{1}{2}(0)^2 + 5(0) > -8$
$-4.5 > -8$	$-10.5 > -8$	$0 > -8$
true	false	true

Vertex

Use $-\frac{b}{2a}$ to find the vertex.

$y = -2x^2 - 4x + 7$

$a = -2 \quad b = -4$

$h = \frac{-b}{2a} = \frac{-(-4)}{2(-2)} = \frac{4}{-4} = -1$

$k = -2(-1)^2 - 4(-1) + 7 = 9$

Vertex = (-1,9)

Graph Quadratics

$f(x) = (x - 3)(x + 1)$ intercept form $y = a(x - p)(x - q)$

$a = 1 \quad p = 3 \quad q = -1$

$h = \frac{p+q}{2} = \frac{3+(-1)}{2} = \frac{2}{2} = 1$

$k = (1 - 3)(1 + 1) = (-2)(2) = -4$

x-intercept = (3,0)(-1,0)

vertex = (1,-4)

axis of symetry x = 1

opens up

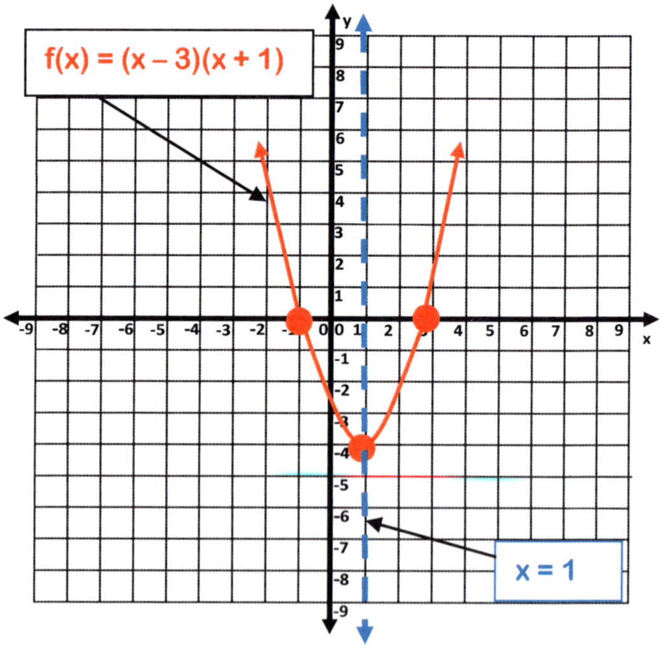

Vocabulary

Product of Powers Property
Power of a Power Property
Power of a Quotient Property
Quotient of Powers Property
Power of a Product Property
Negative Exponent Property
Zero Exponent Property

Zero Exponent Property ____________ $a^0 = 1 \quad a \neq 0$

Quotient of Powers Property ____________ $\frac{a^m}{a^n} = a^{m-n} \quad a \neq 0$

Product of Powers Property ____________ $a^m a^n = a^{m+n}$

Power of a Product Property ____________ $(ab)^m = a^m b^m$

Algebra 2 Builder # 46

Name:_______________________________

Vertex Form

Write in vertex form.

$y = -\frac{1}{3}x^2 + 2x - 5$

$y = -\frac{1}{3}(x^2 - 6x + 9) - 5 + 3$

$y = -\frac{1}{3}(x - 3)^2 - 2$

$-6 \cdot \frac{1}{2}$

$(-3)^2$

9

Exponent Rules

$(2xy^{-2})(3x^2y^{-3})^{-2}$

$\frac{2xy^{-2}}{(3x^2y^{-3})^2}$

$\frac{2xy^{-2}}{9x^4y^{-6}}$

$\frac{2y^4}{9x^3}$

$(x^{1/2}y^{1/4})^2$

$x^{(\frac{1}{2})(2)}y^{(\frac{1}{4})(2)}$

$xy^{1/2}$

Solve Quadratic Inequalities

Solve algebraically.

$2x^2 < 6x + 20$

$2x^2 - 6x - 20 < 0$

$2(x^2 - 3x - 10) < 0$

$2(x - 5)(x + 2) < 0$

$x - 5 = 0$ or $x + 2 = 0$

+5 +5   -2 -2

$x = 5$ $x = -2$

$\{x \mid -2 < x < 5\}$

(-2,5)

Test Points -3, 0, 6

$x = -3$	$x = 0$	$x = 6$
$2(-3)^2 < 6(-3) + 20$	$2(0)^2 < 6(0) + 20$	$2(6)^2 < 6(6) + 20$
$18 < 2$	$0 < 20$	$72 < 56$
false	true	false

Vertex

Use $-\frac{b}{2a}$ to find the vertex.

$f(x) = x^2 + 3x + 8$

a = 1   b = 3

$h = \frac{-b}{2a} = \frac{-(3)}{2(1)} = \frac{-3}{2}$

$k = \left(\frac{-3}{2}\right)^2 + 3\left(\frac{-3}{2}\right) + 8 = \frac{23}{4}$

$\text{Vertex} = \left(\frac{-3}{2}, \frac{23}{4}\right)$

Graph Quadratics

$y = -(x - 1)^2 - 3$ vertex form $y = a(x - h)^2 + k$

a = -1   h = 1   k = -3

Vertex = (1,-3)

Axis of Symmetry x = 1

Opens down

x	$-(x - 1)^2 - 3$	y
2	$-(2 - 1)^2 - 3$	-4
3	$-(3 - 1)^2 - 3$	-7

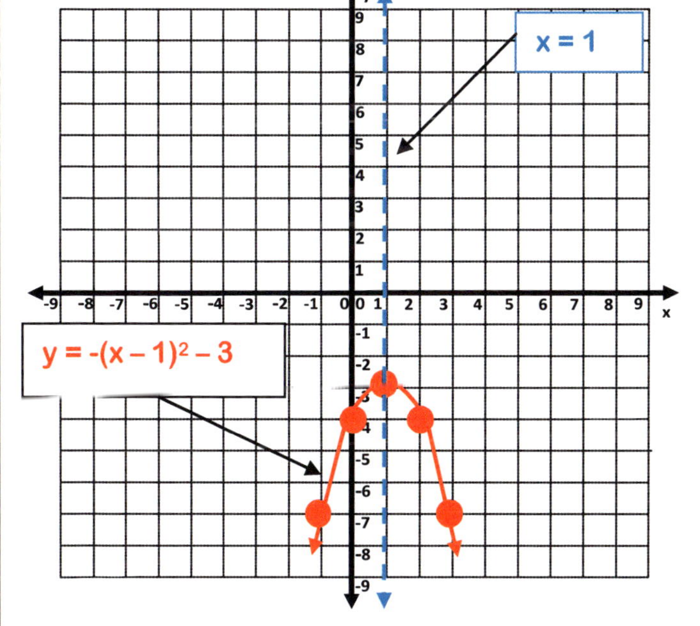

Vocabulary

Product of Powers Property
Power of a Power Property
Power of a Quotient Property
Quotient of Powers Property
Power of a Product Property
Negative Exponent Property
Zero Exponent Property

Negative Exponent Property ________ $a^{-n} = \frac{1}{a^n}$ or $\frac{1}{a^{-n}} = a^n$ $a \neq 0$

Quotient of Powers Property ________ $\frac{a^m}{a^n} = a^{m-n}$ $a \neq 0$

Power of a Quotient Property ________ $\left(\frac{a}{b}\right)^n = \frac{a^n}{b^n}$ $b \neq 0$

Power of a Power Property ________ $(a^m)^n = a^{mn}$

Algebra 2 Builder # 47

Name:______________________________

Vertex Form

Write in vertex form.

$f(x) = x^2 - 5x + 7$

$f(x) = 1(x^2 - 5x + \frac{25}{4}) + 7 - \frac{25}{4}$

$f(x) = (x - \frac{5}{2})^2 + \frac{3}{4}$

$-5 \cdot \frac{1}{2}$

$(-\frac{5}{2})^2$

$\frac{25}{4}$

Exponent Rules

$(5x^0y^3)(-3x^{-3}y^{-2})^{-2}$

$\frac{5y^3}{(-3x^{-3}y^{-2})^2}$

$\frac{5y^3}{9x^{-6}y^{-4}}$

$\frac{5x^6y^7}{9}$

$(x^{-4})^{1/2}$

x^{-2}

$\frac{1}{x^2}$

Solve Quadratic Inequalities

Solve algebraically.

$4x^2 - 5x + 4 \leq 3x^2 - 7x + 7$

-3 1

$x^2 + 2x - 3 \leq 0$

$(x + 3)(x - 1) \leq 0$

$x + 3 = 0$ or $x - 1 = 0$

$-3 \quad -3$ $\qquad +1 \quad +1$

$x = -3$ $\qquad x = 1$

$\{x \mid -3 \leq x \leq 1\}$

[-3,1]

Test Points -4, 0, 2

$x = -4$	$4(-4)^2 - 5(-4) + 4 \leq 3(-4)^2 - 7(-4) + 7$ $88 \leq 83$ False
$x = 0$	$4(0)^2 - 5(0) + 4 \leq 3(0)^2 - 7(0) + 7$ $4 \leq 7$ True
$x = 2$	$4(2)^2 - 5(2) + 4 \leq 3(2)^2 - 7(2) + 7$ $10 \leq 5$ False

Vertex

Use $-\frac{b}{2a}$ to find the vertex.

$f(x) = \frac{1}{2}x^2 - 4x + 2$

$a = \frac{1}{2} \quad b = -4$

$h = \frac{-b}{2a} = \frac{-(-4)}{2(1/2)} = \frac{4}{1} = 4$

$k = \frac{1}{2}(4)^2 - 4(4) + 2 = -6$

Vertex = (4,-6)

Graph Quadratics

$y = x^2 - 2x - 3$ standard form $\qquad y = ax^2 + bx = c$

$a = 1 \quad b = -2 \quad c = -3$

$h = \frac{-b}{2a} = \frac{-(-2)}{2(1)} = \frac{2}{2} = 1$

$k = (1)^2 - 2(1) - 3 = -4$

Vertex = (1,-4)

Axis of Symmetry x = 1

Opens up

x	$x^2 - 2x - 3$	y
2	$(2)^2 - 2(2) - 3$	-3
3	$(3)^2 - 2(3) - 3$	0

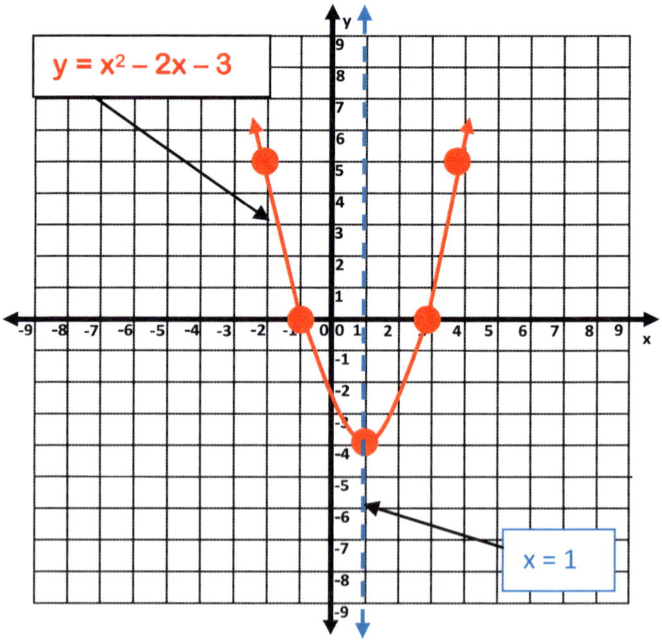

Vocabulary

Product of Powers Property
Power of a Power Property
Power of a Quotient Property
Quotient of Powers Property
Power of a Product Property
Negative Exponent Property
Zero Exponent Property

Product of Powers Property ______ $a^ma^n = a^{m+n}$

Zero Exponent Property ______ $a^0 = 1 \quad a \neq 0$

Quotient of Powers Property ______ $\frac{a^m}{a^n} = a^{m-n} \quad a \neq 0$

Power of a Product Property ______ $(ab)^m = a^mb^m$

Algebra 2 Builder # 48

Name:______________________________

Vertex Form

Write in vertex form.

$f(x) = 2x^2 - 3x + 5$

$f(x) = 2(x^2 - \frac{3}{2}x + \frac{9}{16}) + 5 - \frac{9}{8}$

$f(x) = 2(x - \frac{3}{4})^2 + \frac{31}{8}$

$\frac{-3}{2} \cdot \frac{1}{2}$

$(-\frac{3}{4})^2$

$\frac{9}{16}$

Exponent Rules

$\left(\frac{x^2y^{-3}}{4x^3y^2}\right)^{-2}$

$\left(\frac{1}{4xy^5}\right)^{-2}$

$(4xy^5)^2$

$16x^2y^{10}$

$\frac{x^{2/3}\ y}{4x^{1/3}\ y^{1/2}}$

$\frac{x^{\frac{2}{3}-\frac{1}{3}}y^{1-\frac{1}{2}}}{4}$

$\frac{x^{\frac{1}{3}}y^{\frac{1}{2}}}{4}$

Solve Quadratic Inequalities

Solve algebraically.

$2x^2 + 7x + 1 \geq 2x + 4$

$2x^2 + 5x - 3 \geq 0$

$(2x - 1)(x + 3) \geq 0$

$2x - 1 = 0$

$2x = 1$ or $x + 3 = 0$

$\frac{2x}{2} = \frac{1}{2}$ $-3 \ \ -3$

$x = ½$ $x = -3$

$\{x \mid x \leq -3 \text{ or } x \geq ½\}$

$(-\infty, -3] \cup [½, \infty)$

Test Points -4, 0, 1

x = -4	$2(-4)^2 + 7(-4) + 1 \geq 2(-4) + 4$ $5 \geq -4$ True
x = 0	$2(0)^2 + 7(0) + 1 \geq 2(0) + 4$ $1 \geq 4$ False
x = 1	$2(1)^2 + 7(1) + 1 \geq 2(1) + 4$ $10 \geq 6$ True

Vertex

Use $-\frac{b}{2a}$ to find the vertex.

$f(x) = -\frac{1}{4}x^2 + 8x + 2$

$a = -\frac{1}{4}$ $b = 8$

$h = \frac{-b}{2a} = \frac{-(8)}{2(-\frac{1}{4})} = \frac{-8}{-\frac{1}{2}} = 16$

$k = -\frac{1}{4}(16)^2 + 8(16) + 2 = 66$

Vertex = (16,66)

Graph Quadratics

$f(x) = -2(x-3)^2 + 1$ vertex form $y = a(x - h)^2 + k$

a = -2   h = 3   k = 1

Vertex = (3,1)

Axis of Symmetry x = 3

Opens down

x	$-2(x-3)^2 + 1$	y
4	$-2(4 - 3)^2 + 1$	-1
5	$-2(5 - 3)^2 + 1$	-7

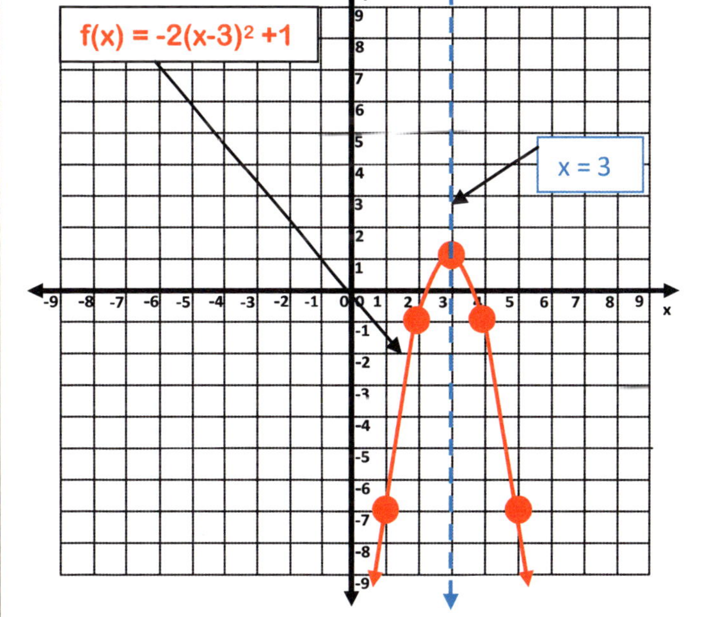

Vocabulary

Product of Powers Property
Power of a Power Property
Power of a Quotient Property
Quotient of Powers Property
Power of a Product Property
Negative Exponent Property
Zero Exponent Property

Negative Exponent Property ____ $a^{-n} = \frac{1}{a^n}$ or $\frac{1}{a^{-n}} = a^n$ $a \neq 0$

Power of a Power Property ____ $(a^m)^n = a^{mn}$

Quotient of Powers Property ____ $\frac{a^m}{a^n} = a^{m-n}$ $a \neq 0$

Power of a Quotient Property ____ $\left(\frac{a}{b}\right)^n = \frac{a^n}{b^n}$ $b \neq 0$

Algebra 2 Builder # 49

Name:______________________________

Solve Radicals by Graphing

Use a graphing calculator. Round to the nearest hundredth.

$\sqrt{x+2} = 3$

$x = 7$

Solve Radicals Algebraically

Check for extraneous solutions.

$(\sqrt{x+2})^2 = (4)^2$

$x + 2 = 16$
$-2 \quad -2$
$x = 14$

CHECK

$\sqrt{x+2} = 4$

$\sqrt{14+2} = 4$

$\sqrt{16} = 4$

$4 = 4$

Square Root Inequalities

Solve using a table on the calculator.

$3\sqrt{x} - 1 \geq 8$

$\{x|x \geq 9\}$

$[9, \infty)$

x	y_1	y_2
3	4.1962	8
4	5	8
5	5.7082	8
6	6.3485	8
7	6.9373	8
8	7.4853	8
9	8	8
10	8.4868	8

Rational Expressions

Simplify.

$\dfrac{x^2 - 5x + 6}{x^2 - 6x + 8}$

$\dfrac{(x-2)(x-3)}{(x-2)(x-4)}$

$\dfrac{x-3}{x-4}$

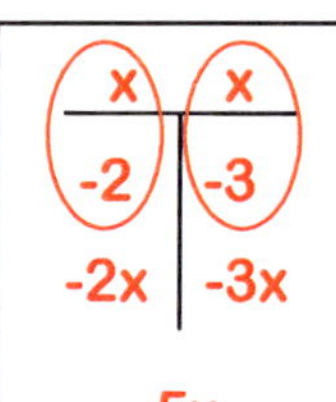

x x
-2 -4
-2x -4x
- 6x

Inverse Functions

Find $f^{-1}(x)$. Find the domain and range of f(x) and $f^{-1}(x)$. Write in set builder and interval notation.

$f(x) = \sqrt{x+3}$

$y = \sqrt{x+3}$

$(x)^2 = (\sqrt{y+3})^2$

$x^2 = y + 3$
$-3 \quad -3$
$x^2 - 3 = y$

$f^{-1}(x) = x^2 - 3$

f(x)

domain = $\{x|x \geq -3\}$
$[-3, \infty)$

range = $\{f(x)|f(x) \geq 0\}$
$[0, \infty)$

f^{-1}(x)

domain = $\{x|x \geq 0\}$
$[0, \infty)$

range = $\{f(x)|f(x) \geq -3\}$
$[-3, \infty)$

Long Division

$(3x^4 + 4x^3 - 3x + 1) \div (3x + 4)$

$$
\begin{array}{r}
x^3 \qquad - 1 \\
3x+4 \overline{)\, 3x^4 + 4x^3 - 3x + 1} \\
-(3x^4 + 4x^3) \qquad\qquad \\
-3x + 1 \\
-(-3x - 4) \\
5
\end{array}
$$

$x^3 - 1 + \dfrac{5}{3x+4}$

Vocabulary

Zero(s) of a Function
Domain
Range
Extraneous Solution
Radical
Radicand
End Behavior
Inverse Function

Inverse Function — a function that results from interchanging the domain and range values of a one to one function.

Domain — is the set of first elements in ordered pair or table.

Range — is the set of second elements in ordered pair or table.

Zero(s) of a Function — value(s) of x for which f(x) = 0.

Algebra 2 Builder # 50

Name:______________________________

Solve Radicals by Graphing

Use a graphing calculator. Round to the nearest hundredth.

$\sqrt{2x-8} = 2.3$

$x \approx 6.65$

Solve Radicals Algebraically

Check for extraneous solutions.

$\sqrt{4x+2} - 5 = 3$

$+5 \quad +5$

$(\sqrt{4x+2})^2 = (8)^2$

$4x + 2 = 64$

$-2 \quad -2$

$4x = 62$

$4 \quad 4$

$x = \frac{31}{2}$

CHECK

$\sqrt{4(\frac{31}{2})+2} - 5 = 3$

$\sqrt{62+2} - 5 = 3$

$\sqrt{64} - 5 = 3$

$8 - 5 = 3$

$3 = 3$

Square Root Inequalities

Solve using a table on the calculator.

$\sqrt{x-3} \leq 1$

$\{x|3 \leq x \leq 4\}$

$[3,4]$

x	y_1	y_2
0	ERROR	1
1	ERROR	1
2	ERROR	1
3	0	1
4	1	1
5	1.4142	1
6	1.7321	1

Rational Expressions

Simplify.

$\frac{x^2-1}{x^2+3x-4} \cdot \frac{x^2+6x+8}{x^3-1}$

$\frac{(x-1)(x+1)}{(x+4)(x-1)} \cdot \frac{(x+2)(x+4)}{(x-1)(x^2+x+1)}$

$\frac{(x+1)(x+2)}{(x-1)(x^2+x+1)}$

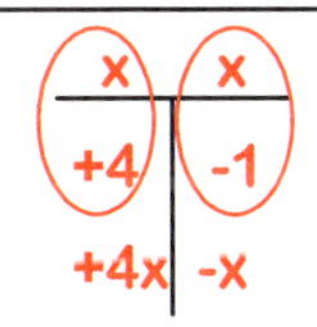

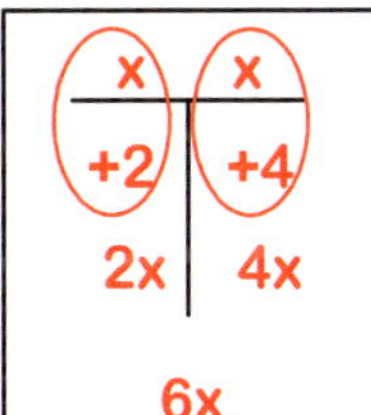

Inverse Functions

Find $f^{-1}(x)$. Find the domain and range of f(x) and $f^{-1}(x)$. Write in set builder and interval notation.

$f(x) = \sqrt{x} + 1$

$y = \sqrt{x} + 1$

$x = \sqrt{y} + 1$

$-1 \quad -1$

$(x-1)^2 = (\sqrt{y})^2$

$(x-1)^2 = y$

$x^2 - 2x + 1 = y$

$f^{-1}(x) = x^2 - 2x + 1$

f(x)

domain = $\{x|x \geq 0\}$
$[0,\infty)$

range = $\{f(x)|f(x) \geq 1\}$
$[1,\infty)$

$f^{-1}(x)$

domain = $\{x|x \geq 1\}$
$[1,\infty)$

range = $\{f(x)|f(x) \geq 0\}$
$[0,\infty)$

Long Division

$(x^3 - 3x^2 + 2x - 5) \div (x^2 - 1)$

$$
\begin{array}{r}
x - 3 \\
x^2 - 1 \,\big)\, x^3 - 3x^2 + 2x - 5 \\
-(x^3 \qquad\quad - x) \\
-3x^2 + 3x - 5 \\
-(-3x^2 \qquad + 3) \\
3x - 8
\end{array}
$$

$x - 3 + \frac{3x-8}{x^2-1}$

Vocabulary

Zero(s) of a Function
Domain
Range
Extraneous Solutions
Radical
Radicand
End Behavior
Inverse Function

Extraneous Solutions solutions that do not check.

Radicand the number or expression under the radical sign.

End Behavior the behavior of the graph of a function as x approaches negative infinity or positive infinity.

Radical an expression of the form $\sqrt{b}$ or $\sqrt[n]{b}$ where b is a number or expression.

Algebra 2 Builder # 51

Name:__________________________

Solve Radicals by Graphing

Use a graphing calculator. Round to the nearest hundredth.

$\sqrt[3]{x-5} = 1.3$

$x \approx 7.20$

Solve Radicals Algebraically

Check for extraneous solutions.

$\sqrt[3]{2x+3} = -2$

$(\sqrt[3]{2x+3})^3 = (-2)^3$

$2x + 3 = -8$

$-3 \quad -3$

$\frac{2x}{2} = \frac{-11}{2}$

$x = -\frac{11}{2}$

CHECK

$\sqrt[3]{2(-\frac{11}{2}) + 3} = -2$

$\sqrt[3]{-11+3} = -2$

$\sqrt[3]{-8} = -2$

$-2 = -2$

Square Root Inequalities

Solve using a table on the calculator.

$\sqrt{x+4} - 1 < 2$

$\{x \mid -5 < x < 5\}$

$(-5, 5)$

x	y_1	y_1
-6	ERROR	2
-5	ERROR	2
-4	-1	2
-3	0	2
-2	0.41421	2
-1	0.73205	2
0	1	2
1	1.2361	2
2	1.4495	2
3	1.6458	2
4	1.8284	2
5	2	2
6	2.1623	2

Rational Expressions

Simplify.

$\frac{x^2 - 5x + 6}{x^2 - 9} \div \frac{x^3 - 8}{x^2 + x - 6}$

$\frac{x^2 - 5x + 6}{x^2 - 9} \cdot \frac{x^2 + x - 6}{x^3 - 8}$

$\frac{(x-2)(x-3)}{(x-3)(x+3)} \cdot \frac{(x-2)(x+3)}{(x-2)(x^2 + 2x + 4)}$

$\frac{(x-2)}{(x^2 + 2x + 4)}$

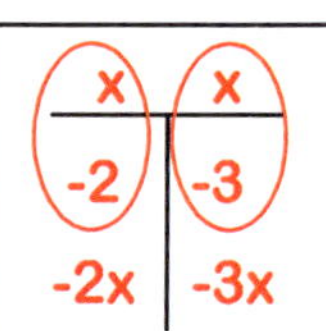

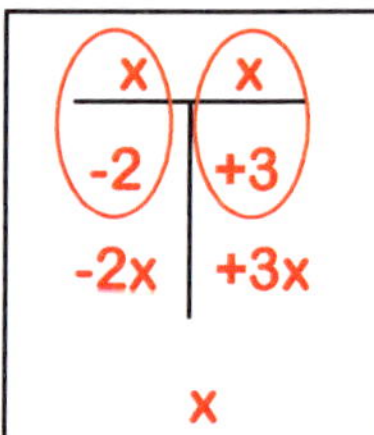

Inverse Functions

Find $f^{-1}(x)$. Find the domain and range of f(x) and $f^{-1}(x)$. Write in set builder and interval notation.

$f(x) = \sqrt{2x+3}$

$y = \sqrt{2x+3}$

$(x)^2 = (\sqrt{2y+3})^2$

$x^2 = 2y + 3$

$-3 \quad -3$

$\frac{x^2 - 3}{2} = \frac{2y}{2}$

$\frac{x^2-3}{2} = y$

$f^{-1}(x) = \frac{x^2-3}{2}$

f(x)

domain = $\{x \mid x \geq -\frac{3}{2}\}$

$[-\frac{3}{2}, \infty)$

range = $\{f(x) \mid f(x) \geq 0\}$

$[0, \infty)$

$f^{-1}(x)$

domain = $\{x \mid x \geq 0\}$

$[0, \infty)$

range = $\{f(x) \mid f(x) \geq -\frac{3}{2}\}$

$[-\frac{3}{2}, \infty)$

Long Division

$(2x^4 - 14x^3 + 22x^2 - 2x + 1) \div (2x - 4)$

$$\begin{array}{r} x^3 - 5x^2 + x + 1 \\ 2x - 4 \overline{)\, 2x^4 - 14x^3 + 22x^2 - 2x + 1} \\ \underline{-(2x^4 - 4x^3)} \\ -10x^3 + 22x^2 \\ \underline{-(-10x^3 + 20x^2)} \\ 2x^2 - 2x \\ \underline{-(2x^2 - 4x)} \\ 2x + 1 \\ \underline{-(2x - 4)} \\ 5 \end{array}$$

$x^3 - 5x^2 + x + 1 + \frac{5}{2x-4}$

Vocabulary

Zero(s) of a Function
Domain
Range
Extraneous Solutions
Radical
Radicand
End Behavior
Inverse Function

Range is the set of second elements in ordered pair or table.

Zero(s) of a Function value(s) of x for which f(x) = 0.

Inverse Function a function that results from interchanging the domain and range values of a one to one function.

Domain is the set of first elements in ordered pair or table.

Algebra 2 Builder # 52

Name:____________________________

Solve Radicals by Graphing

Use a graphing calculator. Round to the nearest hundredth.

$\sqrt{3x-2}=\sqrt{2x+5}$

$x = 7$

Solve Radicals Algebraically

Check for extraneous solutions.

$\sqrt[3]{3x}-2=2$

$+2 \quad +2$

$\sqrt[3]{3x}=4$

$(\sqrt[3]{3x})^3=(4)^3$

$3x = 64$

$\frac{3x}{3}=\frac{64}{3}$

$x=\frac{64}{3}$

CHECK

$\sqrt[3]{3\left(\frac{64}{3}\right)}-2=2$

$\sqrt[3]{64}-2=2$

$4-2=2$

$2=2$

Square Root Inequalities

Solve using a table on the calculator.

$\sqrt{x-2}>3$

$\{x|x>11\}$

$(11,\infty)$

x	y_1	y_1
8	2.4495	3
9	2.6458	3
10	2.8284	3
11	3	3
12	3.1623	3
13	3.3166	3
14	3.4641	3

Rational Expressions

Simplify.

$\frac{1}{x+2}+\frac{2}{x-3}$

$\frac{1}{x+2}\frac{(x-3)}{(x-3)}+\frac{2}{x-3}\frac{(x+2)}{(x+2)}$

$\frac{x-3}{(x+2)(x-3)}+\frac{2x+4}{(x+2)(x-3)}$

$\frac{3x+1}{(x+2)(x-3)}$

Inverse Functions

Find $f^{-1}(x)$. Find the domain and range of f(x) and $f^{-1}(x)$. Write in set builder and interval notation.

$f(x)=\sqrt{x-2}+1$

$y=\sqrt{x-2}+1$

$x=\sqrt{y-2}+1$

$-1 \qquad -1$

$(x-1)^2=(\sqrt{y-2})^2$

$x^2-2x+1=y-2$

$+2 \qquad +2$

$x^2-2x+3=y$

$f^{-1}(x)=x^2-2x+3$

f(x)

domain = $\{x|x\geq 2\}$
$[2,\infty)$

range = $\{f(x)|f(x)\geq 1\}$
$[1,\infty)$

$f^{-1}(x)$

domain = $\{x|x\geq 1\}$
$[1,\infty)$

range = $\{f(x)|f(x)\geq 2\}$
$[2,\infty)$

Long Division

$(x^4+4x^3-4x+6)\div(x^2+4x+1)$

$$
\begin{array}{r}
x^2 \qquad -1 \\
x^2+4x+1\,\overline{)\,x^4+4x^3+0x^2-4x+6} \\
-(x^4+4x^3+x^2) \\
-x^2-4x+6 \\
-(-x^2-4x-1) \\
7
\end{array}
$$

$x^2-1+\frac{7}{x^2+4x+1}$

Vocabulary

Zero(s) of a Function
Domain
Range
Extraneous Solutions
Radical
Radicand
End Behavior
Inverse Function

End Behavior the behavior of the graph of a function as x approaches negative infinity or positive infinity.

Radical an expression of the form $\sqrt{b}$ or $\sqrt[n]{b}$ where b is a number or expression.

Extraneous Solutions solutions that do not check.

Radicand the number or expression under the radical sign.

Algebra 2 Builder # 53

Name:____________________________

Solve Radicals by Graphing

Use a graphing calculator. Round to the nearest hundredth.

$\sqrt{2x+3} - 3 = \sqrt{x+4} - 2$

$x \approx 9.29$

Solve Radicals Algebraically

Check for extraneous solutions.

$\sqrt{x+2} = x - 4$

$(\sqrt{x+2})^2 = (x-4)^2$

$x + 2 = (x-4)(x-4)$

$x + 2 = x^2 - 8x + 16$

$-x - 2 \quad\quad -x \quad -2$

$0 = x^2 - 9x + 14$

$0 = (x-7)(x-2)$

$x - 7 = 0 \quad x - 2 = 0$

$\boxed{x = 7}$ or $x = 2$

x	x
-7	-2
-7x	-2x

-9x

CHECK

$\sqrt{(7)+2} = (7) - 4$

$\sqrt{9} = 3$

$3 = 3$

$\sqrt{(2)+2} = (2) - 4$

$\sqrt{4} = -2$

$2 \neq -2$

Square Root Inequalities

Solve using a graphing calculator.

In y1 type left side of the inequality
in y2 type the right side of the inequality.
2nd Calc then
5 intersect.

$3\sqrt{x} - 2 < 7$

$\{x | 0 \leq x < 9\}$

$[0, 9)$

Rational Expressions

Simplify.

$\frac{1}{x} - \frac{3}{x+3}$

$\frac{1}{x}\frac{(x+3)}{(x+3)} - \frac{3}{(x+3)}\frac{(x)}{(x)}$

$\frac{x+3}{x(x+3)} - \frac{3x}{x(x+3)}$

$\frac{-2x+3}{x(x+3)}$

Inverse Functions

Find $f^{-1}(x)$. Find the domain and range of f(x) and $f^{-1}(x)$. Write in set builder and interval notation.

$f(x) = x^2 - 5 \quad x \leq 0$

$y = x^2 - 5$

$x = y^2 - 5$

$+5 \quad\quad +5$

$\sqrt{x+5} = \sqrt{y^2}$

$-\sqrt{x+5} = y$

$f^{-1}(x) = -\sqrt{x+5}$

f(x)

domain = $\{x | x \leq 0\}$
$[0, \infty)$

range = $\{f(x) | f(x) \geq -5\}$
$[-5, \infty)$

$f^{-1}(x)$

domain = $\{x | x \geq -5\}$
$[-5, \infty)$

range = $\{f(x) | f(x) \leq 0\}$
$[0, \infty)$

Synthetic Division

$(x^3 + 4x^2 + 5x + 7) \div (x - 3)$

3	1	4	5	7
	↓	3	21	78
	1	7	26	85

$x^2 + 7x + 26 + \frac{85}{x-3}$

Vocabulary

Zero(s) of a Function
Domain
Range
Extraneous Solutions
Radical
Radicand
End Behavior
Inverse Function

Range ____ is the set of second elements in ordered pair or table.

Domain ____ is the set of first elements in ordered pair or table.

Zero(s) of a Function ____ value(s) of x for which f(x) = 0.

Inverse Function ____ a function that results from interchanging the domain and range values of a one to one function.

Algebra 2 Builder # 54

Name:____________________

Solve Radicals by Graphing

Use a graphing calculator. Round to the nearest hundredth.

$\sqrt[3]{2x+1} = x + 5$

$x \approx -7.40$

Solve Radicals Algebraically

Check for extraneous solutions.

$\sqrt{x+3} + 3 = x$

$\quad -3 \quad -3$

$(\sqrt{x+3})^2 = (x-3)^2$

$x + 3 = (x-3)(x-3)$

$x + 3 = x^2 - 6x + 9$

$-x - 3 \quad -x \quad -3$

$0 = x^2 - 7x + 6$

$0 = (x-6)(x-1)$

$x - 6 = 0 \quad x - 1 = 0$

$x = 6$ or $x = 1$

CHECK

$\sqrt{(6)+3} + 3 = (6)$

$\sqrt{9} + 3 = 6$

$3 + 3 = 6$

$6 = 6$

$\sqrt{(1)+3} + 3 = (1)$

$\sqrt{4} + 3 = 1$

$2 + 3 = 1$

$5 \neq 1$

Square Root Inequalities

Solve using a graphing calculator.

In y1 type left side of the inequality
in y2 type the right side of the inequality.
2nd Calc then
5 intersect.

$\sqrt{x+1} > 10$

$\{x | x > 99\}$

$(99, \infty)$

Rational Expressions

Simplify.

$\frac{x}{x^2-9} + \frac{2}{x^2+5x+6}$

$\frac{x(x+2)}{(x\quad 3)(x+3)(x+2)} + \frac{2(x-3)}{(x+3)(x+2)(x-3)}$

$\frac{x^2+2x}{(x-3)(x+3)(x+2)} + \frac{2x-6}{(x-3)(x+3)(x+2)}$

$\frac{x^2+4x-6}{(x-3)(x+3)(x+2)}$

Inverse Functions

Find $f^{-1}(x)$. Find the domain and range of f(x) and $f^{-1}(x)$. Write in set builder and interval notation.

$f(x) = (x+2)^2 \quad x \geq -2$

$y = (x+2)^2$

$\sqrt{x} = \sqrt{(y+2)^2}$

$\sqrt{x} = y + 2$

$-2 \quad -2$

$\sqrt{x} - 2 = y$

$f^{-1}(x) = \sqrt{x} - 2$

f(x)

domain = $\{x | x \geq -2\}$
$[-2, \infty)$

range = $\{f(x) | f(x) \geq 0\}$
$[0, \infty)$

$f^{-1}(x)$

domain = $\{x | x \geq 0\}$
$[0, \infty)$

range =
$\{f(x) | f(x) \geq -2\}$
$[-2, \infty)$

Synthetic Division

$(x^4 - 3x^2 + 2x + 4) \div (x + 2)$

-2	1	0	-3	2	4
	↓	-2	4	-2	0
	1	-2	1	0	4

$x^3 - 2x^2 + x + \frac{4}{x+2}$

Vocabulary

Zero(s) of a Function
Domain
Range
Extraneous Solutions
Radical
Radicand
End Behavior
Inverse Function

Radicand the number or expression under the radical sign.

Radical an expression of the form $\sqrt{b}$ or $\sqrt[n]{b}$ where b is a number or expression.

Extraneous Solutions solutions that do not check.

End Behavior the behavior of the graph of a function as x approaches negative infinity or positive infinity.

Algebra 2 Builder # 55

Name:______________________

Solve Radicals by Graphing

Use a graphing calculator. Round to the nearest hundredth.

$\sqrt[3]{4x-5}+3=x$

$x \approx 5.59$

Solve Radicals Algebraically

Check for extraneous solutions.

$\sqrt{5x-5}=\sqrt{2x+4}$

$(\sqrt{5x-5})^2=(\sqrt{2x+4})^2$

$5x-5=2x+4$

$-2x+5 \quad -2x+5$

$3x=9$

$\frac{3x}{3}=\frac{9}{3}$

$x=3$

CHECK

$\sqrt{5(3)-5}=\sqrt{2(3)+4}$

$\sqrt{10}=\sqrt{10}$

Square Root Inequalities

Solve using graphing calculator.

$\sqrt{x+1}+3\geq 5$

$\{x|x\geq 3\}$

$[3,\infty)$

Rational Expressions

Simplify.

$\frac{x+4}{2x^2-2x-12}-\frac{x}{x^2-4}$

$\frac{x+4}{2(x^2-x-6)}-\frac{x}{(x-2)(x+2)}$

$\frac{(x+4)(x-2)}{2(x-3)(x+2)(x-2)}-\frac{(x)(2)(x-3)}{(x-2)(x+2)(2)(x-3)}$

$\frac{x^2-2x+4x-8}{2(x-3)(x+2)(x-2)}-\frac{2x^2-6x}{2(x-3)(x+2)(x-2)}$

$\frac{-x^2+8x-8}{2(x-3)(x+2)(x-2)}$

Inverse Functions

Find $f^{-1}(x)$. Find the domain and range of f(x) and $f^{-1}(x)$. Write in set builder and interval notation.

$f(x)=(x-3)^2+4 \qquad x\leq 3$

$y=(x-3)^2+4$

$x=(y-3)^2+4$

$-4 \qquad -4$

$\sqrt{x-4}=\sqrt{(y-3)^2}$

$-\sqrt{x-4}=y-3$

$+3 \qquad +3$

$-\sqrt{x-4}+3=y$

$f^{-1}(x)=-\sqrt{x-4}+3$

f(x)

domain = $\{x|x\leq 3\}$

$[-\infty,3)$

range = $\{f(x)|f(x)\geq 4\}$

$[4,\infty)$

$f^{-1}(x)$

domain = $\{x|x\geq 4\}$

$[4,\infty)$

range = $\{f(x)|f(x)\leq 3\}$

$[-\infty,3)$

Synthetic Division

$(2x^3-3x^2+x)\div(x-4)$

$(2x^3-3x^2+x+0)\div(x-4)$

4	2	-3	1	0
	↓	8	20	84
	2	5	21	84

$2x^2+5x+21+\frac{84}{x-4}$

Vocabulary

Zero(s) of a Function
Domain
Range
Extraneous Solutions
Radical
Radicand
End Behavior
Inverse Function

Domain is the set of first elements in ordered pair or table.

Zero(s) of a Function value(s) of x for which f(x) = 0.

Range is the set of second elements in ordered pair or table.

Inverse Function a function that results from interchanging the domain and range values of a one to one function.

Algebra 2 Builder # 56

Name:________________________

Solve Radicals by Graphing

Use a graphing calculator. Round to the nearest hundredth.

$\sqrt{2x} - 1 = \sqrt{3x+1} - 4$

$x \approx 87.27$

Solve Radicals Algebraically

Check for extraneous solutions.

$\sqrt{23x+12} = 2x + 3$

$(\sqrt{23x+12})^2 = (2x+3)^2$

$23x + 12 = (2x+3)(2x+3)$

$23x + 12 = 4x^2 + 6x + 6x + 9$

$23x + 12 = 4x^2 + 12x + 9$

$-23x - 12 \quad -23x - 12$

$0 = 4x^2 - 11x - 3$

$0 = (4x+1)(x-3)$

$4x + 1 = 0$ or $x - 3 = 0$

$4x = -1 \qquad x = 3$

$x = -\frac{1}{4}$

$4x$	x
$+1$	-3
$+x$	$-12x$

$-11x$

CHECK

$\sqrt{23(-\frac{1}{4}) + 12} = 2(-\frac{1}{4}) + 3$

$\sqrt{6.25} = 2.5$

$2.5 = 2.5$

CHECK

$\sqrt{23(3) + 12} = 2(3) + 3$

$\sqrt{81} = 9$

$9 = 9$

Square Root Inequalities

Solve using graphing calculator.

$\sqrt{x+3} < 5$

$\{x \mid -3 \le x < 22\}$

$[-3, 22)$

Rational Expressions

Simplify.

$\frac{3}{x-2} - \frac{4}{x^2 - 4x + 4}$

$\frac{3}{x-2} \cdot \frac{(x-2)}{(x-2)} - \frac{4}{(x-2)^2}$

$\frac{3x-6}{(x-2)^2} - \frac{4}{(x-2)^2}$

$\frac{3x-10}{(x-2)^2}$

x	x
-2	-2
$-2x$	$-2x$

$-4x$

Inverse Functions

Find $f^{-1}(x)$. Find the domain and range of f(x) and $f^{-1}(x)$. Write in set builder and interval notation.

$f(x) = x^2 + 6 \quad x \ge 0$

$y = x^2 + 6$

$x = y^2 + 6$

$-6 \qquad -6$

$\sqrt{x-6} = \sqrt{y^2}$

$\sqrt{x-6} = y$

$f^{-1}(x) = \sqrt{x-6}$

f(x)

domain = $\{x \mid x \ge 0\}$

$[0, \infty)$

range = $\{f(x) \mid f(x) \ge 6\}$

$[6, \infty)$

$f^{-1}(x)$

domain = $\{x \mid x \ge 6\}$

$[6, \infty)$

range = $\{f(x) \mid f(x) \ge 0\}$

$[0, \infty)$

Synthetic Division

$(3x^4 - 5x + 2) \div (x + 3)$

$(3x^4 + 0x^3 + 0x^2 - 5x + 2) \div (x + 3)$

-3	3	0	0	-5	2
	↓	-9	27	-81	258
	3	-9	27	-86	260

$2x^3 - 9x^2 + 27x - 86 + \frac{260}{x+3}$

Vocabulary

Zero(s) of a Function
Domain
Range
Extraneous Solutions
Radical
Radicand
End Behavior
Inverse Function

Radicand the number or expression under the radical sign.

End Behavior the behavior of the graph of a function as x approaches negative infinity or positive infinity.

Radical an expression of the form $\sqrt{b}$ or $\sqrt[n]{b}$ where b is a number or expression.

Extraneous Solutions solutions that do not check.

Algebra 2 Builder # 57

Name:________________________

Direct/Inverse Variation

If y varies directly with x, and y = 30 when x = 6, find the equation relating x and y. Then find y when $x = \frac{3}{2}$.

$y = kx$

$\frac{30}{6} = \frac{k(6)}{6}$

$5 = k$

$y = 5x$

$y = 5(\frac{3}{2})$

$y = \frac{15}{2}$

Rational Equations

Solve and then check for extraneous solutions.

$\frac{1}{x} = \frac{2x}{x+3}$

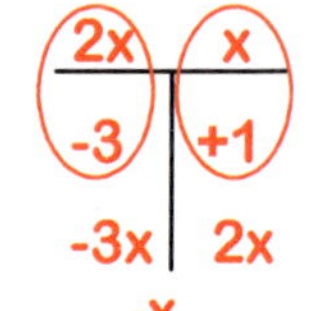

$x(2x) = 1(x + 3)$
$2x^2 = x + 3$
$-x -3 \quad -x -3$
$2x^2 - x - 3 = 0$
$(2x - 3)(x + 1) = 0$
$2x - 3 = 0$ or $x + 1 = 0$
$2x = 3 \qquad x = -1$

$x = \frac{3}{2}$

CHECK

$\frac{1}{(\frac{3}{2})} = \frac{2(\frac{3}{2})}{(\frac{3}{2}) + 3}$

$\frac{2}{3} = \frac{3}{\frac{9}{2}}$

$\frac{2}{3} = \frac{2}{3}$

CHECK

$\frac{1}{(-1)} = \frac{2(-1)}{(-1) + 3}$

$\frac{1}{-1} = \frac{-2}{2}$

$-1 = -1$

Rational Inequalities

Solve the inequality algebraically.

$\frac{2}{x-3} > 0$

$x - 3 = 0$
$x = 3$
Test Points 2 , 4

$\frac{2}{(2)-3} > 0 \qquad \frac{2}{(4)-3} > 0$

$-2 > 0 \qquad 2 > 0$

FALSE TRUE

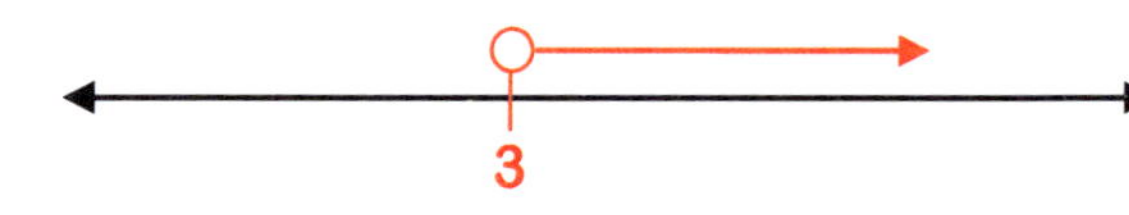

$\{x|x > 3\}$

$(3, \infty)$

Graph Rational Functions

Find the vertical and horizontal asymptotes, the x and y intercepts, the domain and range, then graph the equation.

$y = \frac{1}{x}$

Vertical Asymptote $x = 0$

Horizontal Asymptote $y = 0$

x-intercept none

y-intercept none

Domain = $\{x|\text{all real numbers except zero}\}$
$(-\infty, 0) \cup (0, \infty)$

Range = $\{y|\text{all real numbers except zero}\}$
$(-\infty, 0) \cup (0, \infty)$

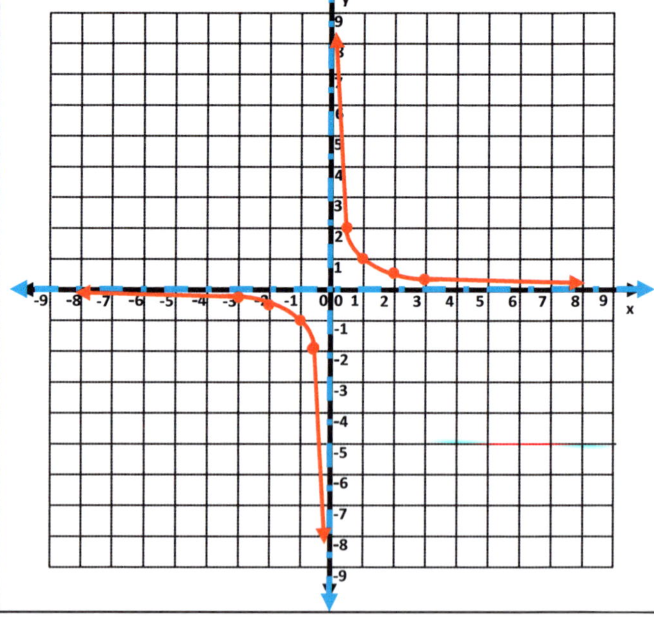

Vocabulary

Extraneous Solutions
Asymptote
Discontinuity
Complex Fraction
Rational Function
Least Common Denominator
Direct Variation
Inverse Variation

Asymptote a line that a graph closely approaches.

Inverse Variation the relationship of two variables x and y where there is some constant k such that xy = k or $y = \frac{k}{x}$.

Discontinuity a break in the continuity of a function.

Extraneous Solutions solutions that do not check.

Algebra 2 Builder # 58

Name:_______________________________

Direct/Inverse Variation

If y varies inversely with x, and y = 30 when x = 6, find the equation relating x and y. Then find y when x = $\frac{3}{2}$.

$y = \frac{k}{x}$

$\frac{30}{1} = \frac{k}{6}$

k = 180

$y = \frac{180}{x}$

$y = \frac{180}{\frac{3}{2}}$

y = 120

Rational Equations

Solve and then check for extraneous solutions.

$\frac{x-1}{x+3} = \frac{x-5}{x+4}$

(x + 3)(x – 5) = (x – 1)(x + 4)

$x^2 - 5x + 3x - 15 = x^2 + 4x - x - 4$

$x^2 - 2x - 15 = x^2 + 3x - 4$

$-x^2 - 3x + 15 \quad -x^2 - 3x + 15$

$\frac{-5x}{-5} = \frac{11}{-5}$

$x = -\frac{11}{5}$

CHECK

$\frac{(-\frac{11}{5}) - 1}{(-\frac{11}{5}) + 3} = \frac{(-\frac{11}{5}) - 5}{(-\frac{11}{5}) + 4}$

$\frac{-\frac{16}{5}}{\frac{4}{5}} = \frac{-\frac{36}{5}}{\frac{9}{5}}$

-4 = -4

Rational Inequalities

Solve the inequality algebraically.

$\frac{2}{x-1} < -2$

+2 +2

$\frac{2}{x-1} + \frac{2}{1}\frac{(x-1)}{(x-1)} < 0$

$\frac{2}{x-1} + \frac{2x-2}{x-1} < 0$

$\frac{2x}{x-1} < 0$

2x = 0 or x – 1 = 0

x = 0 x = 1

TEST POINTS -1, 0.5, 2

$\frac{2}{(-1)-1} < -2$	$\frac{2}{(0.5)-1} < -2$	$\frac{2}{(2)-1} < -2$
$-1 < -2$	$\frac{2}{-0.5} < -2$	$2 < -2$
False	$-4 < -2$	False
	True	

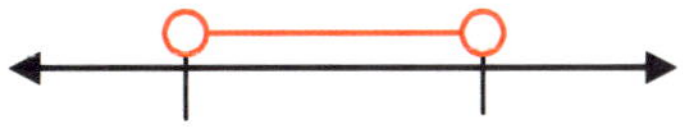

$\{x | 0 < x < 1\}$

(0,1)

Graph Rational Functions

Find the vertical and horizontal asymptotes, the x and y intercepts, the domain and range, then graph the equation.

$y = \frac{1}{x} + 2$

Vertical Asymptote x = 0

Horizontal Asymptote y = 2

x-intercept (-0.5,0)

y-intercept none

Domain = $\{x | \text{all real numbers except } 0\}$

$(-\infty, 0) \cup (0, \infty)$

Range = $\{x | \text{all real numbers except } 2\}$

$(-\infty, 2) \cup (2, \infty)$

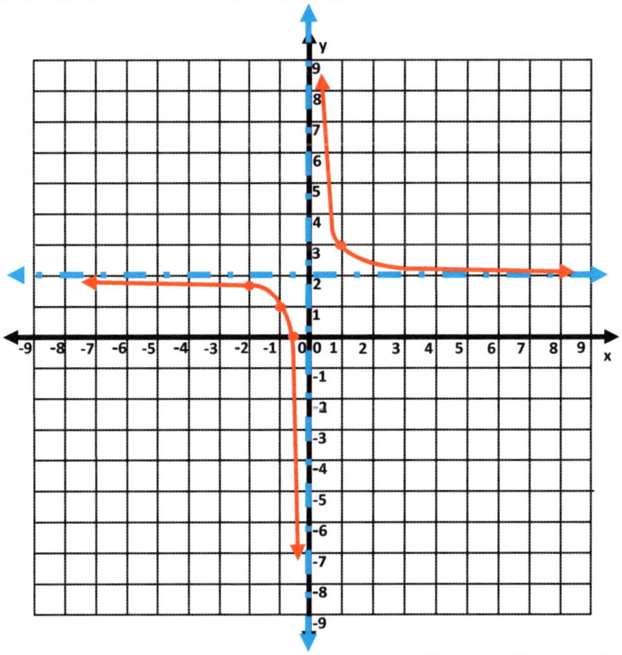

Vocabulary

Extraneous Solutions
Asymptote
Discontinuity
Complex Fraction
Rational Function
Least Common Denominator
Direct Variation
Inverse Variation

Complex Fraction a fraction that contains a fraction in the numerator or denominator.

Rational Function a ratio of two polynomial functions where the denominator cannot equal zero.

Least Common Denominator the smallest factor that each denominator can divide into evenly.

Direct Variation the relationship of 2 variables x and y where there is some constant k such that y = kx.

Algebra 2 Builder # 59

Name:______________________

Direct/Inverse Variation

If y varies directly with x, and y = 1/2 when x = 3/2, find the equation relating x and y. Then find y when x = 8.

y = kx

$\left(\frac{2}{3}\right)\frac{1}{2} = k\left(\frac{3}{2}\right)\left(\frac{2}{3}\right)$

$\frac{1}{3} = k$

$y = \frac{1}{3}(x)$

$y = \frac{1}{3}(8)$

$y = \frac{8}{3}$

Rational Equations

Solve and then check for extraneous solutions.

$\frac{1}{x} + \frac{1}{2x} = 3$

$(2x)\frac{1}{x} + \frac{1}{2x}\ (2x) = 3\ (2x)$

$2 + 1 = 6x$

$\frac{3}{6} = \frac{6x}{6}$

$x = \frac{1}{2}$

CHECK

$\frac{1}{\left(\frac{1}{2}\right)} + \frac{1}{2\left(\frac{1}{2}\right)} = 3$

2 + 1 = 3

3 = 3

Rational Inequalities

Solve the inequality algebraically.

$\frac{3}{x-2} \leq 0$

$x - 2 = 0$

$x = 2$

TEST POINTS 0 , 3

$\frac{3}{(0)-2} \leq 0$

$-\frac{3}{2} \leq 0$

True

$\frac{3}{(3)-2} \leq 0$

$\frac{3}{1} \leq 0$

$3 \leq 0$

False

$\{x|x < 2\}$

$(-\infty, 2)$

Graph Rational Functions

Find the vertical and horizontal asymptotes, the x and y intercepts, the domain and range, then graph the equation.

$f(x) = \frac{3}{x} - 2$

Vertical Asymptote x = 0

Horizontal Asymptote f(x) = -2

x-intercept $\left(\frac{3}{2}, 0\right)$

y-intercept none

Domain = $\{x|\text{all real numbers except zero}\}$

$(-\infty, 0) \cup (0, \infty)$

Range = $\{f(x)|\text{all real numbers except } -2\}$

$(-\infty, -2) \cup (-2, \infty)$

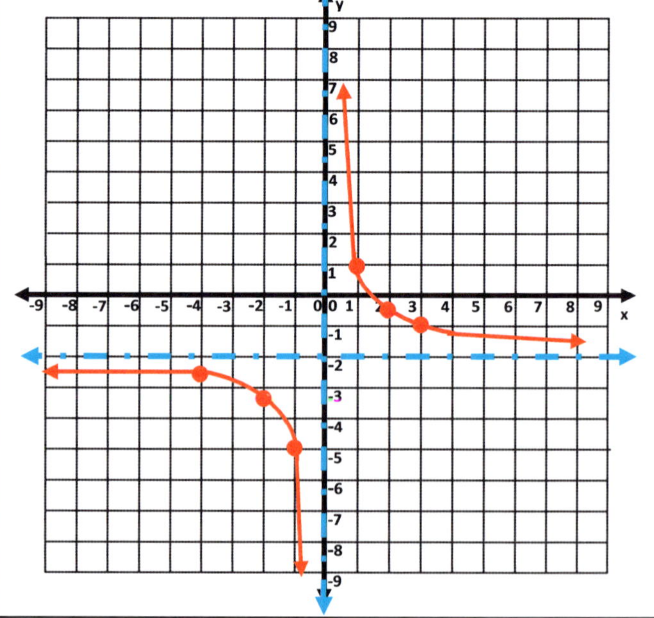

Vocabulary

Extraneous Solutions
Asymptote
Discontinuity
Complex Fraction
Rational Function
Least Common Denominator
Direct Variation
Inverse Variation

Extraneous Solutions solutions that do not check.

Asymptote a line that a graph closely approaches.

Inverse Variation the relationship of two variables x and y where there is some constant k such that xy = k or $y = \frac{k}{x}$.

Discontinuity a break in the continuity of a function.

Algebra 2 Builder # 60

Name:______________________

Direct/Inverse Variation

If y varies inversely with x, and $y = 1/2$ when $x = 3/2$, find the equation relating x and y. Then find y when x = 8.

$y = \frac{k}{x}$

$\left(\frac{2}{3}\right)\frac{1}{2} = \frac{k}{\frac{3}{2}}\left(\frac{2}{3}\right)$

$k = \frac{1}{3}$

$y = \frac{\frac{1}{3}}{x}$

$y = \frac{1}{3x}$

$y = \frac{1}{3(8)}$

$y = \frac{1}{24}$

Rational Equations

Solve and then check for extraneous solutions.

$\frac{2}{3x} + \frac{4}{6x} = \frac{x}{3}$

$(6x)\frac{2}{3x} + \frac{4}{6x}(6x) = \frac{x}{3}(6x)$

$4 + 4 = 2x^2$

$\frac{8}{2} = \frac{2x^2}{2}$

$4 = x^2$

$0 = x^2 - 4$

$0 = (x - 2)(x + 2)$

$x - 2 = 0$ or $x + 2 = 0$

$x = 2$ $x = -2$

CHECK

$\frac{2}{3(2)} + \frac{4}{6(2)} = \frac{(2)}{3}$

$\frac{1}{3} + \frac{1}{3} = \frac{2}{3}$

$\frac{2}{3} = \frac{2}{3}$

CHECK

$\frac{2}{3(-2)} + \frac{4}{6(-2)} = \frac{(-2)}{3}$

$-\frac{1}{3} - \frac{1}{3} = -\frac{2}{3}$

$-\frac{2}{3} = -\frac{2}{3}$

Rational Inequalities

Solve the inequality algebraically.

$\frac{3}{x^2 - 4} \geq 0$

$x^2 - 4 = 0$

$(x - 2)(x + 2) = 0$

$x - 2 = 0$ or $x + 2 = 0$

$x = 2$ $x = -2$

TEST POINTS -3, 0, 3

$\frac{3}{(-3)^2 - 4} \geq 0$	$\frac{3}{(0)^2 - 4} \geq 0$	$\frac{3}{(3)^2 - 4} \geq 0$
$\frac{3}{5} \geq 0$	$-\frac{3}{4} \geq 0$	$\frac{3}{5} \geq 0$
True	False	True

-2 2

$\{x | x < -2 \text{ or } x > 2\}$

$(-\infty, -2) \cup (2, \infty)$

Graph Rational Functions

Find the vertical and horizontal asymptotes, the x and y intercepts, the domain and range, then graph the equation.

$y = \frac{2}{x - 3} + 2$

Vertical Asymptote $x = 3$

Horizontal Asymptote $y = 2$

x-intercept $(2, 0)$

y-intercept $\left(0, \frac{4}{3}\right)$

Domain = $\{x | \text{all real numbers except } 3\}$

$(-\infty, 3) \cup (3, \infty)$

Range = $\{y | \text{all real numbers except } 2\}$

$(-\infty, 2) \cup (2, \infty)$

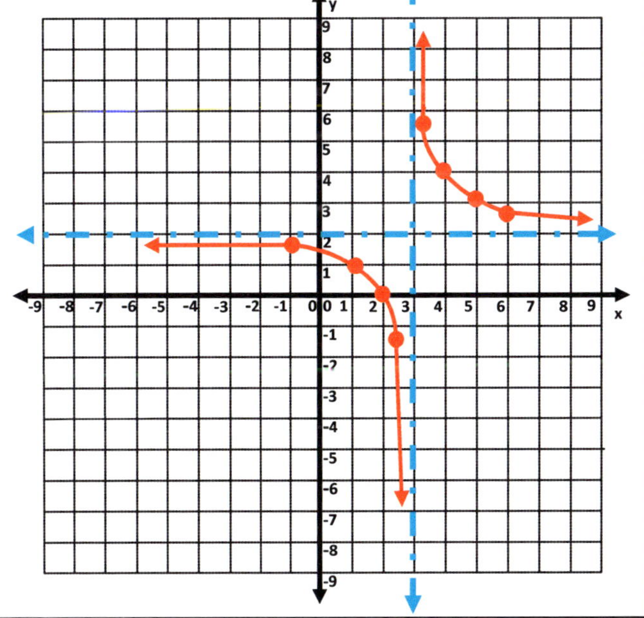

Vocabulary

Extraneous Solutions
Asymptote
Discontinuity
Complex Fraction
Rational Function
Least Common Denominator
Direct Variation
Inverse Variation

Direct Variation the relationship of two variables x and y where there is some constant k such that y = kx.

Complex Fraction a fraction that contains a fraction in the numerator or denominator.

Rational Function a ratio of two polynomial functions where the denominator cannot equal zero.

Least Common Denominator the smallest factor that each denominator can divide into evenly.

Algebra 2 Builder # 61

Name:____________________

Direct/Inverse Variation

Use k as the constant of variation and write an equation for the given relationship

When w varies directly as x and inversely as z.

$$w = \frac{kx}{z}$$

Rational Equations

Solve and then check for extraneous solutions.

$$\frac{3}{x-2} - 4 = \frac{4}{x-7}$$

$$\frac{3(x-2)(x-7)}{x-2} - \frac{4(x-2)(x-7)}{1} = \frac{4(x-2)(x-7)}{x-7}$$

$3x - 21 - 4(x^2 - 9x + 14) = 4x - 8$

$3x - 21 - 4x^2 + 36x - 56 = 4x - 8$

$-4x + 8 \quad -4x + 8$

$-4x^2 + 35x - 69 = 0$

$4x^2 - 35x + 69 = 0$

$(4x - 23)(x - 3) = 0$

$4x - 23 = 0$ or $x - 3 = 0$

$4x = 23 \qquad x = 3$

$x = \frac{23}{4}$

CHECK

$$\frac{3}{(\frac{23}{4}) - 2} - 4 = \frac{4}{(\frac{23}{4}) - 7}$$

$$\frac{3}{\frac{15}{4}} - 4 = \frac{4}{\frac{-5}{4}}$$

$$\frac{4}{5} - 4 = \frac{-16}{5}$$

$$\frac{-16}{5} = \frac{-16}{5}$$

CHECK

$$\frac{3}{3-2} - 4 = \frac{4}{3-7}$$

$$3 - 4 = \frac{4}{-4}$$

$$-1 = -1$$

Rational Inequalities

Solve the inequality using a table.

$$\frac{-2x-4}{x-3} < 0$$

x	y
-5	-.75
-4	-.5714
-3	-.3333
-2	0
-1	.5
0	1.3333
1	3
2	8
3	ERROR
4	-12
5	-7

$\{x | x < -2 \text{ or } x > 3\}$

$(-\infty, -2) \cup (3, \infty)$

Graph Rational Functions

Find the vertical and horizontal asymptotes, the x and y intercepts, the domain and range, then graph the equation.

$$g(x) = \frac{2x+3}{x-4}$$

Vertical Asymptote $x = 4$

Horizontal Asymptote $g(x) = 2$

x-intercept $(-1.5, 0)$

y-intercept $(0, -0.75)$

Domain = $\{x | \text{all real numbers except } 4\}$

$(-\infty, 4) \cup (4, \infty)$

Range = $\{g(x) | \text{all real numbers except } 2\}$

$(-\infty, 2) \cup (2, \infty)$

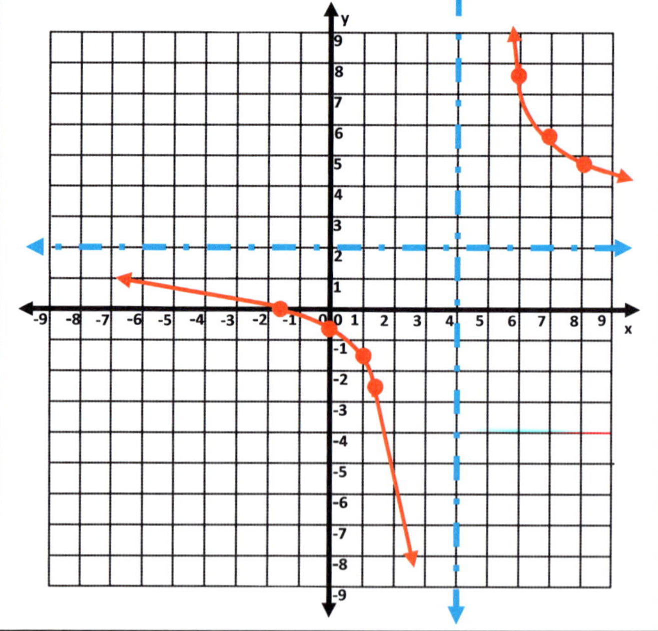

Vocabulary

Extraneous Solutions
Asymptote
Discontinuity
Complex Fraction
Rational Function
Least Common Denominator
Direct Variation
Inverse Variation

Discontinuity a break in the continuity of a function.

Extraneous Solutions solutions that do not check.

Asymptote a line that a graph closely approaches.

Inverse Variation the relationship of two variables x and y where there is some constant k such that xy = k or $y = \frac{k}{x}$.

Algebra 2 Builder # 62

Name:______________________

Direct/Inverse Variation

Use k as the constant of variation and write an equation for the given relationship

When q varies directly as the square of x and inversely as the cube of y.

$q = \frac{kx^2}{y^3}$

Rational Equations

Solve and then check for extraneous sol

$\frac{2x}{x^2-4x} = \frac{2}{x-4} + \frac{x-1}{x}$

$x(x-4)\frac{2x}{x^2-4x} = \frac{2}{x-4}x(x-4) + \frac{x-1}{x}x(x-4)$

$2x = 2x + x^2 - 5x + 4$

$-2x \quad -2x$

$0 = x^2 - 5x + 4$

$0 = (x-1)(x-4)$

$x - 1 = 0$ or $x - 4 = 0$

$x = 1$ (boxed) $\quad x = 4$

Check

$\frac{2(1)}{(1)^2-4(1)} = \frac{2}{(1)-4} + \frac{(1)-1}{(1)}$

$-\frac{2}{3} = -\frac{2}{3} + \frac{0}{1}$

$-\frac{2}{3} = -\frac{2}{3}$

Check

$\frac{2(4)}{(4)^2-4(4)} = \frac{2}{(4)-4} + \frac{(4)-1}{(4)}$

$\frac{8}{0} = \frac{2}{0} + \frac{1}{4}$

Undefined

Rational Inequalities

Solve the inequality using a table.

$\frac{-2x-3}{x-4} \geq 0$

x	y
-3	-.4286
-2.5	-.3077
-2	-.1667
-1.5	0
-1	.2
-.5	.4444
0	.75
.5	1.1429
1	1.6667

x	y
1.5	2.4
2	3.5
2.5	5.333
3	9
3.5	20
4	ERROR
4.5	-24
5	-13

$\{x \mid -1.5 \leq x < 4\}$

$[-1.5, 4)$

Graph Rational Functions

Find the vertical and horizontal asymptotes, the x and y intercepts, the domain and range, then graph the equation.

$y = \frac{6}{x^2 - x - 6}$

Vertical Asymptote $x = -2, x = 3$

Horizontal Asymptote $y = 0$

x-intercept none

y-intercept $(0, -1)$

Domain = $\{x \mid \text{all real numbers except } -2 \text{ and } 3\}$

$(-\infty, -2) \cup (-2, 3) \cup (3, \infty)$

Range = $\{g(x) \mid \text{all real numbers except } 0\}$

$(-\infty, 0) \cup (0, \infty)$

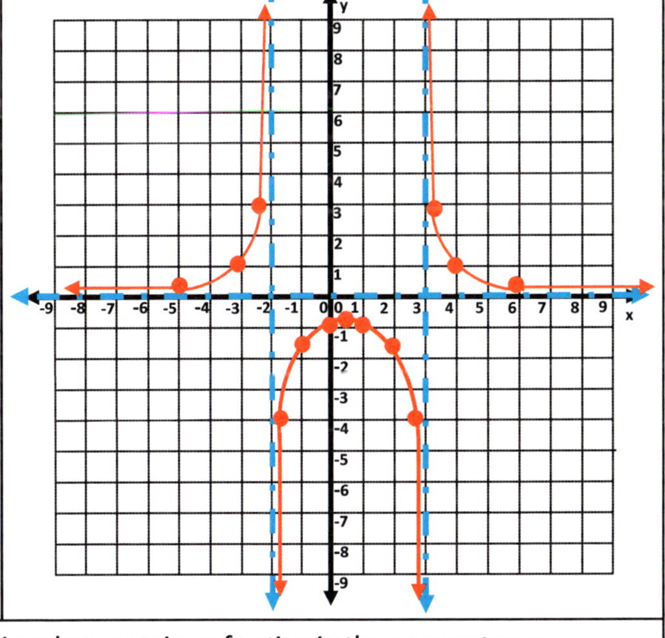

Vocabulary

Extraneous Solutions
Asymptote
Discontinuity
Complex Fraction
Rational Function
Least Common Denominator
Direct Variation
Inverse Variation

Complex Fraction a fraction that contains a fraction in the numerator or denominator.

Direct Variation the relationship of two variables x and y where there is some constant k such that y = kx.

Rational Function a ratio of two polynomial functions where the denominator cannot equal zero.

Least Common Denominator the smallest factor that each denominator can divide into evenly.

Algebra 2 Builder # 63 Name:________________________

Direct/Inverse Variation

Use k as the constant of variation and write an equation for the given relationship

The area of a square varies directly as the square of the length of the side.

$A = ks^2$

Rational Equations

Solve and then check for extraneous solutions.

$$\frac{1}{x-1} + \frac{2}{x+2} = \frac{3}{2}$$

$$\frac{1(2)(x+2)(x-1)}{x-1} + \frac{2(2)(x-2)(x-1)}{x+2} = \frac{3(2)(x+2)(x-1)}{2}$$

$2(x + 2) + 4(x - 1) = 3(x - 1)(x + 2)$

$2x + 4 + 4x - 4 = 3(x^2 + x - 2)$

$6x = 3x^2 + 3x - 6$

$0 = 3x^2 - 3x - 6$

$0 = 3(x^2 - x - 2)$

$0 = (x - 2)(x + 1)$

$x - 2 = 0$ or $x + 1 = 0$

$x = 2$ $x = -1$

-1,2

CHECK

$$\frac{1}{(-1)-1} + \frac{2}{(-1)+2} = \frac{3}{2}$$

$$-\frac{1}{2} + 2 = \frac{3}{2}$$

$$\frac{3}{2} = \frac{3}{2}$$

$$\frac{1}{(2)-1} + \frac{2}{(2)+2} = \frac{3}{2}$$

$$1 + \frac{1}{2} = \frac{3}{2} \qquad \frac{3}{2} = \frac{3}{2}$$

Rational Inequalities

Solve the inequality by graphing.

$$\frac{4x-3}{x-2} > 3$$

$\{x | x < -3 \text{ or } x > 2\}$

$(-\infty, -3) \cup (2, \infty)$

Graph Rational Functions

Find the vertical and horizontal asymptotes, the x and y intercepts, the domain and range, then graph the equation.

$$f(x) = \frac{x^2 - 5x - 6}{x^2 - 4}$$

Vertical Asymptote	x = -2, x = 2
Horizontal Asymptote	f(x) = 1
x-intercepts	(-1 , 0)(6 , 0)
y-intercept	(0 , 1.5)

Domain = $\{x | \text{all real numbers except } -2 \text{ and } 2\}$

$(-\infty, -2) \cup (-2, 2) \cup (2, \infty)$

Range = $\{f(x) | \text{all real numbers}\}$

$(-\infty, \infty)$

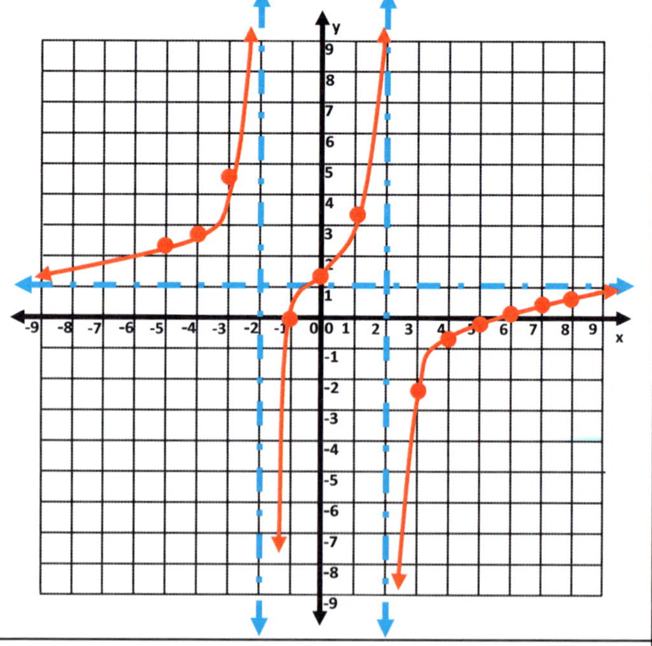

Vocabulary

Extraneous Solutions
Asymptote
Discontinuity
Complex Fraction
Rational Function
Least Common Denominator
Direct Variation
Inverse Variation

Asymptote a line that a graph closely approaches.

Extraneous Solutions solutions that do not check.

Inverse Variation the relationship of two variables x and y where there is some constant k such that xy = k or $y = \frac{k}{x}$.

Discontinuity a break in the continuity of a function.

Algebra 2 Builder # 64

Name:_________________________

Direct/Inverse Variation

Use k as the constant of variation and write an equation for the given relationship

The resistance of an electrical wire and the passage of the current, varies directly as the length of the wire, and inversely as the square of the wire's diameter.

$$R = \frac{kl}{d^2}$$

Rational Equations

Solve and then check for extraneous solutions.

$$\frac{3}{x+4} + \frac{x-2}{x} = \frac{5x+1}{7x}$$

$$\frac{3(7x)(x+4)}{x+4} + \frac{(x-2)(7x)(x+4)}{x} = \frac{(5x+1)(7x)(x+4)}{7x}$$

$7x(3) + 7(x-2)(x+4) = (5x+1)(x+4)$

$21x + 7(x^2 + 2x - 8) = 5x^2 + 21x + 4$

$21x + 7x^2 + 14x - 56 = 5x^2 + 21x + 4$

$7x^2 + 35x - 56 = 5x^2 + 21x + 4$

$2x^2 + 14x - 60 = 0$

$2(x^2 + 7x - 30) = 0$

$2(x+10)(x-3) = 0$

$x + 10 = 0$ or $x - 3 = 0$

$x = -10$ $\quad$ $x = 3$

CHECK

$$\frac{3}{(-10)+4} + \frac{(-10)-2}{(-10)} = \frac{5(-10)+1}{7(-10)}$$

$$\frac{3}{-6} + \frac{-12}{-10} = \frac{-49}{-70}$$

$$\frac{-1}{2} + \frac{6}{5} = \frac{7}{10}$$

$$\frac{7}{10} = \frac{7}{10}$$

$$\frac{3}{(3)+4} + \frac{(3)-2}{(3)} = \frac{5(3)+1}{7(3)}$$

$$\frac{3}{7} + \frac{1}{3} = \frac{16}{21}$$

$$\frac{16}{21} = \frac{16}{21}$$

Rational Inequalities

Solve the inequality by graphing.

$$\frac{3}{x+2} \le 1$$

$$\{x | x < -2 \text{ or } x \ge 1\}$$

$$(-\infty, -2) \cup [1, \infty)$$

Graph Rational Functions

Find the vertical and horizontal asymptotes, the x and y intercepts, the domain and range, then graph the equation.

$$y = \frac{x^2 - 9}{x^2}$$

Vertical Asymptote $x = 0$

Horizontal Asymptote $y = 1$

x-intercept $(-3, 0)\ (3, 0)$

y-intercept none

Domain = $\{x | \text{all real numbers except } 0\}$

$(-\infty, 0) \cup (0, \infty)$

Range = $\{y | y < 1\}$

$(-\infty, 1)$

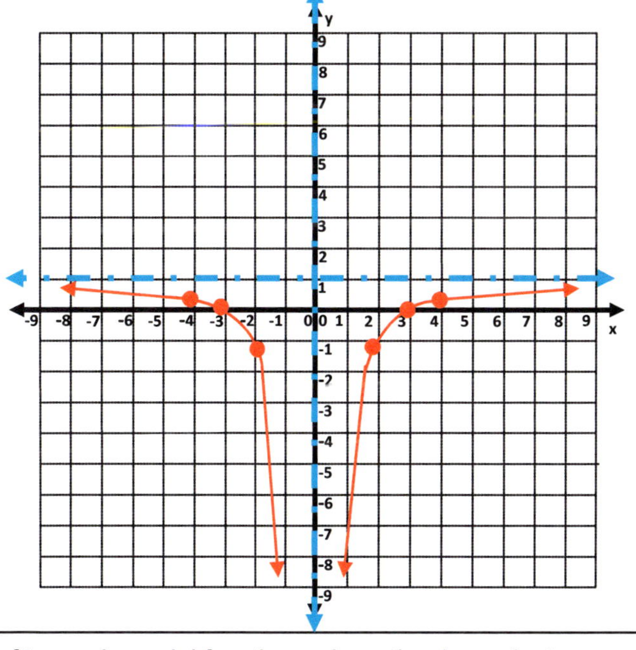

Vocabulary

Extraneous Solutions
Asymptote
Discontinuity
Complex Fraction
Rational Function
Least Common Denominator
Direct Variation
Inverse Variation

Rational Function a ratio of two polonomial functions where the denominator cannot equal zero.

Direct Variation the relationship of two variables x and y where there is some constant such that y = kx.

Complex Fraction a fraction that contains a fraction in the numerator or denominator.

Least Common Denominator the smallest factor that each denominator can divide into evenly.

Algebra 2 Builder # 65

Name:________________________________

Evaluate Logarithms

Evaluate without a calculator.

$\log_6 36$

$\log_6 6^2$

2

$12^{\log_{12} 3}$

3

Expand Logarithms

Use properties of logarithms to expand the expression.

$\log xy$

$\log x + \log y$

Condense Logarithms

Use properties of logarithms to condense the expression.

$\log_7 x - \log_7 y$

$\log_7 \frac{x}{y}$

Inverse Functions

Find the inverse of the function.

y = 3^x

x = 3^y

$\log_3 x = y$

Exponential / Log Equations

Solve.

$2^{2x-4} = 16^{x-2}$

$2^{2x-4} = (2^4)^{x-2}$

$2^{2x-4} = 2^{4x-8}$

$2x - 4 = 4x - 8$
$-2x + 8 \quad -2x + 8$
$4 = 2x$
$\frac{4}{2} = \frac{2x}{2}$
$2 = x$

Note: Set exponents equal

Exponential / Log Application

Write an exponential growth model for the given situation.

Sam deposits $700.00 in an account that pays 1.5% annual interest compounded weekly.

$I(t) = 700\left(1 + \frac{0.015}{52}\right)^{52t}$

$I(t) = 700(1.000288)^{52t}$

Graph Exponential Functions

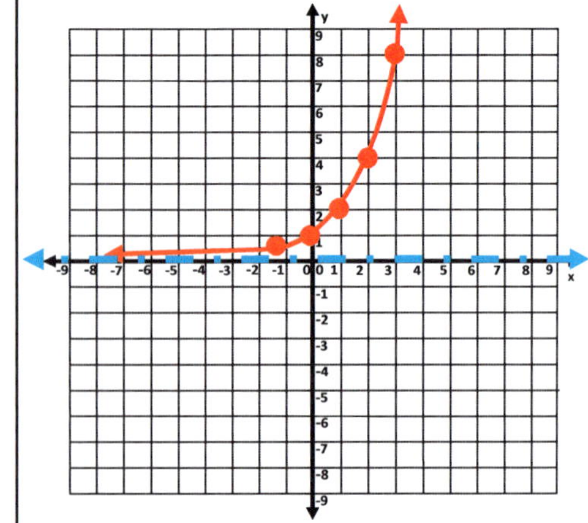

Find the asymptote, intercepts, the domain and range, then graph.

y = 2^x

Horizontal Asymptote y = 0

Y-intercept (0 , 1)

Domain $\{x \mid x \in R\}$ $(-\infty, \infty)$

Range $\{y \mid y > 0\}$ $(0, \infty)$

Vocabulary

Asymptote
Exponential Function
Exponential Growth
Exponential Decay
Logarithmic Function
Common Logarithm
Natural Logarithm
Natural Base e

Exponential Function a function in which the independent variable is the exponent.

Logarithmic Function The inverse of an exponential function.

Exponential Growth An exponential function y = ab^x, where a > 0 and b > 1

Exponential Decay An exponential function y = ab^x, where a > 0 and 0 < b < 1

Algebra 2 Builder # 66

Name:______________________

Evaluate Logarithms

Evaluate without a calculator.

$\log_8 1$ $e^{\ln 5}$

0   5

Expand Logarithms

Use properties of logarithms to expand the expression.

$\ln x^2 y^3$

$\ln x^2 + \ln y^3$

$2\ln x + 3\ln y$

Condense Logarithms

Use properties of logarithms to condense the expression.

$2\log x + 3\log y$

$\log x^2 + \log y^3$

$\log(x^2 y^3)$

Inverse Functions

Find the inverse of the function.

$y = \log_3 x$

$x = \log_3 y$

$3^x = y$

Exponential / Log Equations

Solve.

$3^{x+1} = \frac{1}{9}^x$

$3^{x+1} = (3^{-2})^x$

$3^{x+1} = 3^{-2x}$

$x + 1 = -2x$

$-x \quad -x$

$1 = -3x$

$x = -\frac{1}{3}$

Exponential / Log Application

Write an exponential decay model for the given situation.

A new car cost $25,000. The value of the car depreciates at a rate of 14% per year.

$c(t) = 25000(1 - 0.14)^t$

$c(t) = 25000(0.86)^t$

Graph Exponential Functions

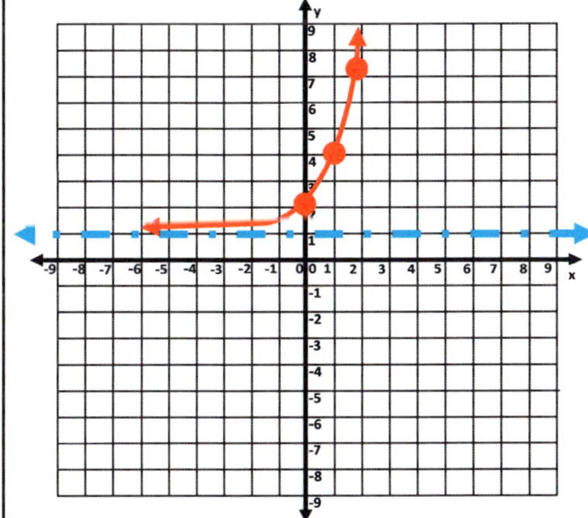

Find the asymptote, intercepts, the domain and range, then graph.

$y = 3^x + 1$

Horizontal Asymptote $y = 1$

Y-intercept $(0, 2)$

Domain $\{x \mid x \in R\}$ $(-\infty, \infty)$

Range $\{y \mid y > 1\}$ $(1, \infty)$

Vocabulary

Asymptote
Exponential Function
Exponential Growth
Exponential Decay
Logarithmic Function
Common Logarithm
Natural Logarithm
Natural Base *e*

Natural Base *e* The Euler number, $e \approx 2.718281828$.

Common Logarithm A base 10 logarithm.

Natural Logarithm A base *e* logarithm denoted by ln.

Asymptote A line that a graph closely approaches.

Algebra 2 Builder # 67

Name:____________________________

Evaluate Logarithms

Evaluate without a calculator.

$\log_3 \frac{1}{27}$ | $\log_2 64$

$\log_3 3^{-3}$ | $\log_2 2^6$

-3 | 6

Expand Logarithms

Use properties of logarithms to expand the expression.

$\ln 2xy^3$

$\ln 2 + \ln x + \ln y^3$

$\ln 2 + \ln x + 3\ln y$

Condense Logarithms

Use properties of logarithms to condense the expression.

$3\log_3 x + 2\log_3 y + \log_3 z$

$\log_3 x^3 + \log_3 y^2 + \log_3 z$

$\log_3(x^3 y^2 z)$

Inverse Functions

Find the inverse of the function.

$y = 2^{x-1}$

$x = 2^{y-1}$

$\log_2 x = y - 1$

$+1 \quad +1$

$\log_2 x + 1 = y$

Exponential / Log Equations

Solve. $3^{x+1} = 7$

$\log 3^{x+1} + \log 7$

$\frac{(x+1)\log 3}{\log 3} = \frac{\log 7}{\log 3}$

$x + 1 = \frac{\log 7}{\log 3}$

$x + 1 = \frac{\log 7}{\log 3} - 1$

$x \approx 0.7712$

Exponential / Log Application

You deposit $5000.00 in an account that pays 1.25% interest compounded quarterly. After 20 years, what is the balance of the account?

$b(20) = 5000(1 + \frac{0.0125}{4})^{4(20)}$

$b(20) = 5000(1.003125)^{80}$

$b(20) = 6417.62$

After 20 years the balance of the account will be $6417.62.

Graph Exponential Functions

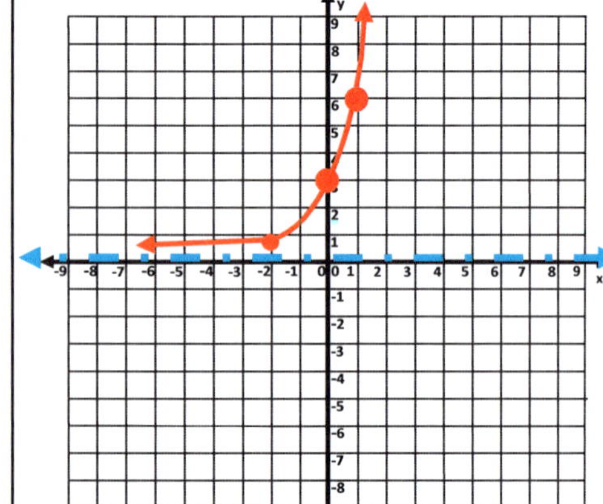

Find the asymptote, intercepts, the domain and range, then graph.

$f(x) = 3 \cdot 2^x$

Horizontal Asymptote $f(x) = 0$

Y-intercept (0 , 3)

Domain $\{x \mid x \in R\}\ (-\infty, \infty)$

Range $\{f(x) \mid f(x) > 0\}\ (0, \infty)$

Vocabulary

Asymptote
Exponential Function
Exponential Growth
Exponential Decay
Logarithmic Function
Common Logarithm
Natural Logarithm
Natural Base *e*

Exponential Function — a function in which the independent variable is the exponent.

Exponential Decay — An exponential function $y = ab^x$, where $a > 0$ and $0 < b < 1$

Logarithmic Function — The inverse of an exponential function.

Exponential Growth — An exponential function $y = ab^x$, where $a > 0$ and $b > 1$

Algebra 2 Builder # 68

Name:______________________

Evaluate Logarithms

Evaluate without a calculator.

$\log_{\frac{1}{3}} 27$

$\log_{\frac{1}{3}} (\frac{1}{3})^{-3}$

-3

$\log_8 4$

$\log_8 8^{\frac{2}{3}}$

$\frac{2}{3}$

Expand Logarithms

Use properties of logarithms to expand the expression.

$\ln \sqrt{xy}$

$\ln(xy)^{1/2}$

$\frac{1}{2}\ln(xy)$

$\frac{1}{2}(\ln x + \ln y)$

$\frac{1}{2}\ln x + \frac{1}{2}\ln y$

Condense Logarithms

Use properties of logarithms to condense the expression.

$\ln x - \ln y - \ln z$

$\ln \frac{x}{yz}$

Inverse Functions

Find the inverse of the function.

$y = \log x + 1$

$x = \log y + 1$

$\underline{-1 \qquad -1}$

$x - 1 = \log y$

$10^{x-1} = y$

Exponential / Log Equations

Solve.

$5^{x-3} = 6^x$

$\log 5^{x-3} = \log 6^x$

$(x-3)\log 5 = x \log 6$

$x\log 5 - 3\log 5 = x\log 6$

$\underline{-x\log 6 + 3\log 5 \quad -x\log 6 + 3\log 5}$

$x\log 5 - x\log 6 = 3\log 5$

$\frac{x(\log 5 - \log 6)}{\log 5 - \log 6} = \frac{3\log 5}{\log 5 - \log 6}$

$x = \frac{3\log(5)}{(\log(5) - \log(6))}$

x = -26.48

Exponential / Log Application

A new car cost $35,000. The value of the car depreciates at a rate of 12% per year. What is the value of the car in five years?

$c(5) = 35000(1 - 0.12)^5$

$c(5) = 35000(0.88)^5$

$c(5) = 18470.62$

The car is valued at $18470.62 in five years.

Graph Exponential Functions

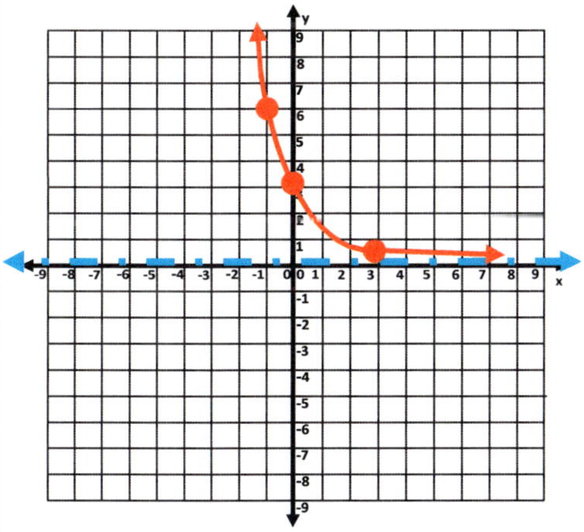

Find the asymptote, intercepts, the domain and range, then graph.

$f(x) = 3\left(\frac{1}{2}\right)^x$

Horizontal Asymptote $f(x) = 0$

Y-intercept $(0, 3)$

Domain $\{x \mid x \in R\}$ $(-\infty, \infty)$

Range $\{f(x) \mid f(x) > 0\}$ $(0, \infty)$

Vocabulary

Asymptote
Exponential Function
Exponential Growth
Exponential Decay
Logarithmic Function
Common Logarithm
Natural Logarithm
Natural Base *e*

Natural Base *e* — The Euler number, $e \approx 2.718281828$.

Asymptote — A line that a graph closely approaches.

Common Logarithm — A base 10 logarithm.

Natural Logarithm — A base *e* logarithm denoted by ln.

Algebra 2 Builder # 69

Name:______________________________

Evaluate Logarithms

Evaluate using a calculator, round to 4 decimal places.

$\log 5$ — **0.6990**

$\ln 7$ — **1.9459**

Expand Logarithms

Use properties of logarithms to expand the expression.

$\log \frac{2x}{y}$

$\log 2 + \log x - \log y$

Condense Logarithms

Use properties of logarithms to condense the expression.

$2\ln a - 3\ln b + \ln c$

$\ln a^2 - \ln b^3 + \ln c$

$\ln\left(\frac{a^2}{b^3}\right) + \ln c$

$\ln\left(\frac{a^2 c}{b^3}\right)$

Inverse Functions

Find the inverse of the function.

$y = 3^x + 2$

$x = 3^y + 2$

$-2 \quad -2$

$x - 2 = 3^y$

$\log_3(x-2) = y$

Exponential / Log Equations

Solve and check for extraneous solutions.

$\log_5(x-2) = 2$

$5^2 = x - 2$

$25 = x - 2$

$+2 \quad +2$

$27 = x$

CHECK

$\log_5(27-2) = 2$

$\log_5 25 = 2$

$2 = 2$

Exponential / Log Application

You deposit $6000.00 in an account that pays 1.2% interest compounded quarterly. How long will it take for the account to reach $8000.00?

$\frac{8000}{6000} = \frac{6000(1 + \frac{0.012}{4})^{4t}}{6000}$

$\frac{4}{3} = 1.003^{4t}$

$\log\left(\frac{4}{3}\right) = \log(1.003^{4t})$

$\frac{\log\left(\frac{4}{3}\right)}{(4\log(1.003))} = \frac{4t\log 1.003}{4\log(1.003)}$

$24 \approx t$

It will take approximately 24 years for the account to reach $8000.00.

Graph Logarithmic Functions

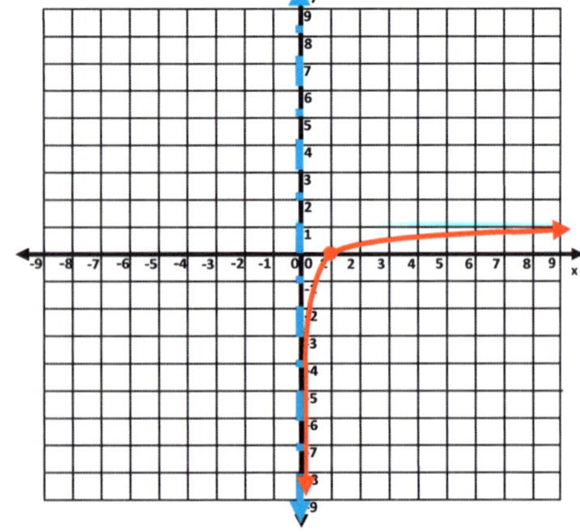

Find the asymptote, intercepts, the domain and range, then graph.

$y = \log x$

Vertical Asymptote $x = 0$

x-intercept $(1, 0)$

Domain $\{x \mid x > 0\}$ $(0, \infty)$

Range $\{y \mid y \in R\}$ $(-\infty, \infty)$

Vocabulary

Asymptote
Exponential Function
Exponential Growth
Exponential Decay
Logarithmic Function
Common Logarithm
Natural Logarithm
Natural Base *e*

Exponential Decay — An exponential function $y = ab^x$, where $a > 0$ and $0 < b < 1$

Exponential Function — a function in which the independent variable is the exponent.

Logarithmic Function — The inverse of an exponential function.

Exponential Growth — An exponential function $y = ab^x$, where $a > 0$ and $b > 1$

Algebra 2 Builder # 70

Name:______________________________

Evaluate Logarithms

Evaluate using a calculator, round to 4 decimal places.

$\log 4 + \log 7$

1.4472

$\ln 3 - \ln 6$

-0.6931

Expand Logarithms

Use properties of logarithms to expand the expression.

$\log_3 \frac{3x^2}{y}$

$\log_3 3 + \log_3 x^2 - \log_3 y$

$\log_3 3 + 2\log_3 x - \log_3 y$

Condense Logarithms

Use properties of logarithms to condense the expression.

$\frac{1}{2}\log_2 a + 2\log_2 3$

$\log_2 a^{\frac{1}{2}} + \log_2 3^2$

$\log_2 a^{\frac{1}{2}} + \log_2 9$

$\log_2 9a^{\frac{1}{2}}$

$\log_2(9\sqrt{a}\ )$

Inverse Functions

Find the inverse of the function.

$y = e^x - 1$

$x = e^y - 1$

$+1 \qquad +1$

$x + 1 = e^y$

$\ln(x + 1) = y$

Exponential / Log Equations

Solve and check for extraneous solutions.

$\log_3(2x - 5) = \log_3(x + 7)$

$2x - 5 = x + 7$

$-x + 5 \quad -x + 5$

$x = 12$

CHECK

$\log_3(2(12) - 5) = \log_3(12 + 7)$

$\log_3 19 = \log_3 19$

Exponential / Log Application

You deposit $7000.00 in an account that pays 1.25% interest compounded continuously. How long will it take for the account to double?

$14000 = 7000e^{0.0125t}$

$2 = e^{0.0125t}$

$\ln 2 = \ln e^{0.0125t}$

$\ln 2 = 0.0125t$

$0.0125 \qquad 0.0125$

$55.45 \approx t$

It will take appoximately 55 years for the account to double.

Graph Logarithmic Functions

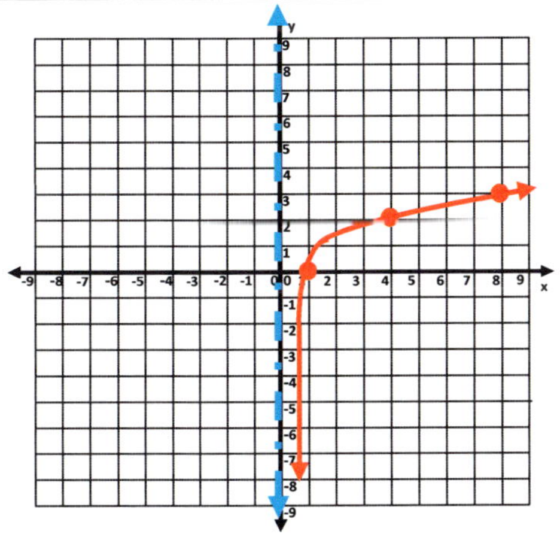

Find the asymptote, intercepts, the domain and range, then graph.

$y = \log_2 x$

Vertical Asymptote $x = 0$

x-intercept $(1, 0)$

Domain $\{x \mid x > 0\}\ (0, \infty)$

Range $\{y \mid y \in R\}\ (-\infty, \infty)$

Vocabulary

- Asymptote
- Exponential Function
- Exponential Growth
- Exponential Decay
- Logarithmic Function
- Common Logarithm
- Natural Logarithm
- Natural Base e

Asymptote A line that a graph closely approaches.

Natural Base e The Euler number, $e \approx 2.718281828$.

Common Logarithm A base 10 logarithm.

Natural Logarithm A base e logarithm denoted by ln.

Algebra 2 Builder # 71

Name:________________________

Evaluate Logarithms

Evaluate using a calculator, round to 4 decimal places.

$\frac{\log 5}{\log 6 + \log 7}$ **0.4306**

$\frac{\ln 3 + \ln 4}{2 \ln 5}$ **0.7720**

Expand Logarithms

Use properties of logarithms to expand the expression.

$\log_5\left(\frac{x^2\ y^3}{z^4}\right)$

$\log_5 x^2 + \log y^3 - \log_5 z^4$

$2\log_5 x + 3\log_5 y - 4\log_5 z$

Condense Logarithms

Use properties of logarithms to condense the expression.

$\ln x - 2\ln 4$

$\ln x - \ln 4^2$

$\ln x - \ln 16$

$\ln\left(\frac{x}{16}\right)$

Inverse Functions

Find the inverse of the function.

y = $\ln(x+2)$

x = $\ln(y+2)$

$e^x = y + 2$

-2 -2

$e^x - 2 = y$

Exponential / Log Equations

Solve and check for extraneous solutions.

$\log_3(x+2) - \log_3(x-1) = 2$

$\log_3 \frac{x+2}{x-1} = 2$

$3^2 = \frac{x+2}{x-1}$

$\frac{9}{1} = \frac{x+2}{x-1}$

9x – 9 = x + 2

-x +9 -x +9

8x = 11

x = $\frac{11}{8}$

CHECK

$\log_3(\frac{11}{8} + 2) - \log_3(\frac{11}{8} - 1) = 2$

$\log_3(\frac{27}{8}) - \log_3(\frac{3}{8}) = 2$

$\log_3 \frac{\frac{27}{8}}{\frac{3}{8}} = 2$

$\log_3 9 = 2$ 2 = 2

Exponential / Log Application

A new car cost $35,000.00. The value of the car depreciates at a rate of 12% per year. When will the car be worth $5000.00?

5000 = 35000(1– 0.12)^t

35000 35000

$\frac{1}{7} = 0.88^t$

$\log(\frac{1}{7}) = \log(0.88)^t$

$\log(\frac{1}{7}) = t\log(0.88)$

$\log(0.88)$ $\log(0.88)$

15.22 ≈ t

It will take appoximately 15 years the car will be worth $500.00

Graph Logarithmic Functions

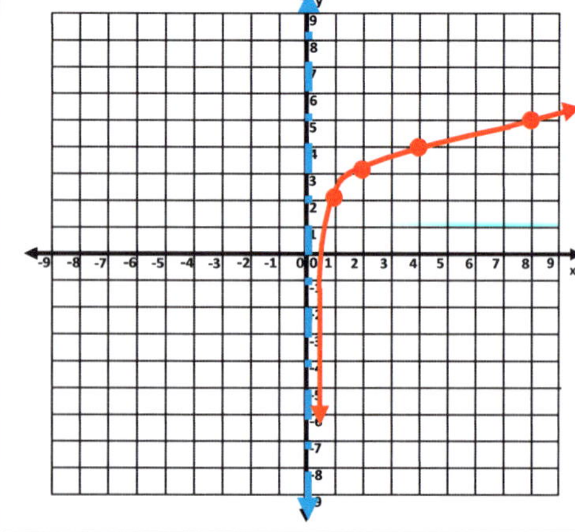

Find the asymptote, intercepts, the domain and range, then graph.

y = $\log_2 x + 2$

Vertical Asymptote x = 0

x-intercept (0.25 , 0)

Domain $\{x \mid x > 0\}$ $(0, \infty)$

Range $\{y \mid y \in R\}$ $(-\infty, \infty)$

Vocabulary

Asymptote
Exponential Function
Exponential Growth
Exponential Decay
Logarithmic Function
Common Logarithm
Natural Logarithm
Natural Base *e*

Exponential Decay — An exponential function y = ab^x, where a > 0 and 0 < b < 1

Exponential Function — a function in which the independent variable is the exponent.

Exponential Growth — An exponential function y = ab^x, where a > 0 and b > 1

Logarithmic Function — The inverse of an exponential function.

Algebra 2 Builder # 72

Name:______________________________

Evaluate Logarithms

Evaluate using a calculator, round to 4 decimal places.

$\log_3 7$

$\dfrac{\log 7}{\log 3}$

1.7712

$\log_9 \frac{2}{3}$

$\dfrac{\log\left(\frac{2}{3}\right)}{\log 9}$

-0.1846

Expand Logarithms

Use properties of logarithms to expand the expression.

$\log \sqrt{\dfrac{x^3y^5}{z}}$

$\log\left(\dfrac{x^3y^5}{z}\right)^{\frac{1}{2}}$

$\log \dfrac{x^{3/2}y^{5/2}}{z^{1/2}}$

$\log x^{3/2} + \log y^{5/2} - \log z^{1/2}$

$\frac{3}{2}\log x + \frac{5}{2}\log y - \frac{1}{2}\log z$

Condense Logarithms

Use properties of logarithms to condense the expression.

$3\log 2 + 3\log 4 + \frac{1}{2}\log x$

$\log 2^3 + \log 4^3 + \log x^{\frac{1}{2}}$

$\log 8 + \log 64 + \log x^{\frac{1}{2}}$

$\log(8 \cdot 64) + \log x^{\frac{1}{2}}$

$\log 512 + \log x^{\frac{1}{2}}$

$\log(512\, x^{\frac{1}{2}}) = \mathbf{\log(512\sqrt{x})}$

Inverse Functions

Find the inverse of the function.

$y = 3^{x-2}$

$x = 3^{y-2}$

$\log_3 x = y - 2$

$\quad +2 \qquad +2$

$\log_3 x + 2 = y$

Exponential / Log Equations

Solve and check for extraneous solutions.

$\log_3(3x-2) = \log_3(5x-7)$

$3x - 2 = 5x - 7$

$-3x + 7 \quad -3x + 7$

$5 = 2x$

$2 \quad 2$

$x = \frac{5}{2}$

CHECK

$\log_3\left(3\left(\frac{5}{2}\right) - 2\right) = \log_3\left(5\left(\frac{5}{2}\right) - 7\right)$

$\log_3\left(\frac{11}{2}\right) = \log_3\left(\frac{11}{2}\right)$

Exponential / Log Application

A new car cost $40,000.00. The value of the car depreciates at a rate of 10% per year. When will the car be worth half of its original cost?

$20000 = 40000(1 - 0.10)^t$

$40000 \quad 40000$

$0.5 = 0.9^t$

$\log 0.5 = \log 0.9^t$

$\log 0.5 = t\log 0.9$

$\log 0.9 \quad \log 0.9$

$6.5788 = t$

In about $6\frac{1}{2}$ years the car would be worth half of its original cost.

Graph Logarithmic Functions

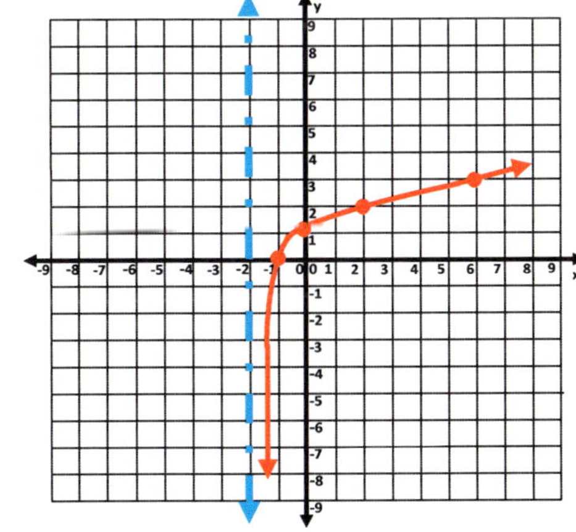

Find the asymptote, intercepts, the domain and range, then graph.

$y = \log_2(x + 2)$

Vertical Asymptote $x = -2$

x-intercept $(-1, 0)$

y-intercept $(0, 1)$

Domain $\{x \mid x > -2\}$ $(-2, \infty)$

Range $\{y \mid y \in R\}$ $(-\infty, \infty)$

Vocabulary

- Asymptote
- Exponential Function
- Exponential Growth
- Exponential Decay
- Logarithmic Function
- Common Logarithm
- Natural Logarithm
- Natural Base *e*

Natural Logarithm A base *e* logarithm denoted by ln.

Asymptote A line that a graph closely approaches.

Natural Base *e* The Euler number, $e \approx 2.718281828$.

Common Logarithm A base 10 logarithm.

Algebra 2 Builder # 73 Name:______________________________

Graph Parabolas

Write the equation in standard form, find the vertex, how it opens, the focus, the directrix and the length of the latus rectum and graph.

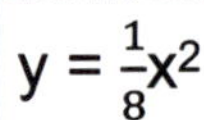

$y = \frac{1}{8}x^2$

$(8)(y) = \left(\frac{1}{8}x^2\right)(8)$

$8y = x^2$

$x^2 = 8y$

$h = 0 \quad 4p = 8 \quad k = 0$

$p = 2$

vertex = (0,0)

opens up

focus = (0,2)

directrix $y = -2$

length of latus rectum = 8

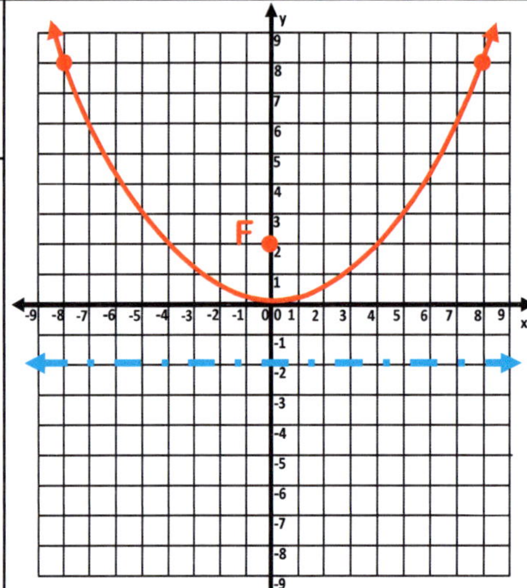

Equations of Parabolas

Write the equation given these conditions.

Vertex (0,0); focus (0,4)

vertex = (0,0) focus = (0,4)

h k

opens up

$p = 4$

$(x - h)^2 = 4p(y - k)$

$(x - 0)^2 = 4(4)(y - 0)$

$x^2 = 16y$

Graph Circles

Write the equation in standard form, find the center and the radius.

$x^2 + y^2 = 25$

Center (0,0)

Radius = 5

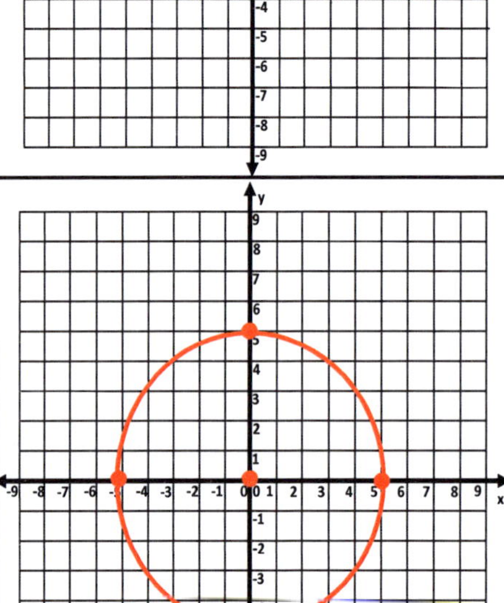

Equations of Circles

Write the equation given these conditions.

Center at the origin; radius is 6

$x^2 + y^2 = 36$

Systems of Equations

Solve.

$x^2 + y^2 = 25$

$y - x = 1$

$\quad +x \quad +x$

$y = x + 1$

$x^2 + (x + 1)^2 = 25$

$x^2 + x^2 + 2x + 1 = 25$

$2x^2 + 2x + 1 = 25$

$\quad -25 \quad -25$

$2x^2 + 2x - 24 = 0$

$2(x^2 + x - 12) = 0$

$2(x + 4)(x - 3) = 0$

$x + 4 = 0$ or $x - 3 = 0$

$x = -4$ or $x = 3$

x	x
+4	-3
4x	-3x

x

$y = x + 1$

$x = -4 \qquad x = 3$

$y = -4 + 1 \qquad y = 3 + 1$

$y = -3 \qquad y = 4$

Solutions

(-4,-3)

(3,4)

Vocabulary

- Conics
- Circle
- Center of a Circle
- Radius of a Circle
- Parabola
- Latus Rectum of a Parabola
- Focus of a Parabola
- Vertex of a Parabola

Conics A curved formed by the intersection of a plane and double napped cone.

Parabola A locus of points equal distance from a point called the focus and a line called the directrix.

Circle The locus of points that is equal distance from the center.

Focus of the Parabola The fixed point on the inside of the parabola.

Algebra 2 Builder # 74

Name:

Graph Parabolas

Write the equation in standard form, find the vertex, how it opens, the focus, the directrix and the length of the latus rectum and graph.

$x = \frac{1}{4}y^2$

$(4)(x) = \left(\frac{1}{4}y^2\right)(4)$

$4x = y^2$

$y^2 = 4x$

h = 0 4p = 4 k = 0

p = 1

vertex = (0,0)

opens right

focus = (1,0)

directrix x = -1

length of latus rectum = 4

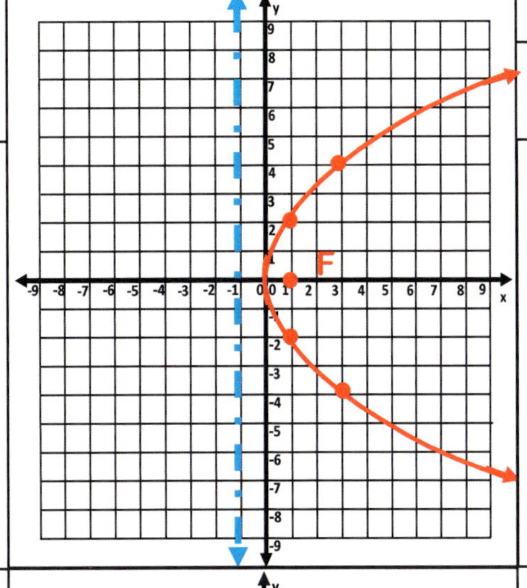

Equations of Parabolas

Write the equation given these conditions.

Vertex (0,0); directrix x = 2

vertex = (0,0) directrix x = 2

h k

opens left

p = -2

$(x - h)^2 = 4p(y - k)$

$(x - 0)^2 = 4(-2)(y - 0)$

$x^2 = -8y$

Graph Circles

Write the equation in standard form, find the center and the radius.

$(x - 1)^2 + (y + 2)^2 = 16$

h = 1 k = -2 $r^2 = 16$

r = 4

Center (1,-2)

Radius = 4

Equations of Circles

Write the equation given these conditions.

Center at (-4,5); radius is 5

h k

$(x + 4)^2 + (y - 5)^2 = 25$

Systems of Equations

Solve.

$x^2 + y^2 = 13$

$x - y = 5$

+y +y

x = y + 5

$(y + 5)^2 + y^2 = 13$

$y^2 + 10y + 25 + y^2 = 13$

-13 -13

$2y^2 + 10y + 12 = 0$

$2(y^2 + 5y + 6) = 0$

$2(y + 3)(y + 2) = 0$

y + 3 = 0 or y + 2 = 0

y = -3 or y = -2

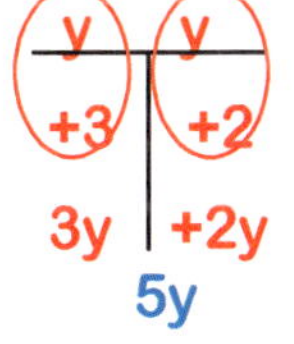

x = y + 5

y = -3	y = -2
x = -3 + 5	x = -2 + 5
x = 2	x = 3

Solutions

(2,-3)

(3,-2)

Vocabulary

- Conics
- Circle
- Center of a Circle
- Radius of a Circle
- Parabola
- Latus Rectum of a Parabola
- Focus of a Parabola
- Vertex of a Parabola

Latus Rectum of a Parabola A chord of a parabola that passes through the focus and is parallel to the directrix.

Center of a Circle A point inside the circle that is the same distance from each point on the circle.

Vertex of a Parabola The turning point on the graph of a parabola.

Radius of a Circle The distance from the center of the circle to any point on a circle.

Algebra 2 Builder # 75

Name:______________________

Graph Parabolas

Write the equation in standard form, find the vertex, how it opens, the focus, the directrix and the length of the latus rectum and graph.

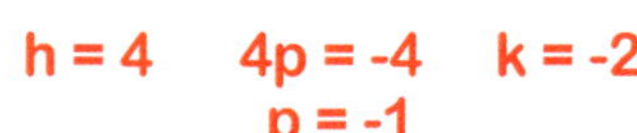

$(y + 2)^2 = -4(x - 4)$

$h = 4$ $4p = -4$ $k = -2$

$p = -1$

vertex = (4,-2)
opens left
focus = (3,-2)
directrix $x = 5$
length of latus rectum = 4

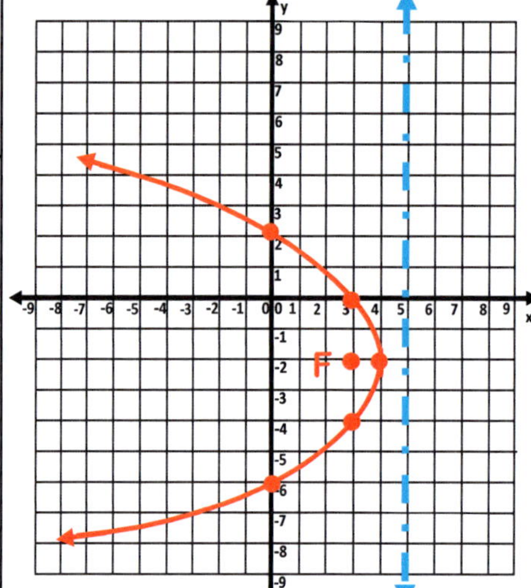

Equations of Parabolas

Write the equation given these conditions.
Vertex (2,1); focus (2,-3)

vertex = (2,1) focus = (2,-3)
h k

opens down
$p = -4$

$(x - h)^2 = 4p(y - k)$

$(x - 2)^2 = 4(-4)(y - 1)$

$(x - 2)^2 = -16(y - 1)$

Graph Circles

Write the equation in standard form, find the center and the radius.

$x^2 + y^2 + 2x - 4y - 4 = 0$

$(x^2 + 2x + 1) + (y^2 - 4y + 4) = 4 + 1 + 4$

$(x + 1)^2 + (y - 2)^2 = 9$

Center (-1,2)

Radius = 3

$(2)(\frac{1}{2})$ $-4 \cdot \frac{1}{2}$

$(1)^2$ $(-2)^2$

1 4

Equations of Circles

Write the equation given these conditions.
Center at (2,3); and passes through the point (3,-1)

$r = \sqrt{(3-2)^2 + (-1-3)^2}$

$r = \sqrt{1^2 + (-4)^2}$

$r = \sqrt{1 + 16}$

$r = \sqrt{17}$

$(x - 2)^2 + (y - 3)^2 = 17$

Systems of Equations

Solve.

$4x + y^2 = 0$

$3x + y = -1$

$y = -3x - 1$

$x = -\frac{1}{9}$	$x = -1$
$y = -3(-\frac{1}{9}) - 1$	$y = -3(-1) - 1$
$y = \frac{1}{3} - 1$	$y = 3 - 1$
$y = -\frac{2}{3}$	$y = 2$

$4x + (-3x - 1)^2 = 0$

$4x + (-3x - 1)(-3x - 1) = 0$

$4x + 9x^2 + 3x + 3x + 1 = 0$

$9x^2 + 10x + 1 = 0$

$(9x + 1) = 0$ $(x + 1) = 0$

$9x + 1 = 0$ or $x + 1 = 0$

$x = -\frac{1}{9}$ or $x = -1$

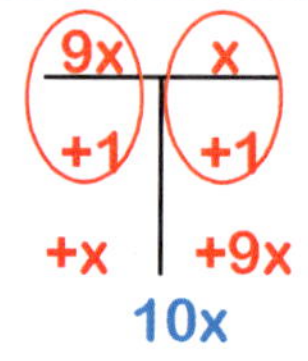

Solutions

$(-\frac{1}{9}, -\frac{2}{3})$

$(-1, 2)$

Vocabulary

Conics
Circle
Center of a Circle
Radius of a Circle
Parabola
Latus Rectum of a Parabola
Focus of a Parabola
Vertex of a Parabola

Conics ________ A curved formed by the intersection of a plane and double napped cone.

Parabola ________ A locus of points equal distance from a point called the focus and a line called the directrix.

Circle ________ The locus of points that is equal distance from the center.

Focus of a Parabola ________ The fixed point on the inside of the parabola.

Algebra 2 Builder # 76

Name:______________________________

Graph Parabolas

Write the equation in standard form, find the vertex, how it opens, the focus, the directrix and the length of the latus rectum and graph.

$x^2 - 6x - 8y + 25 = 0$

$-6 \cdot \frac{1}{2}$
$(-3)^2$
9

$(x^2 - 6x + 9) = 8y - 25 + 9$
$(x - 3)^2 = 8y - 16$
$(x - 3)^2 = 8(y - 2)$

$h = 3 \quad 4p = 8 \quad k = 2$
$p = 2$

vertex = (3,2)
opens up
focus = (3,4)
directrix y = 0
length of latus rectum = 8

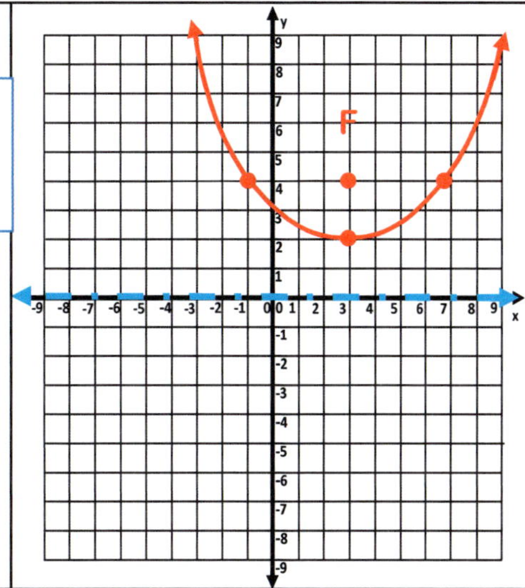

Equations of Parabolas

Write the equation given these conditions.
Focus (2,3); directrix x = -6

vertex = (-2,3) focus = (2,3)
h k

opens right
p = 4

$(y - k)^2 = 4p(x - h)$
$(y - 3)^2 = 4(4)(x + 2)$
$(y - 3)^2 = 16(x + 2)$

Graph Circles

Write the equation in standard form, find the center and the radius.

$\dfrac{2x^2 + 2y^2 - 12x + 4y - 12 = 0}{2}$

$x^2 + y^2 - 6x + 2y - 6 = 0$
$+6 \quad +6$
$(x^2 - 6x + 9) + (y^2 + 2y + 1) = 6 + 9 + 1$

$(x - 3)^2 + (y + 1)^2 = 16$

Center (3,-1)
Radius = 4

$-6(\frac{1}{2})$ $2 \cdot \frac{1}{2}$
$(-3)^2$ $(1)^2$
9 1

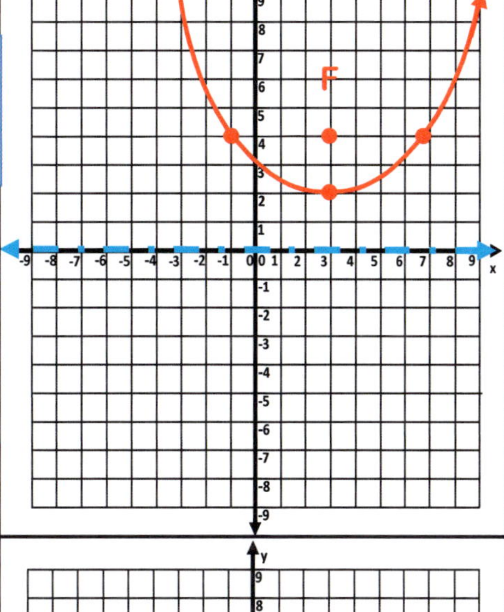

Equations of Circles

Write the equation given these conditions.
Center at (4,-2); and tangent to the x-axis.

Radius = 4
$(x - 4)^2 + (y + 2)^2 = 16$

Systems of Equations

Solve.

$-1(x^2 + y^2 = 13)$
$(x - 5)^2 + y^2 = 18$

$-x^2 - y^2 = -13$
$(x - 5)^2 + y^2 = 18$

$(x - 5)^2 - x^2 = 5$

$x^2 - 10x + 25 - x^2 = 5$
$-10x + 25 = 5$
$-25 \quad -25$
$\frac{-10x}{-10} = \frac{-20}{-10} \quad x = 2$

$(2)^2 + y^2 = 13$
$4 + y^2 = 13$
$-4 \quad -4$
$y^2 = 9$
$\sqrt{y^2} = \sqrt{9}$
$y = \pm 3$

Solutions
(2, -3)
(2 , 3)

Vocabulary

- Conics
- Circle
- Center of a Circle
- Radius of a Circle
- Parabola
- Latus Rectum of a Parabola
- Focus of a Parabola
- Vertex of a Parabola

Radius of a Circle The distance from the center of the circle to any point on a circle.

Latus Rectum of a Parabola A chord of a parabola that passes through the focus and is parallel to the directrix.

Vertex of a Parabola The turning point on the graph of a parabola.

Center of a Circle A point inside the circle that is the same distance from each point on the circle.

Algebra 2 Builder # 77

Name:__________________________________

Graph Ellipse

Write the equation in standard form, find the center, vertices, co-verticies, foci and length of the major and minor axis, then graph.

$$\frac{x^2}{9} + \frac{y^2}{4} = 1$$

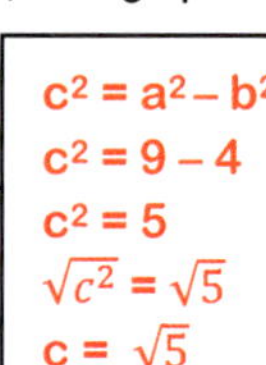

$c^2 = a^2 - b^2$
$c^2 = 9 - 4$
$c^2 = 5$
$\sqrt{c^2} = \sqrt{5}$
$c = \sqrt{5}$

h = 0 k = 0
a = 3 b = 2

Center =(0,0)
vertices = (-3,0)(3,0)
Co-vertices = (0,-2)(0,2)

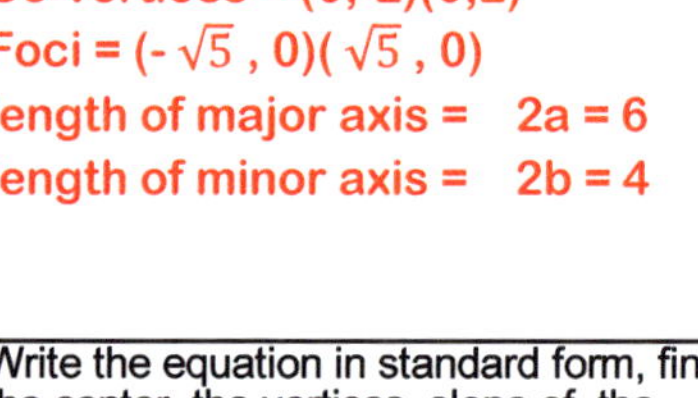

Foci = $(-\sqrt{5}, 0)(\sqrt{5}, 0)$
length of major axis = 2a = 6
length of minor axis = 2b = 4

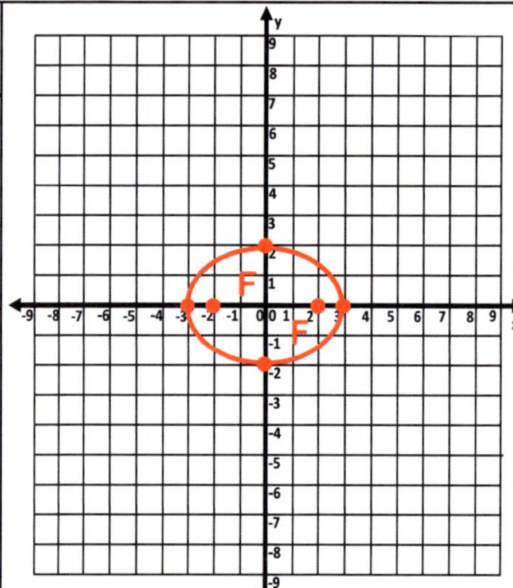

Equations of Ellipse

Write the equation given these conditions.
Center at (0,0); length of the horizontal major axis 16; length of the minor axis 6

2a = 16 2b = 6
a = 8 b = 3

$$\frac{x^2}{64} + \frac{y^2}{9} = 1$$

Graph Hyperbolas

Write the equation in standard form, find the center, the vertices, slope of the asymptotes, foci, length of transverse axis, then graph.

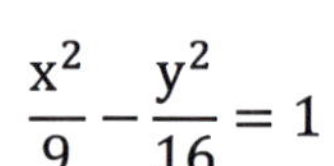

$$\frac{x^2}{9} - \frac{y^2}{16} = 1$$

$c^2 = a^2 + b^2$
$c^2 = 9 + 16$
$c^2 = 25$
$\sqrt{c^2} = \sqrt{25}$
$c = 5$

h = 0 k = 0
a = 3 b = 4

Center =(0,0)
vertices = (-3,0)(3,0)
Slope of asymptote = $\pm\frac{4}{3}$
Foci = (- 5, 0)(5 , 0)
length of transverse = 6

Equations of Hyperbolas

Write the equation given these conditions.
Center at (0,0);
a = 5, c = 7
Vertical transverse axis

$c^2 = a^2 + b^2$
$49 = 25 + b^2$
$24 = b^2$

$$\frac{y^2}{25} - \frac{x^2}{24} = 1$$

Systems of Equations

Solve.

$x^2 + y^2 = 10$
$x^2 - y^2 = -8$

$\frac{2x^2}{2} = \frac{2}{2}$

$\sqrt{x^2} = \sqrt{1}$

$x = \pm 1$

x = -1
$(-1)^2 + y^2 = 10$
$1 + y^2 = 10$
$-1 \quad -1$
$\sqrt{y^2} = \sqrt{9}$
$y = \pm 3$

(-1,-3)(-1,3)

x = 1
$(1)^2 + y^2 = 10$
$1 + y^2 = 10$
$-1 \quad -1$
$\sqrt{y^2} = \sqrt{9}$
$y = \pm 3$

(1,-3)(1,3)

Vocabulary

Ellipse
Major Axis of an Ellipse
Minor Axis of an Ellipse
Vertices of an Ellipse
Foci of an Ellipse
Co-Vertices of an Ellipse
Hyperbola
Transverse Axis of a Hyperbola

Hyperbola ______ A locus of points P, the difference of whose distance to the foci is constant.

Transverse Axis of a Hyperbola The line segment between the vertices of a hyperbola.

Major Axis of an Ellipse The line segment joining the vertices of an ellipse.

Ellipse ______ A locus of points P, the sum of whose distance to the foci is constant.

Algebra 2 Builder # 78

Name:______________________________

Graph Ellipse

Write the equation in standard form, find the center, vertices, co-verticies, foci and length of the major and minor axis, then graph.

$$\frac{9x^2}{225} + \frac{25y^2}{225} = \frac{225}{225}$$

$$\frac{x^2}{25} + \frac{y^2}{9} = 1$$

$c^2 = a^2 - b^2$
$c^2 = 25 - 9$
$c^2 = 16$
$\sqrt{c^2} = \sqrt{16}$
$c = 4$

Center =(0,0)
vertices = (-5,0)(5,0)
Co-vertices = (0,-3)(0,3)
Foci = (-4, 0)(4,0)
length of major axis = 10
length of minor axis = 6

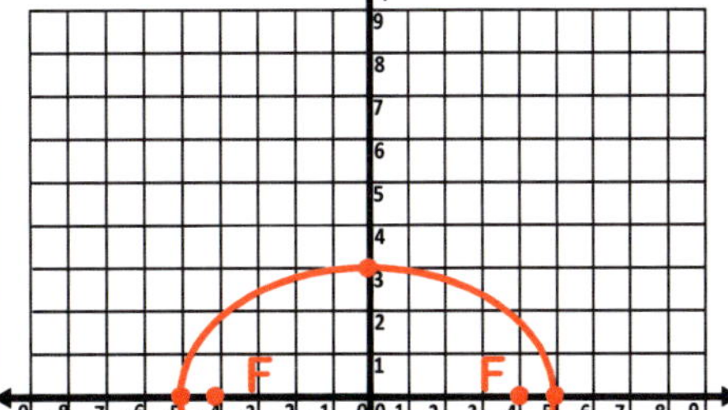

Equations of Ellipse

Write the equation given these conditions.
Center at (-2,3);
a = 4, b = 3
major axis is vertical

$$\frac{(y-3)^2}{16} + \frac{(x+2)^2}{9} = 1$$

Graph Hyperbolas

Write the equation in standard form, find the center, the vertices, slope of the asymptotes, foci, length of transverse axis, then graph.

$$\frac{-16x^2}{144} + \frac{9y^2}{144} = \frac{144}{144}$$

$$\frac{-x^2}{9} + \frac{y^2}{16} = 1$$

$$\frac{y^2}{16} - \frac{x^2}{9} = 1$$

$c^2 = a^2 + b^2$
$c^2 = 16 + 9$
$c^2 = 25$
$\sqrt{c^2} = \sqrt{25}$
$c = 5$

Center =(0,0)
vertices = (0,-4)(0,4)
Foci = (0, -5)(0,5)
length of transverse axis = 8
Slope of asymptote = $\pm\frac{4}{3}$

Equations of Hyperbolas

Write the equation given these conditions.
Foci (5,0) and (-5,0)
Vertices (4,0) and (-4,0)

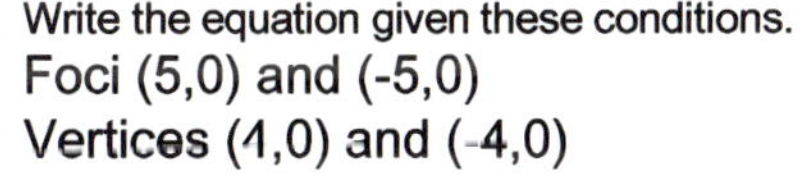

Center = (0,0)

a = 4 c = 5
$c^2 = a^2 + b^2$
$25 = 16 + b^2$
$9 = b^2$

$$\frac{x^2}{16} - \frac{y^2}{9} = 1$$

Systems of Equations

Solve.

$2x^2 - y^2 = -7$

$y = 2x - 5$

$2x^2 - (2x-5)^2 = -7$
$2x^2 - (4x^2 - 20x + 25) = -7$
$2x^2 - 4x^2 + 20x - 25 = -7$
$\quad +7 \quad +7$
$-2x^2 + 20x - 18 = 0$
$-2(x^2 - 10x + 9) = 0$
$-2(x-9)(x-1) = 0$

$x - 9 = 0$ or $x - 1 = 0$
$x = 9 \qquad x = 1$

$y = 2x - 5$
$x = 9$
$y = 2(9) - 5$
$y = 18 - 5$
$y = 13$

$x = 1$
$y = 2(1) - 5$
$y = 2 - 5$
$y = -3$

(9,13)(1,-3)

Vocabulary

- Ellipse
- Major Axis of an Ellipse
- Minor Axis of an Ellipse
- Vertices of an Ellipse
- Foci of an Ellipse
- Co-Vertices of an Ellipse
- Hyperbola
- Transverse Axis of a Hyperbola

Minor Axis of an Ellipse The line segment between the co-vertices of an ellipse.

Vertices of and Ellipse Where the major axis intersects the ellipse.

Co-Vertices of an Ellipse Where the minor axis intersects the ellipse.

Foci of an Ellipse Two fixed points inside the ellipse on the major axis.

Algebra 2 Builder # 79 Name:_______________

Graph Ellipse

Write the equation in standard form, find the center, vertices, co-verticies, foci and length of the major and minor axis, then graph.

$$\frac{(x-3)^2}{25}+\frac{(y+1)^2}{16}=1$$

$c^2 = a^2 - b^2$
$c^2 = 25 - 16$
$c^2 = 9$
$\sqrt{c^2} = \sqrt{9}$
$c = 3$

Center =(3,-1)
vertices = (-2,-1)(8,-1)
Co-vertices = (3,-5)(3,3)
Foci = (0, -1)(6,-1)
length of major axis = 10
length of minor axis = 8

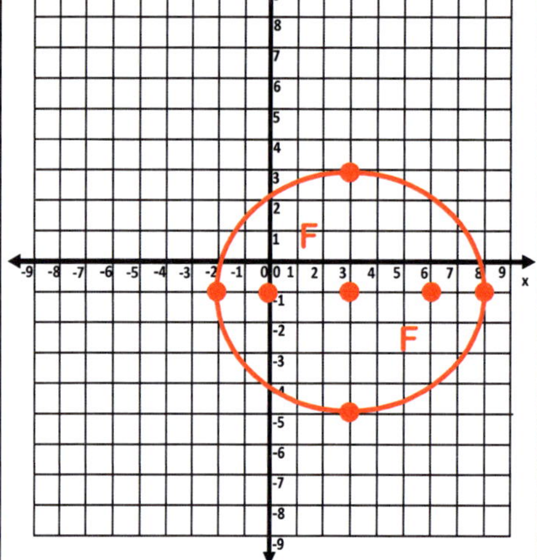

Equations of Ellipse

Write the equation given these conditions.
Foci (0,4) and (0,-4)
Length of major axis 10

Center = (0,0)
2a = 10
a = 5

$c^2 = a^2 - b^2$
$16 = 25 - b^2$
$-9 = -b^2$
$b^2 = 9$
$\frac{y^2}{25}+\frac{x^2}{9}=1$

Graph Hyperbolas

Write the equation in standard form, find the center, the vertices, slope of the asymptotes, foci, length of transverse axis, then graph.

$$\frac{(y-1)^2}{4}-\frac{(x+2)^2}{4}=1$$

$c^2 = a^2 + b^2$
$c^2 = 4 + 4$
$c^2 = 8$
$\sqrt{c^2} = \sqrt{8}$
$c = 2\sqrt{2}$

Center =(-2,1)
vertices = (-2,3)(-2,-1)
Foci = $(-2, 1-2\sqrt{2})(-2, 1+2\sqrt{2})$
length of transverse axis = 4
Slope of asymptote = $\pm\frac{2}{2}$

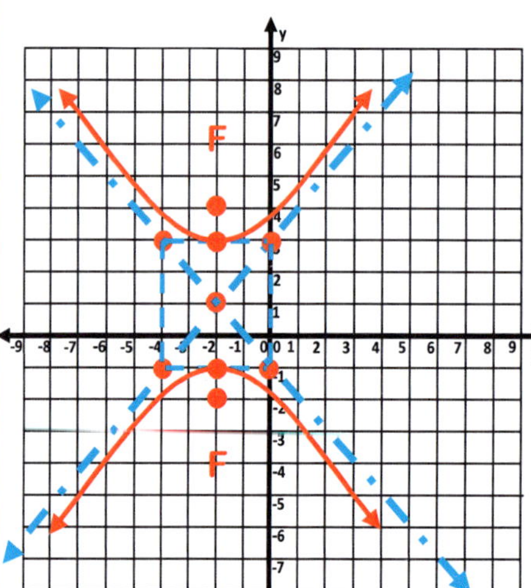

Equations of Hyperbolas

Write the equation given these conditions.
Foci (0,7) and (0,-7);
Vertices (0,5) and (0,-5)

Center = (0,0)
c = 7 a = 5

$c^2 = a^2 + b^2$
$49 = 25 + b^2$
$24 = b^2$

$\frac{y^2}{25}-\frac{x^2}{24}=1$

Systems of Equations

Solve.

$x^2 - y^2 = -4$
$x^2 + y^2 = 4$
$2x^2 = 0$
$x^2 = 0$
$x = 0$

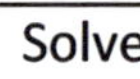

x = 0

$x^2 + y^2 = 4$
$(0)^2 + y^2 = 4$
$y^2 = 4$
$\sqrt{y^2} = \sqrt{4}$
$y = \pm 2$

Solutions

(0,-2)(0,2)

Vocabulary

Ellipse
Major Axis of an Ellipse
Minor Axis of an Ellipse
Vertices of an Ellipse
Foci of an Ellipse
Co-Vertices of an Ellipse
Hyperbola
Transverse Axis of a Hyperbola

Hyperbola: A locus of points P, the difference of whose distance to the foci is constant.

Transverse Axis of a Hyperbola: The line segment between the vertices of a hyperbola.

Major Axis of an Ellipse: The line segment joining the vertices of an ellipse.

Ellipse: A locus of points P, the sum of whose distance to the foci is constant.

Algebra 2 Builder # 80

Name:______________________________

Graph Ellipse

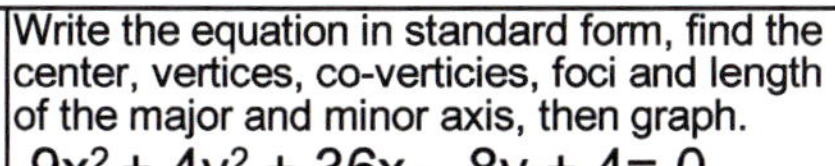

Write the equation in standard form, find the center, vertices, co-verticies, foci and length of the major and minor axis, then graph.

$9x^2 + 4y^2 + 36x - 8y + 4 = 0$

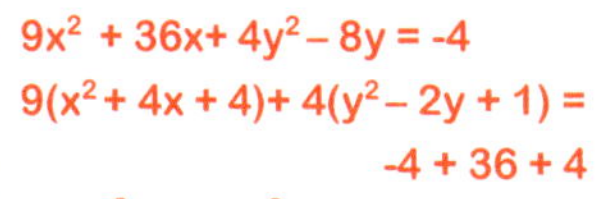

$9x^2 + 36x + 4y^2 - 8y = -4$

$9(x^2 + 4x + 4) + 4(y^2 - 2y + 1) = -4 + 36 + 4$

$\frac{9(x+2)^2}{36} + \frac{4(y-1)^2}{36} = \frac{36}{36}$

$\frac{(x+2)^2}{4} + \frac{(y-1)^2}{9} = 1$

$c^2 = a^2 - b^2$
$c^2 = 9 - 4$
$c^2 = 5$
$\sqrt{c^2} = \sqrt{5}$
$c = \sqrt{5}$

Center =(-2,1)
vertices = (-2,-2)(-2,4)
Co-vertices = (-4,1)(0,1)
Foci = $(-2, 1-\sqrt{5})(-2, 1+\sqrt{5})$
length of major axis = 6
length of minor axis = 4

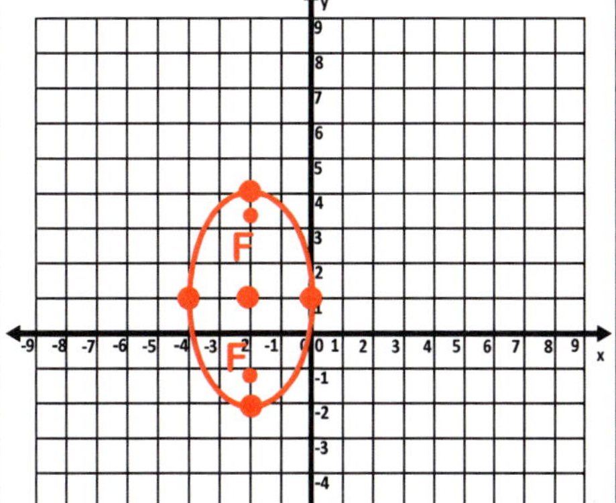

Equations of Ellipse

Write the equation given these conditions.

Vertices (-2,4) and (-2,-2);
Foci (-2,3) and (-2,-1)

Center = (-2,1)
a = 3 c = 2

$c^2 = a^2 - b^2$
$4 = 9 - b^2$
$-5 = -b^2$
$5 = b^2$

$\frac{(y-1)^2}{9} + \frac{(x+2)^2}{5} = 1$

Graph Hyperbolas

Write the equation in standard form, find the center, the vertices, slope of the asymptotes, foci, length of transverse axis, then graph.

$16x^2 - 25y^2 - 64x - 50y - 361 = 0$

$16x^2 - 64x - 25y^2 - 50y = 361$

$16(x^2 - 4x + 4) - 25(y^2 + 2y + 1) = 361 + 64 - 25$

$\frac{16(x-2)^2}{400} - \frac{25(y+1)^2}{400} = \frac{400}{400}$

$\frac{(x-2)^2}{25} - \frac{(y+1)^2}{16} = 1$

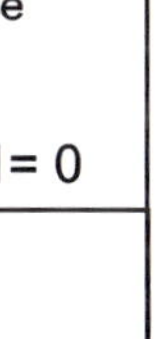

$c^2 = a^2 + b^2$
$c^2 = 25 + 16$
$c^2 = 41$
$\sqrt{c^2} = \sqrt{41}$
$c = \sqrt{41}$

Center =(2,-1)
vertices = (-3,-1)(7,-1)
Foci = $(2 - \sqrt{41}, -1)(2 + \sqrt{41}, -1)$
Slope of asymptote = $\pm\frac{4}{5}$

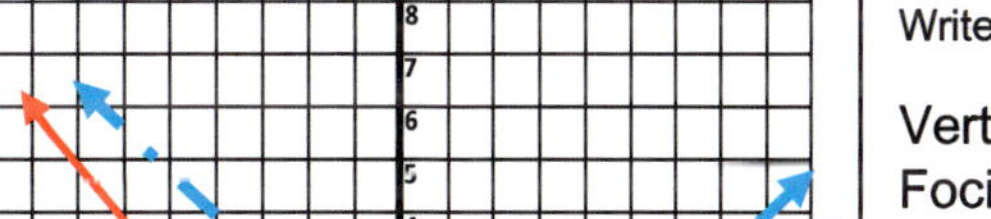

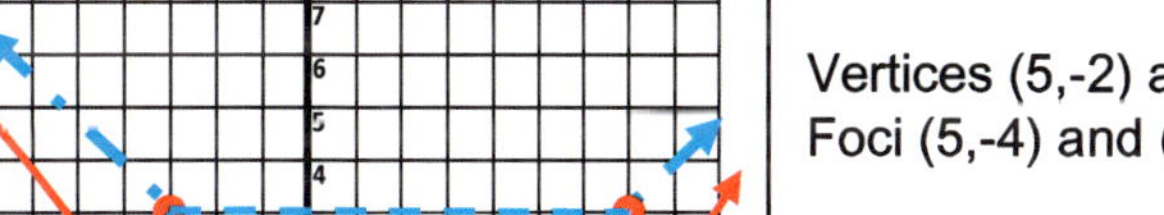

Equations of Hyperbolas

Write the equation given these conditions.

Vertices (5,-2) and (5,4);
Foci (5,-4) and (5,6)

Center = (5,1)
a = 3 c = 5

$c^2 = a^2 + b^2$
$25 = 9 + b^2$
$16 = b^2$

$\frac{(y-1)^2}{9} - \frac{(x-5)^2}{16} = 1$

Systems of Equations

Solve.

$6x^2 + y^2 = 10$
$-3(2x^2 + 4y^2 = 18)$

$6x^2 + y^2 = 10$
$-6x^2 - 12y^2 = -54$
$\frac{-11y^2}{-11} = \frac{-44}{-11}$

$y^2 = 4$
$\sqrt{y^2} = \sqrt{4}$
$y = \pm 2$

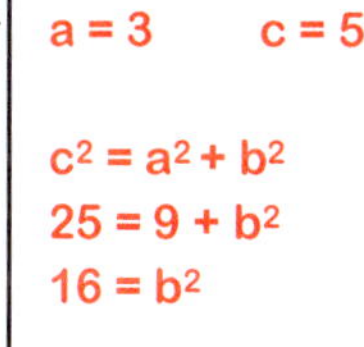

y = -2

$6x^2 + (-2)^2 = 10$
$6x^2 + 4 = 10$
$-4 \quad -4$
$\frac{6x^2}{6} = \frac{6}{6}$

$x^2 = 1$
$\sqrt{x^2} = \sqrt{1}$
$x = \pm 1$

y = 2

$6x^2 + (2)^2 = 10$
$6x^2 + 4 = 10$
$-4 \quad -4$
$\frac{6x^2}{6} = \frac{6}{6}$

$x^2 = 1$
$\sqrt{x^2} = \sqrt{1}$
$x = \pm 1$

Solutions

(1,-2)(-1,-2) (1,2)(-1,2)

Vocabulary

Ellipse
Major Axis of an Ellipse
Minor Axis of an Ellipse
Vertices of an Ellipse
Foci of an Ellipse
Co-Vertices of an Ellipse
Hyperbola
Transverse Axis of a Hyperbola

Minor Axis of an Ellipse The line segment between the co-vertices of an ellipse.

Vertices of an Ellipse Where the major axis intersects the ellipse.

Co-Vertices of an Ellipse Where the minor axis intersects the ellipse.

Foci of an Ellipse Two fixed points inside the ellipse on the major axis.

Vocabulary

ALGEBRA READINESS BUILDERS

Algebra 2

Algebra Readiness Builders Algebra 2 Vocabulary

Additive Inverse Property- For all real numbers a, a + (-a) = 0.

Associative Property- For all real numbers a, b, and c, (a + b) + c = a + (b + c) or (ab)c = a(bc)

Asymptote-a line that a graph closely approaches.

Axis of Symmentry-The line that divides the graph into equal halves.

Center of a Circle- A point inside the circle that is the same distance from each point on the circle.

Circle-The locus of points that is equal distance from the center.

Common Logarithm-A base 10 logarithm.

Commutative Property-For all real numbers a and b, a + b = b + a or ab = ba.

Complex Fraction-a fraction that contains a fraction in the numerator or denominator.

Complex Number-a number written in the form a + bi where a and b are real numbers and i = $\sqrt{-1}$.

Conics-A curved formed by the intersection of a plane and double napped cone.

Conjugate-Two binomials that are the same except the middle signs are opposite.

Continuous Function-A function whose graph has no gaps or breaks.

Co-Vertices of an Ellipse-Where the minor axis intersects the ellipse.

Direct Variation-the relationship of 2 variables x and y where there is some constant k such that y = kx.

Discontinuity-a break in the continuity of a function.

Discrete Function-A function whose graph consist of separate points.

Discriminant-a part of the quadratic formula that is used to determine the number and type of roots of a quadratic equation.

Discriminant-For a quadratic equation, the expression under the radical in the quadratic formula.

Distributive Property-For all real numbers a, b and c, a(b + c) = ab + ac.

Algebra Readiness Builders Algebra 2 Vocabulary

Domain-is the set of first elements in ordered pair or table.

Ellipse-A locus of points P, the sum of whose distance to the foci is constant.

End Behavior-the behavior of the graph of a function as x approaches negative infinity or positive infinity.

Equation-a mathematical statement that shows two expressions are equivalent.

Exponential Decay-An exponential function $y = ab^x$, where $a > 0$ and $0 < b < 1$.

Exponential Function-a function in which the independent variable is the exponent.

Exponential Growth-An exponential function $y = ab^x$, where $a > 0$ and $b > 1$.

Extraneous Solutions-solutions that do not check.

Foci of an Ellipse-Two fixed points inside the ellipse on the major axis.

Focus of the Parabola-The fixed point on the inside of the parabola.

Function-a relation in which every input has exactly one output.

Hyperbola-A locus of points P, the difference of whose distance to the foci is constant.

Inequality- is a type of problem that often has a set of answers and can be written in interval notation.

Inverse Function-A function that results from interchanging the domain and range values of a one to one function.

Inverse Variation-the relationship of two variables x and y where there is some constant k such that $xy = k$ or $y = \frac{k}{x}$.

Irrational Number-A number that neither repeats or terminates.

Latus Rectum of a Parabola- A chord of a parabola that passes through the focus and is parallel to the directrix.

Least Common Denominator-the smallest factor that each denominator can divide into evenly.

Linear Programming-a method of finding a minimum or maximum value of a linear function, that satisfies a given set of constraints.

Logarithmic Function-The inverse of an exponential function.

Algebra Readiness Builders Algebra 2 Vocabulary

Major Axis of an Ellipse-The line segment joining the vertices of an ellipse.

Minor Axis of an Ellipse-The line segment between the co- vertices of an ellipse.

Multiplicative Inverse Property-For all real number a, $a \cdot \frac{1}{a} = 1, \quad a \neq 0.$

Natural Base *e*-The Euler number, $e \approx 2.718281828$.

Natural Logarithm-A base *e* logarithm denoted by ln.

Negative Exponent Property-$a^{n} = \frac{1}{a^n}$ or $\frac{1}{a^{-n}} = a^n \quad a \neq 0$

Parabola-The shape of the graph of a quadratic function.

Parabola-A locus of points equal distance from a point called the focus and a line called the directrix.

Parallel Lines-Lines that have the same slope.

Parent Function-The most basic function in a family of functions.

Perpendicular Lines-Lines whose slopes are negative reciprocals.

Polynomial-a monomial or a sum of monomials.

Power of a Power Property-$(a^m)^n = a^{mn}$

Power of a Product Property-$(ab)^m = a^m b^m$

Power of a Quotient Property-$\left(\frac{a}{b}\right)^n = \frac{a^n}{b^n} \quad b \neq 0$

Product of Powers Property-$a^m a^n = a^{m+n}$

Quotient of Powers Property-$\frac{a^m}{a^n} = a^{m-n} \quad a \neq 0$

Quotient of Powers Property-$\frac{a^m}{a^n} = a^{m-n} \quad a \neq 0$

Radical-an expression in the form $\sqrt{b}$ or the $\sqrt[n]{b}$ where b is a number or an expression, and n is an integer greater than 2.

Radicand-the number or expression under the radical sign.

Radius of a Circle-The distance from the center of the circle to any point on a circle.

Range-is the set of second elements in ordered pair or table.

Algebra Readiness Builders Algebra 2 Vocabulary

Rational Function-a ratio of two polynomial functions where the denominator cannot equal zero.

Rational Number-A number that can be expressed as the ratio of two integers and the denominator cannot equal zero.

Representations-Models, graphs, equations, tables and verbal descriptions of data.

Scatter Plot-A graph with points plotted to find the relationship between two sets of data.

Slope-The ratio of the vertical change (rise) to the horizontal change (run).

Solution-a value for the variable or an ordered pair that makes an equation true.

Standard Form of a Quadratic Function-a quadratic function written in the form $f(x) = ax^2 + bx + c$.

Systems of Equations-a set of two or more equations that have two or more variables.

Transformations-Ways to manipulate a graphs, size, shape, position or orientation.

Transverse Axis of a Hyperbola-The line segment between the vertices of a hyperbola.

Vertex Form of a Quadratic Function-a quadratic function written in the form $f(x) = a(x - h)^2 + k$.

Vertex of a Parabola-The turning point on the graph of a parabola.

Vertex of the Parabola-The maximum or minimum point on a parabola.

Vertices of and Ellipse-Where the major axis intersects the ellipse.

Zero Exponent Property-$a^0 = 1 \quad a \neq 0$

Zero(s) of a Function-Value(s) of x for which $f(x) = 0$.

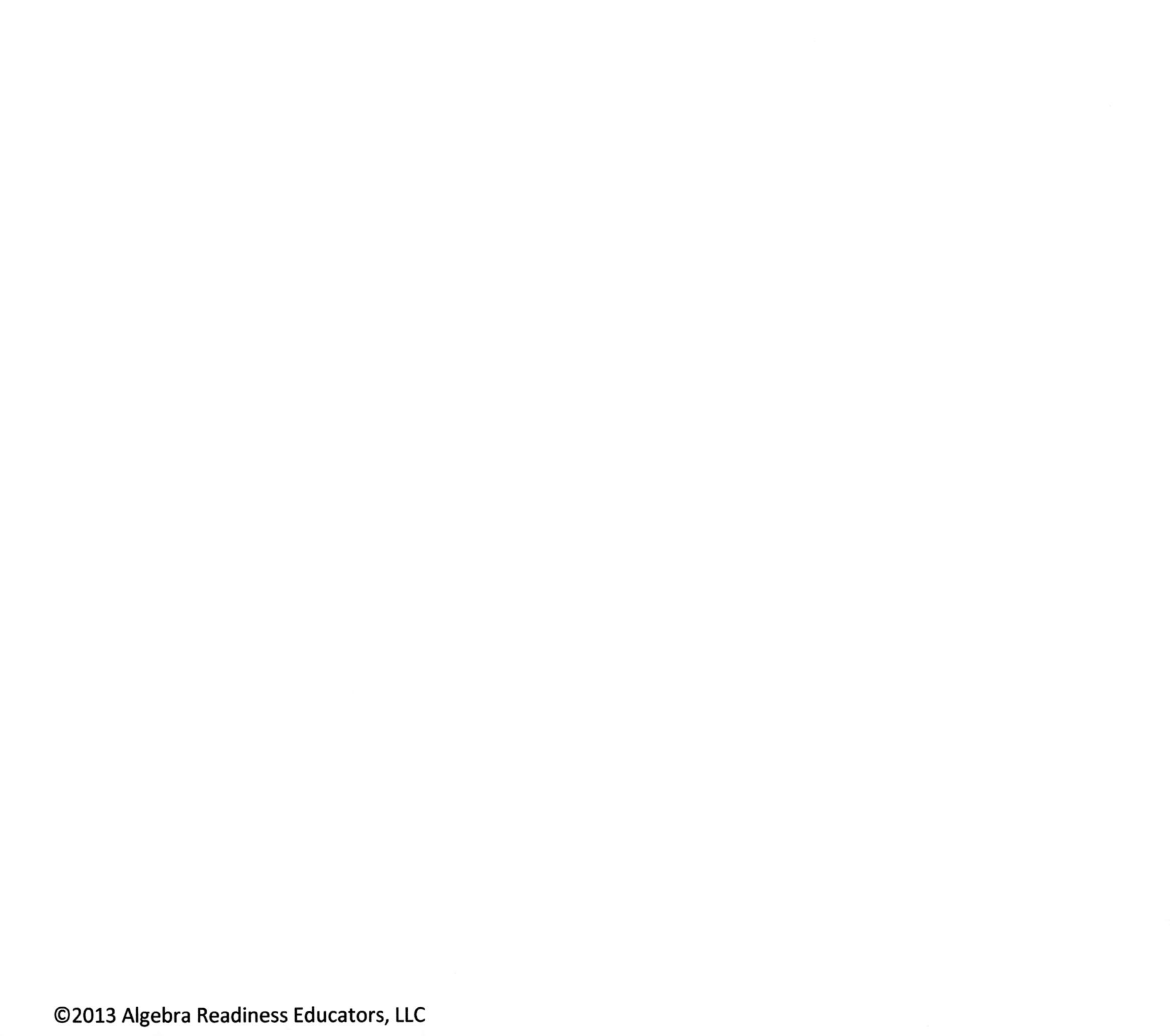

Authors

Having spent several years searching for a resource that spirals the necessary skills for success in math, we decided to write our own. Our students' scores on the state mandated test improved dramatically after the implementation of our builders.

Enjoy the same success by implementing builders as your daily homework assignments.

Katherine LaChance and Rhonda Brady

Made in the USA
San Bernardino, CA
12 March 2014